THE CLASSICS OF WESTERN SPIRITUALITY

JOHN DONNE

SELECTIONS FROM *DIVINE POEMS*, SERMONS, *DEVOTIONS*, AND PRAYERS

EDITED AND INTRODUCED BY
JOHN BOOTY

PREFACE BY
P.G. STANWOOD

PAULIST PRESS
NEW YORK • MAHWAH

Cover art: A great admirer of John Donne's poetry, Karen Laub-Novak is also a sculptor, painter and printmaker. She has published numerous articles on art and has exhibited and lectured throughout the United States.

Library of Congress Cataloging-in-Publication Data

Donne, John, 1572–1631.
    [Selections]
    Divine poems, sermons, devotions, and prayers/John Donne;
edited with an introduction by John Booty.
        p.   cm.—(The Classics of Western spirituality)
    ISBN 0-8091-0435-0 —ISBN 0-8091-3160-9 (pbk.)
    1. Christian literature, English. I. Booty, John E. II. Title. III. Series.
PR2246.B6   1990
821'.3—dc20   90-34580
                                                                  CIP

Published by Paulist Press
997 Macarthur Boulevard
Mahwah, New Jersey 07430

Printed and bound in the United States of America

Contents

Editor of this Volume

JOHN BOOTY is Professor of Anglican Studies at the School of Theology of the University of the South, Sewanee, Tennessee. Having received his Ph.D. from Princeton University in 1960, he then concentrated his studies on religion and culture in sixteenth and seventeenth century England. His published works include *John Jewel as Apologist of the Church of England* and *The Godly Kingdom* of Tudor England. He has edited *The Book of Common Prayer 1559* and Jewel's *Apology,* and is an editor of the Folger Edition of the *Works* of Richard Hooker. Professor Booty has taught at Virginia Theological Seminary, Yale Divinity School, the Episcopal Divinity School, and Sewanee. A student of spirituality, he has written *Yearning to be Free, Three Anglican Divines on Prayer, Meditating on Four Quartets,* and *The Christ We Know.* An ordained priest, Professor Booty is also Historiographer of the Episcopal Church.

Author of the Preface

P.G. STANWOOD is Professor of English at the University of British Columbia, Vancouver. He has published many articles and reviews on devotional literature, especially that of the earlier seventeenth century. He has edited seven books, including *John Donne and the Theology of Language* (1985), Jeremy Taylor's *Holy Living* and *Holy Dying* (2 volumes, 1989) and, for the Classics of Western Spirituality, William Law's *A Serious Call to a Devout and Holy Life* and *The Spirit of Love* (1978).

Foreword

John Donne is well characterized as an Anglican Divine, one who combines extensive learning with a profound spirituality. Donne combines literary, scholarly, and spiritual gifts in ways which suggest that his poems, sermons, meditations and prayers are inderdependent and best understood in relation to one another. Furthermore, although a deeply spiritual man, Donne was also of the earth, earthy. His spirituality was incarnational, his love poems and his *Holy Sonnets* illuminate one another, his sermons are in touch with the experience of ordinary, fallible human beings, and his meditations written during a serious illness are redolent with the feelings of a man experiencing pain, bedeviled by sundry fears, and yet confident in his God. The spirituality which emerges in reading poems, sermons, and meditations is one with which ordinary folk can identify, and indeed Donne knew this, and recognize that, as is true of Herbert's *The Temple*, his spiritual writings are intended to comfort and instruct those who read them.

These writings are very much products of their time. Words and phrases, concepts and expressions often strike twentieth-century readers as antiquarian and drive many to footnotes, glossaries, and the *Oxford Dictionary* for clarification. But these writings also have something of a timeless quality. They are powerful to move the patient reader and to bring heaven to earth and earth to heaven. Not without reason has Meditation 17 of the *Devotions*, with its magnificent affirmation, "No Man is an Iland, intire of it selfe," caught the imagination and inspired the admiration of moderns concerned with alienation, prejudice, war and terror. And who can read sonnets such as "Death be not proud," and "Batter my heart, three person'd God," without rising excitement and growing gratitude? John Donne belongs to the seventeenth century, and to the twentieth, and to eternity.

I have chosen some of the best of Donne's spiritual writings, most of the *Divine Poems*, some of the sermons, or major portions of some sermons, and some of the *Devotions Upon Emergent Occasions* and prayers. The selection was made with this series in mind and with John Donne in mind, as, I trust, the Introduction demonstrates. I will be satisfied if this selection entices many to read further in Donne's works.

I wish to note my indebtedness to students of the Episcopal Divinity School who participated in my courses on George Herbert, John Donne, and T. S. Eliot. In particular, I think of those who were enrolled in courses on Donne whose contributions through discussions and by means of papers contributed to my understanding of the poet-preacher. Further back in time there was the beneficent influence of Horton Davies, my supervisor at Princeton, who taught me the importance of liturgy and literature to the study of ecclesiastical history. Then too, I am grateful to the Folger Shakespeare Library, to Louis Wright and O. B. Hardison for their support and encouragement. And, clearly, without the support of the School of Theology, and of its dean, Robert Giannini, I would not have been able to do the work this book required. Thanks are due to Paul Stanwood for writing the Preface, to Catherine Louise Booty for her expert secretarial assistance, to James Anderson for his proofreading, and to John Farina of Paulist Press. It has been an honor for me to serve as a member of the editorial board of the series from its inception many years and many volumes ago.

Preface

John Donne belongs to that astonishingly rich period of the English church when theological controversy, worship and liturgy, literature and devotion seem all at once marvelously to burst forth in splendid profusion and abundance. We think immediately of other poet-priests such as George Herbert and Robert Herrick, of the great work of Richard Hooker, the sermons of Lancelot Andrewes, the devotional writing of John Cosin and Jeremy Taylor, the deeply meditative work of such laymen as Sir Thomas Browne—and also of the *Book of Common Prayer* itself and the King James Version of the Bible. Throughout all of this work and translation, we may detect an essentially Anglican character; and this present edition of Donne's religious poetry and selections from his prose well reminds us of that distinctiveness. Within this work, indeed, we may discover one means of understanding and defining Anglican spirituality.

In *The Spirit of Anglicanism*, William J. Wolf writes of "an incarnational piety" that has always dominated Anglicanism (Wilton, CT: Morehouse-Barlow, 1979, p. 178). Anglicanism has, in a way, appropriated the Feast of the Nativity as a celebration of its own particular ethos. Andrewes, for example, preached more sermons for Christmas day than for any other occasion. Of Donne's 160 surviving sermons, the Christmas sermon for 1621, on John 1:8, is one of the most eloquent, and it appropriately begins this present collection. Donne loved to preach and to meditate on those "wingy mysteries of divinity," as Sir Thomas Browne calls the great Christian events: the incarnation, the resurrection and ascension, the trinity, the redemption and atonement, the Last Things—the several doctrines of revealed theology, salvation, and eschatology. But the most fundamental of all doctrines is the incarnation, and for this greatest of Christian paradoxes, the mystery of God made manifest in the flesh, Donne reserves his deepest sympathy.

In a broad sense, the incarnation informs the idea of time and eternity, of finitude and infinity. In expressing his love for "the still point," Donne commonly uses imagery expressing linear progress (lines) or spherical motion (circles); these images, in turn, define the conception and clarify the form of many of his works, which we see illustrated in this edition. Let us briefly reflect on some of them, especially the *La Corona* sonnet sequence (?1608), next "Upon the Annunciation and Passion falling upon one day. 1608," then "Goodfriday, 1613. Riding Westward." In each work, Donne's perception of the doctrine of the incarnation is fundamental to his composition, which exploits the familiar geometrical images. We should first of all recall two passages from the sermons.

In a Lenten sermon of 1621, on 1 Timothy 3:16, "Great is the mystery of godliness: God was manifest in the flesh," Donne declares:

Here is the compass, that the essential Word of God, the Son of God, *Christ Jesus,* went: He was God, *humbled in the flesh;* he was Man, *received into glory.* Here is the compasse that the written Word of God, *went,* the Bible; that begun in *Moses,* in darknesse, in the *Chaos;* and it ends in Saint *John,* in clearnesse, in a Revelation. Here is the compass of all time, as time was distributed in the Creation, *Vespere et mane;* darknesse, and then light: the Evening and the Morning made the Day; Mystery and Manifestation make the Text. (*Sermons,* ed. George R. Potter and Evelyn M. Simpson, Berkeley, Univ. of California Press, 1953–62, 3:206)

In comparing the word of God to a compass, Donne seems to have in mind not only the notion of circumscription and measure, but also the instrument used for describing circumferential figures. But God is also portrayed as the center of all circles, as well as a circle, which is endless: "Fixe upon God any where, and you shall finde him a Circle; He is with you now, when you fix upon him; He was with you before, for he brought you to this fixation; and he will be with you hereafter, for *He is yesterday, and to day, and the same for ever.* (Potter and Simpson, 7:52)

The *La Corona* sonnets are reflections upon events in the life of the

Blessed Virgin Mary from the annunciation to the ascension, offered as a "crown of prayer and praise." Together they form a circlet on the earthly life of Christ and the poet's relationship to that life. The sonnets are formally organized in a circle, the last line of each sonnet forming the first line of the next, so that the first line of sonnet 1 is thus the last line of the final sonnet 7. The events occur in their natural, historical order, beginning with a celebration of the completeness of all the events that crown our ends, "For, at our end begins our endlesse rest." Donne sees the incarnation in terms both of a particular event in which Christ's spatial life becomes conterminous with mankind, and also an event which never has occurred in measurable time. The Crown is circular, but the poet, speaking on behalf of all of us, is straight; yet his aim is to fasten himself in a place where finite and infinite meet.

The poet's prayer is thus to behold this circle and to live within it. While he has carefully portrayed this circle of prayer and praise, it is truly of Christ's describing, who is, after all, at the center. Donne writes of this process in a sermon:

If you carry a Line from the Circumference, to the Circumference againe, as a Diameter, it passes the Center, it flowes from the Center, it looks to the Center both wayes. God is the Center; The Lines above, and the Lines below, still respect and regard the Center; Whether I doe any action honest in the sight of men, or any action acceptable to God, whether I doe things belonging to this life, or to the next, still I must passe all through the Center, and direct all to the glory of God, and keepe my heart right, without variation towards him. (Potter and Simpson, 9:406–07)

The sonnets on "Annunciation" and "Nativitie" (nos. 2 and 3 of the sequence) play wittily on this circumference, "That All, which alwayes is All every where," but which "yeelds himselfe to lye / In prison, in thy wombe; . . . Ere by the spheares time was created, thou / Wast in his minde, who is thy Sonne, and Brother." The last line of this sonnet (and the first of the next) further urge the paradox of "*Immensitie cloysterd in thy deare wombe,*" or, as Richard Crashaw would later say, "Eternity shut in a span." Incarnational time is impossible to understand without recourse to paradox, for "Love's architecture is his own."

"Upon the Annunciation and Passion," which observes the unusual coincidence of Lady Day and Good Friday (that is, March 25), depends upon a similar point, on the incarnational moment both in and out of time. Addressing his soul, Donne realizes that

5

PREFACE

Shee sees him man, so like God made in this,
That of them both a circle embleme is,
Whose first and last concurre. . .

First and last, receiving and giving, rejoicing and grieving, Mary is in "Orbitie," hearing both "Of the'Angels *Ave*'and *Consummatum est.*" Like the *La Corona* sequence, this poem, too, relies on the circle whose informing center is the incarnate Word that radiates the intimate immensity joined "in one / Manhoods extremes," where life and death, time and eternity coalesce, and "As in plaine Maps, the furthest West is East."

Both the sonnets of *La Corona* and the occasional poem, "Upon the Annunciation and Passion" depend so obviously on incarnational time that the familiar paradoxes seem hardly to admit of any additional development. But in "Goodfriday, 1613. Riding Westward," Donne manages to explore these fundamental ideas more elaborately and sensitively. Perhaps this poem succeeds so remarkably well because its doctrine is less obvious and the poet's personal relationship to his material is both more varied and dramatic. "Let mans Soule be a Spheare," Donne begins; for, in such a form, he is affected by influences external to himself. So is it that on this day of Christ's Passion, the poet's business takes him in a direction he would not really wish to go.

In riding west, where God's Son is setting, his inclination is to move east, where he would instead see the Son rising, and "by rising set, / And by that setting endlesse day beget." While Donne's linear motion is west, his real direction is east. But the directions meet, as he has already shown in "Upon the Annunciation and Passion." Donne's achievement in the Good Friday poem grows out of the sense he gives in it of motion, straight and circular, and of the merging of these motions both in the incarnate God and in himself, the poet-traveler who struggles to comprehend God.

In portraying his own time, Donne also expresses the divine time within which he is journeying. The poem is organized in two twenty-line parts, with two lines, in the exact center, separating them:

Could I behold those hands which span the Poles,
And tune all spheares at once, peirc'd with those holes?

One is reminded of the diameter touching the circumference: "I must passe all through the Center, and direct all to the glory of God, and keepe my heart right, without variation towards him." Here equidistant from the beginning and the ending of the poem is the center of the sphere, which figuratively surrounds it and sees in one place the poet's westward journey of the first ten lines along with his eastward direction of the final ten lines; yet both directions meet no matter how one undertakes to measure or describe them. We have discovered the infinite in the finite, the point where the incarnation embraces time, where hands control spheres. Even the final words of the poem support this idea; "I'll turne my face" suggests physical rotation, as if to mark a circle, and the change in direction is not only a "turn" but a conversion, a return to God.

Finally, let us recall *Devotions Upon Emergent Occasions*. Donne's reflections on his own sickness, set out into twenty-three "stations," or steps, and digested into Meditations, Expostulations, and Prayers may profitably be studied in similar terms. In the *Devotions*, Donne contemplates mortality and corruption, but always under the eye of eternity and within the view of the incarnate God. In the first of the prayers, near the beginning of the book, Donne writes:

O Eternal and most gracious God, who, considered in thyself, art a circle, first and last, and altogether; but, considered in thy working upon us, art a direct line, and leadest us from our beginning, through all our ways, to our end, enable me by thy grace to look forward to mine end, and to look backward too, to the considerations of thy mercies afforded me from the beginning. . .

Thus has Donne set out on another pilgrimage, while remembering, nevertheless, that his end may be only the place he would start from, whence he should return again. Donne is writing circumferentially, circumscriptively, comprehensively; and in Meditation XIV, he takes up his common theme:

If we consider eternity, into that time never entered; eternity is not an everlasting flux of time, but time is a short parenthesis in a long period; and eternity had been the same as it is, though time had never been. If we consider, not eternity, but perpetuity; not that which had no time to begin in, but which shall outlive time, and be when time shall be no more, what a minute is the life of the durablest creature compared to that!

Yet the whole work, encompassed by God, is about time and eternity, wherein Donne encounters the incarnate Word which overshadows the ordinary words of his own passing life.

Let us return to another of the sermons, appropriately one for Christmas, where Donne joins eternity and finite time, the everlastingness which contains each one of us; for Donne ever delights in elaborating this incarnational theme with fascination, with longing, and with tenderness. He preached on Christmas day at St. Paul's in 1626, on Luke 2:29–30, "Lord, now lettest thou thy servant depart in peace, according to thy Word: for mine eyes have seen thy salvation":

The whole life of Christ was a continuall Passion; others die Martyrs, but Christ was born a Martyr. He found a *Golgotha,* (where he was crucified) even in Bethlem, where he was born; For, to his tendernesse then, the strawes were almost as sharp as the thornes after; and the Manger as uneasie at first, as his Crosse at last. His birth and his death were but one continuall act, and his Christmas-day and his Good Friday, are but the evening and morning of one and the same day. (Potter and Simpson, VII:279)

So eternity flows into perpetuity. We may leave Donne who, at the conclusion of "Deaths Duell," leaves all of us "in that *blessed dependancy,* to *hang* upon Him that *hangs* upon the Crosse."

Introduction

I

A Brief Life[1]

John Donne was born in 1572, sometime between January 24 and June 19. His father was of Welsh descent, a citizen of London and, before his death in 1576, Warden of the Company of Ironmongers, a position of prominence. Donne's mother, Elizabeth Heywood, was descended from an eminent Roman Catholic family. Her father was John Heywood, the epigrammatist, who married Joan, daughter of John Rastell. Rastell was an author and printer, married to the sister of Sir Thomas More. Donne's grandfather, John Heywood, fled from England to Louvain in 1564, while two of his sons, Ellis and Jasper, became members of the Society of Jesus. Donne's mother was a loyal member of this distinguished, if controversial, family and a devout Roman Catholic. Along with five other children who survived after the death of their father, Donne thus grew up in a recusant family. Shortly after the death of her husband, Donne's mother married John Symadges, an Oxford doctor of physic who had been president of the Royal College of Physicians. Nothing certain is known of Symadges' religious commitments, but given what we know of Donne's mother, there is reason to assume that he was of "the old religion."

In 1581 Jasper Heywood came to England as a Jesuit missionary, was captured and imprisoned in December, 1583. Tried and condemned the following February, he was then committed to the Tower of London. The effect of this on Donne can only be conjectured, but it cannot be doubted that he knew of the travail being endured by the Jesuits, including members of his own family.

On October 23, 1584, John, with his younger brother Henry, matriculated at Hart Hall, Oxford. Such an early matriculation (he was but eleven at the time) was not unusual for children of recusant families. The law required that all pursuing university degrees acknowledge royal supremacy over the church, and Oxford required such subscription of all

11

students over sixteen years of age, something those committed to papal allegiance could not do. Thus the sons of recusants arrived at Oxford young enough to complete their university education before the age of sixteen. At Oxford Donne studied the fundamentals of good learning according to the medieval *trivium* and *quadrivium*. Of that we can be certain, but we know little more of Donne's time at Oxford. It is possible, as Izaak Walton asserts, that Donne studied at Cambridge for a time, but there is no independent evidence to support this claim. His university education seems to have extended to 1589—encompassing the customary five years—ending with travels on the continent between 1589 and 1591.

In 1592, after a year's preparation at Thavies Inn, John Donne was admitted to Lincoln's Inn, to study law. There he stayed until 1594, in a place where his relatives, from Sir Thomas More to John Heywood, had studied before him. In 1593 Donne was dealt a severe blow by the arrest, imprisonment, and death of his brother Henry. The younger Donne, presumably a student at Thavies Inn, was seized when a Roman Catholic priest, William Harrington, was discovered in his rooms. The priest suffered a traitor's death, but Henry died of the plague at Newgate prison.

It was about this time, not surprisingly, that Donne began a serious examination of the controversy between Rome and Canterbury. He was entering upon a time of confusion, separating himself from his recusant heritage but not yet committed to anything else. He examined the religious choices before him and found that neither Roman Catholicism nor the reformed catholicism of the Church of England was satisfactory. As R. C. Bald has commented, "His natural inclination to scepticism was for a time reinforced by a mood of cynicism in which he flaunted his sense of insecurity."[2]

Donne's gradual conversion from his ancestral religion to the Church of England can be dated from his Lincoln's Inn years. The transition was influenced by many things, such as the death of his brother, the onset of scepticism, perhaps in one degree fashionable among educated young men interested in worldly things, and his eventual examination of the controversies of the time. He would have been, so it seems, susceptible to the influence of such powerful figures as King James and such prominent divines as Lancelot Andrewes. Furthermore, the division among English recusants concerning how much loyalty was due to the papacy and how much to the monarch, with many compromising their religious commitments in order to retain their family possessions, would have raised questions in Donne's mind and thus influenced his own convictions. It is to be noted that his recusant mother seemingly suffered no persecution, nor did she leave all her possessions and seek refuge abroad.

During his time at Lincoln's Inn, Donne became known as a man-about-town, a frequenter of theaters and taverns, and an admirer of fair women. He was increasingly known as a poet, the author of verse epistles, elegies, love poems, and the first two of his satires. Ben Jonson admired the elegy called "The Bracelet. Upon the loss of his Mistresses Chaine," which begins:

Not that in colour it was like thy haire,
For Armelets of that thou maist let me weare:
Nor that thy hand it oft embraced and kist,
For so it had that good, which oft I mist:
Nor for that silly old moralitie,
That as these linkes are tyed, our love should bee. . .

Such verse was pointedly secular, but even here the hold of religion upon him is evident, for sceptic though he was, his mind was formed under the influence of strong, dogmatic faith, that of his devout mother. He knew what he meant by "that sillie old moralitie." While writing such verse he studied the law but felt no compulsion to pursue a legal career. If anything, his sights were set higher, on preferment in the royal court rather than in a court of law.

During 1596–1597, Donne pursued this "higher" goal by means of military adventure, in the service of the Earl of Essex. In June of 1596 he was a volunteer on the expedition against Cadiz, and in 1597 he was with Essex in the Azores. Neither was a notable success and the latter expedition was undoubtedly a failure, dogged by poor weather, faulty planning, and bad luck. At the end of these adventures Donne gained neither financial reward nor knighthood. In his poem "The Calme," Donne indicated that he had been moved to engage in the expeditions by "hope of gaine," the need to escape from entrapping amours, and a thirst for adventure. There was little if any financial gain, but there was some escape and some adventure.

By November, 1597, Donne was back in London. Thomas Egerton, whom he had probably known at Lincoln's Inn and who was his companion on the second expedition, now came to Donne's assistance. The eldest son of the Lord Keeper of the Great Seal of England, he informed his father, also Thomas Egerton, of John Donne's desire to enter the great man's service. As a result Donne became secretary to Sir Thomas Egerton, the elder, occupying a post of distinction with a promising future, since the Lord Keeper chose only talented men as his secretaries, men such as he could promote for advancement at court. Egerton presided over the Upper House of Parliament, served as intermediary between the crown and parliament, was engaged as a prominent member of the Queen's Privy Council, passed on all documents requiring the Great Seal, presided over the Court of Star Chamber, and was a member of the Court of High Commission. He was known to be a conscientious, efficient public servant. Donne would have been involved in all aspects of his employer's occupations. He seemingly acquitted himself in an exemplary manner. Donne, the man-about-town, military adventurer, was now becoming a familiar figure at court, still a wit, a versifier, an admirer of fair women, but somewhat more sober and self-contained, as befitted his new station in life.

While in Egerton's employ Donne met Ann More, who was the daughter of Sir George More, one of Queen Elizabeth's favorites. She was the niece of Elizabeth, widow of Sir John Wolley, whom Egerton took as his second wife in October, 1597. Lady Egerton had Ann, then about fourteen, under her care at York House, Egerton's London residence. There Donne met her and the two fell in love. Lady Egerton died in January, 1600, and Ann More left London for her father's estate in the country. Donne could not hope to marry Ann with her father's blessing. His inheritance was gone, his advancement at court was only just beginning (in 1601 he was made a member of Parliament, but this could not be regarded as sufficient by Sir George More), and he had a reputation as a gallant, a womanizer, and the author of risqué love poems.

Determined to marry Ann, Donne planned and plotted and in October, 1601, when Ann accompanied her father to London, the two met secretly, and about three weeks before Christmas were married in a clandestine ceremony. A short time later Ann returned with her father to Losely, his country estate, to await the time when her husband would break the news to her father and claim her as his own. Donne delayed, uncertain how to proceed. He was in danger, having married a minor, the daughter of a prominent and wealthy family, without her father's consent. Both canon law and the rules of society had been violated. When More did at last learn the truth, he was irate. He had Donne imprisoned, saw to it that Sir Thomas Egerton dismissed his secretary, and sought to have the marriage annulled. From the Fleet Donne wrote pleading letters to More and Egerton. The Lord Keeper stood firm. More began to relent. Donne was released from prison, the marriage was declared valid, a final judgment being delivered in April, 1602. But More would not provide financial support and could not convince Egerton to restore Donne to his secretarial position. Man and wife found refuge with Sir Francis Wolley at his estate of Pyrford, not far from Guildford. Save for support from such friends as Wolley, Donne was destitute and without any promising future.

From 1602 until his taking holy orders in 1615, Donne was virtually out of the mainstream of society, living in dignified semi-poverty, supporting a growing family as best he could, courting the good will of the wealthy and the powerful, still driven by ambition, still seeking security. At Pyrford he lived peaceably, studying civil and canon law, among other subjects, corresponding with friends, and assisting Wolley with his estates. In 1605 a third child was born.

In 1606 Donne moved with his family to a house at Mitcham, near London, where he was to make his home for the next five years. This was a time of increasing activity, difficult to chronicle. Bald summarizes:

Donne was in London as often as with his wife and family at Mitcham; he followed the Court and cultivated patrons and patronesses; he devoted laborious hours of study and research to problems of divinity and canon law; and while he addressed poems to great ladies and theological pamphlets to the King, he also cultivated a certain Bohemianism in his leisure hours and liked to relax in the company of wits and writers.[3]

In this period four more children arrived and Ann began to show the strain of frequent childbearing. Donne suffered from ill health and his mind was agitated. Much of his best known religious verse was written during the Mitcham years, including *A Litanie*, written during an illness, his *La Corona*, written for Magdalen Herbert, and most of his *Holy Sonnets*. At the same time his friendship with the influential Lucy, Countess of Bedford, developed, Donne writing flattering verses for her.

During the Mitcham years Donne was immersed in theological conflict. Thomas Morton, Dean of Gloucester, to be Bishop of Durham, a theologian who wrote numerous works in defense of the Church of England against the Church of Rome, encouraged Donne to join him in the cause. Donne wrote his *Pseudo-Martyr* (1610) in which he sought to persuade wavering Roman Catholics to accept the Oath of Allegiance to King James I. In this he showed some sympathy for those related by faith to his own family. But in his *Pseudo-Martyr* and in his next writing, *Ignatius his Conclave* (1611), he vehemently attacked the Jesuits. One should also take into account his *Biathanatos*, written but not published at this time, an exploration of suicide and, like the *Pseudo-Martyr* and the *Ignatius*, a questing for the solution to a knotty theological problem. Writes Bald:

His religious sense was steadily deepening. "If at any time I seem to studie you more inquisitively," he wrote to his friend [Goodyer], "it is for no other end but to know how to present you to God in my prayers, and what to ask of him for you." About the same time he was also asserting that "Two of the most precious things which God hath afforded us here . . . are a thirst and inhiation after the next life, and a frequency of prayer and meditation in this."[4]

The *Pseudo-Martyr* was widely read and admired. Morton and the King urged Donne to seek ordination, to drop his ambition for preferment at court, and to allow the King to prefer him in the church.

Donne was not prepared to take such a decisive step. The memory of past sins, the doubting of present worth, the yearning after worldly glory conspired within him to delay ordination four more years, to allow for the pursuit of fame and fortune and the fulfillment of long-held dreams. In 1611 Donne accepted the patronage of the wealthy and influential Sir Robert Drury of Hawstead in Suffolk, and wrote his famed *Anniversaries* in memory of Sir Robert's daughter Elizabeth, whom Donne had never met. Among the most memorable lines are these:

> Shee, shee is dead; shee's dead: when thou knowest this,
> Thou knowest how poore a triffling thing man is.
> And learn'st thus much of our Anatomee,
> The heart being perish'd, no part can be free.
> And that except thou feed (not banquet) on
> The supernatural food, Religion,
> Thy better Growth growes withered, and scant;
> Be more then man, or thou'rt less than an Ant.[5]

Such verse, written for their daughter, made a profound impression on Sir Robert and Lady Drury.

Donne accompanied Drury to the continent on a journey lasting from July, 1611, to September, 1612. On their return Donne moved his household again, this time to a house owned by Sir Robert in Drury Lane. As time passed his frustration grew. Drury's patronage did nothing to satisfy his ambition. Morton and the King were still pressing him to seek preferment in the church. Donne made one last attempt, this time through the influence of Robert Ker, who in 1611 became Viscount Rochester, but this ultimately was to no avail. In the winter of 1613/14 Donne's plight worsened. He was seriously ill, half-blind, and his children in the grip of an epidemic. Ann miscarried and "confessed herself to be extremely sick." Death was all around and Donne's finances were in a pitiable state. All the while he was studying, concentrating on divinity as if in preparation for ordination, perfecting his knowledge of Hebrew and Greek, and writing, among other things the pieces that were to be his *Essays in Divinity*, completed around 1614. Donne called these essays "sermons" and in them wrote in a style that was meditative, a preparation for worship, concerned with the traditional four-fold interpretation of the scriptures and the rhetoric appropriate to preaching. In writing the essays Donne was beginning his entrance into the priestly vocation.

John Donne was ordained to both the diaconate and the priesthood on January 23, 1615, by John King, Bishop of London. Having taken the decisive step he now looked for the promised preferment. His ambition had not diminished but had rather shifted from court to church. First he was appointed Chaplain-in-Ordinary to the King and thus had an entrance to the court. Next, Donne was made Doctor of Divinity at Cambridge, this by royal mandate, causing some heads of colleges to complain. There followed country benefices, the rectory of Keyston in Huntingdon and the rectory of Sevenoaks in Kent, both in the King's gift.

In the autumn of 1616 Donne received a much more important preferment, being made Divinity Reader of Lincoln's Inn, at the Inns of Court. Twenty-one of his sermons preached there have survived, including the justly praised series of sermons on Psalm 38. But it was as he was beginning his ministry in earnest that his wife, Ann, bore a stillborn child and herself died on August 15, 1617. Mr. Bald comments:

However much he had suffered during the years of his married life, his marriage itself had been a source of sustenance and comfort to him ... He repaid her love not only with his own but with gratitude as well; "we had not one another at so cheap a rate," he wrote in 1614, "as that we should ever be weary with one another."[6]

Donne did not marry again. As we shall have cause to note, Ann's death provided a significant turning point in John Donne's life. Thereafter he possessed a deepening sense of priestly vocation.

In May of 1619 Donne accompanied James Hay, Viscount Doncaster, as chaplain on an embassy to Germany seeking for some settlement of the troubles there which historians now regard as the beginning of the disastrous Thirty Years War. Donne was apprehensive at his departure, knowing that his children were not adequately provided for, and sensing that this time he might depart but not return. He bade farewell to the Benchers at Lincoln's Inn and wrote his "Hymne to Christ, at the Authors last going into Germany," with its expressions of anxiety, fear of shipwreck, and dread of drowning. The embassy accomplished little, ending on January 1, 1620, with the return to London of the considerable entourage.

Donne returned to his duties at Lincoln's Inn to await further promotion. It was thought at one time that he would be made Dean of Salisbury, but instead when Valentine Carey, Dean of St. Paul's Cathedral, London, was consecrated Bishop of Exeter, Donne was installed as Dean of St. Paul's on November 22, 1621. In addition he was presented to the Prebendary of Chiswick, and resigned his position at Lincoln's Inn and the rectory of Keyston. With a decade of his life left to him, Donne had now reached the pinnacle of his clerical career and was relieved of the financial problems that had dogged him most of his life. He did not, however, cease to be concerned about finances. One rather disturbing incident involved his angry treatment of his son-in-law, Edward Alleyn, who kept badgering Donne for money—quite legitimately it seems. Their conflict was one of contrary temperaments but, as Bald says, one can sense "in Donne's behaviour the attitudes of a man who for years had had to struggle to make ends meet and was still not fully used to affluence; hence his reluctance to part easily with even what he had promised to bestow."[7]

During his final years Donne was busy as a well-known preacher at St. Paul's, at St. Dunstan's in the West, which he acquired in 1624, and as a pastor and respected church divine. He was also afflicted, as he had been many times previously, by illness. In 1623 he was the victim of what is now diagnosed as a "relapsing fever." One characteristic of the fever is that in the five to seven days during which it runs its course the victim is mentally alert although physically weak. As he lay in his bed he made notes, and during his convalescence wrote his *Devotions upon Emergent Occasions*. The phases of his illness provided the outline for his spiritual self-examination and meditation. He contemplated his death—his soul, his God—and rejoiced in his faith, the spiritual health that persisted through travail. It was also at this time that Donne wrote two of his most mature and satisfactory religious poems, the "Hymne to God the Father" and his "Hymne to God my God, in my sicknesse." The former implies a resolution of Donne's spiritual turmoil ("And, having done that, Thou haste done, / I have no more") reminiscent of the resolution found in George Herbert's "Love (III)." The latter hymn anticipates the final resolution ("Since I am comming to that Holy roome, / Where, with thy Quire of Saints for evermore, / I shall be made thy Musique").

Donne was never well, but between bouts of sickness from 1625 to his death he was active and involved at court and in the church. He continued a rigorous program of reading and writing. Walton said, "his bed was not able to detain him beyond the hour of four in the morning; and it was no common business that drew him out of his church till past ten. All which time he was employed in study."[8] During the plague in London Donne sought refuge with Sir John and Lady Danvers (Magdalen Herbert) in Chelsea and conversed with George Herbert, who was then struggling with his own vocation to holy orders. While at Chelsea Donne prepared sermons for publication.

On March 27, 1625, King James died. At St. James' Palace, where the king's son and heir, Charles, had been residing, John Donne preached the first sermon heard by Charles after his accession to the throne. On February 2, 1626, the coronation took place and a few days later Parliament assembled. As was customary, a meeting of the Convocation of Canterbury began. Donne served as Prolocutor, presiding over the lower house of Convocation, and delivered a Latin oration before both houses, that of the bishops and that of the other clergy.[9] Shortly after Convocation began, Donne preached his yearly Lenten sermon at court, a sermon well liked by King Charles who urged that it be printed. Thus Donne kept to a busy round of duties. maintaining a moderately high-church tradition in opposition to Puritanism, and saying, "Rituall, and Ceremoniall things move not God, but they exalt that Devotion, and they conserve that Order, which does move him."[10]

From 1628 on Donne contended with numerous bouts of illness. By 1630 his health was seriously impaired and he spent an extended period of time in the country. In December he made his will, providing for his mother and six surviving children. In January, 1631, his mother died. He had cared for her for some time. We do not know how she had adjusted to her son's departure from the faith she held dear, but their life together suggests the possibility of some degree of understanding. In February Donne returned to London to preach at Whitehall on the first Friday in Lent. He was very weak and his friends were alarmed, but he persisted and gave the sermon called "Death's Duell." Donne *"preach't his own Funeral Sermon,"* says Walton. The final words of the most renowned preacher of the day in England were words of hope. He was confident in the promise contained in Christ's resurrection. "There bathe in his [Christ's] tears, there suck at his wounds, and lie down in peace in his grave, till he vouchsafe you a resurrection, and an ascension into that Kingdom, which he hath purchased for you, with the inestimable blood."

Donne died on March 31, 1631, and was buried in his cathedral. Among the many tributes written at the time was "An Elegie upon the death of the Deane of Pauls, Dr. Iohn Donne," which concluded with an epitaph. Thomas Carey, its author, proposed it as appropriate to adorn Donne's tomb. It is memorable for its concise summation of Donne's life and points toward an understanding of the man's spirituality:

> Here lies a King, that rul'd as hee thought fit
> The universall Monarchy of wit;
> Here lie two Flamens, and both those, the best,
> Appollos first, at last, the true Gods Priest.

II

Donne's Spiritual Journey

John Donne's life was a journey marked, as Thomas Carey said, by "two Flamens, and both those, the best, Apollos first, at last, the true Gods Priest." But there was no great gulf fixed between Jack Donne, the poet, would-be courtier, and John Donne, the preacher, man of prayer. Rather there was continuity, as John Chudleigh observed in his elegy on Donne:

> He kept his loves, but not his objects, wit
> He did not banish, but transplanted it,
> Taught in his place and use, and brought it home
> To Pietie, which it doth best become.

His spiritual journey can be likened to an ascent in which there is a gradual conversion of objects. For the early Donne the fire of love was directed toward some earthly object, sometimes in the light of the divine; for the later Donne the fire of love burned for God, understood, often perceived in relation to earthly phenomena.

Murray Rosten writes that in his religious verse Donne had in fact, "not repudiated his earlier concerns, but allowed those themes submerged in his secular verse to rise to the surface and gain a new prominence in their religious setting. For even in the most outrageous and apparently blasphemous gestures of his early poetry, when his lovers, clasped in erotic embrace, had invoked the sacraments of the church to image forth their love, the effect had been, in Donne's delicate handling, a purification of the earthly rather than a sullying of the divine."[1] Rosten rightly perceives in such a poem as "The Expiration," not explicitly but surely there, a profound "concern with death and the eternity of the soul." This should not be surprising given Donne's roots in a devout recusant family and an education which inculcated Counter-Reformation piety.

21

INTRODUCTION

The piety of his youth affected Donne's elegies, songs, and sonnets, as Rosten suggests, and it also influenced his divine poems and his sermons. There is a relationship between such a secular poem as "The Extasie,"

> Where, like a pillow on a bed,
>   A pregnant banke swel'd up, to rest
> The violets reclining head,
>   Sat we two, one anothers best;
>
> Our hands were firmly cimented
>   With a fast balme, which thence did spring,
> Our eye-beames twisted, and did thred
>   Our eyes, upon one double string. . . .

and the *Holy Sonnet*, "Batter my heart three person'd God," with its conclusion:

> Take mee to you, imprison mee, for I
> Except you'enthrall mee, never shall be free,
> Nor ever chast, except you ravish mee.

The connection is in the sexual imagery which draws upon Christian mysticism. In such mysticism, ecstasy figures prominently and concerns the separation of body from soul with a heightened awareness of God, persons, and objects. Teresa of Avila found in sexual ecstasy the most adequate analogy to spiritual ecstasy. Francis de Sales urged Christians to look on human love as a reflection, fainter but nevertheless real, of divine love. That this tradition carried over into Protestant religious thought to some degree at least, is to be seen in Donne's own poetry, but also in the writings of the indubitably Protestant Richard Baxter.

Considering the analogy of human, sexual love to divine love and the Christian spiritual mystical experience, one discerns a profound continuity between Donne and his predecessors. In contrast to Calvinistic theology which sees a great gulf fixed between grace and nature, the catholic tradition emphasized by Lancelot Andrewes, the sixteenth/seventeenth century Anglican divine whose writings influenced Donne, asserted that grace came not to destroy nature but to perfect it.[2] As Richard Hooker taught, nature is God's precious creation, marred by corruption and deficient as a result of human sin, but it is nevertheless God's own beloved possession; the light of reason is dim but it has not been extinguished;

INTRODUCTION

grace presupposes nature and reason.[3] Jackson is right in saying, "the poet's image of the spiritual man is entirely built out of images of the natural man."[4] That, according to the tradition represented by Hooker, is as it should be.

Here we have a major principle in John Donne's spirituality. To be spiritual does not require the negation of the earthly but the cleansing and restoring of it to that condition in which God first created it. Jackson makes a somewhat dubious yet nevertheless intriguing point: In his use of the imagery of human love we have evidence that "Donne lived closer to primitive experience than civilized men have generally since his time."[5] Perhaps it would be best to say that Donne lived vitally, conscious of his entire being, his body and his senses as well as his mind and his soul, and did not absolutely separate the natural and the holy in himself. T. S. Eliot remarked that there was no dissociation of sensibility in Donne. "A thought to Donne was an experience; it modified his sensibility."[6] It was also true that his experience and his natural sensibilities impinged on his thought and his spirituality, and this was to him and to others of his time, as it must be in God's economy for all time.

Another evidence of continuity is indicated by Evelyn Simpson. She writes: "Through all his conflicting moods we can trace a thread of purpose which binds together his youth, manhood, and his later years. He was always the seeker, who pursued the truth."[7] She refers to "Satyre III," a product of his youth, written about 1597. There he wrote:

Cragged, and steep, Truth stands, and hee that will
Reach her, about must, and about must goe . . .   (ll.72–81)

In 1611 he wrote "The Second Anniversary" where he said:

Thirst for that time, O my insatiate soule,
And serve thy thirst, with Gods safe-sealing Bowle.
Be thirsty still, and drinke still till thou goe . . .   (ll.45–47)

After his ordination he was questing still, writing "Show me deare Christ, thy spouse, so bright and cleare." Such verses reflect a point of view prominent in the writings of Richard Hooker who finds God's revelation not only in scripture but in and through all creation and through the writings of the great thinkers of history, both pagans and Christians. He wrote: "Whatsoever either men on earth, or the Angels of heaven do know, it is as a drop of that unemptiable fountaine of wisdom, which wisdom hath diversely imparted her treasure unto the world."[8] The human, endowed with reason is, in relation to such rich and diverse revelation, a seeker, who in searching after truth receives, by God's grace, that for which he seeks. Hooker abided by the rule, "in all things . . . are our consciences best resolved, and in most agreeable sort unto God and nature settled, when they are so far persuaded as those grounds of perswasion which are to be had will beare" (*Laws*, II.7.5.). The spiritual life is a life lived out in quest of truth.

There is another factor involved here. The quest for truth is ultimately the quest for salvation. Having stressed the continuity between the natural and the spiritual in Donne, it is necessary now to emphasize that Donne's spiritual journey involved the quest for the power and understanding needed to escape from the prison of sinful worldliness to enjoy the freedom and virtue of "heavenly worldliness." In these terms the spiritual journey is a battle never concluded, demanding rigor and discipline, evoking impassioned cries of alarm and affliction. Both Bald and Gardner, encountering Donne's preoccupation with sin, speak of his melancholy and Bald, drawing on William James' *Varieties of Religious Experience*, speaks of Donne as a "sick soul . . ."[9] Bald identifies Donne's acute melancholy with the Mitcham years, the most trying time, with the implication that thereafter Donne reaches a spiritual resolution and resting place. Rosten disagrees, arguing to the contrary that the "tortured, dissatisfied, and self-searching mood"—the spiritual battle that Bald identifies with Mitcham—"was to be the permanent motive force of both" Donne's "poetry and prose."[10] The seeking—the imperative quest for salvation—never ends.

Late in his life Donne still felt the weight of his sin and the need for forgiveness, and could preach:

When we looke upon our weaknesse and unworthinesse, we cry out. *Wretched men that wee are, who shall deliver us from the body of death?* For though we have the Spirit of life in us, we have a body of death upon us. How loving soever my Soule be, it will not stay in a diseased soul. . . .[11]

Such a dwelling upon sin and death was not unusual in the seventeenth century nor was serious concern for the ultimate disposition of one's soul a sign of sickness. Such a concern was inculcated by the *Book of Common Prayer*, the book which Donne knew and lived into as a member and then as a priest of the Church of England. In accordance with the Prayer Book he would have confessed *daily:*

INTRODUCTION

Almighty and most merciful Father, we have erred and strayed from thy ways, like lost sheep. We have followed too much the devices and desires of our own hearts. We have offended thy holy laws. We have left undone those things which we ought to have done, and we have done those things which we ought not to have done, and there is no health in us. . . .[12]

The spiritual life involved for Donne, in keeping with the times, the cultivation of sincere contrition through self-examination in the presence of God and in the context of scripture and liturgy. It also involved not only hearing of but receiving God's forgiveness, opening the heart to the healing balm of God's love. As the *Book of Common Prayer* put it, God "pardoneth and absolveth all them which truly repent, and unfeignedly believe his holy gospel."[13] Richard Hooker taught that there could be no holy fear without a previent knowledge of divine love. And therefore true repentance depends on the constant realization of divine forgiveness.

We are here confronting not a once-in-a-lifetime experience but rather an endless rhythm of repentance and forgiveness which has its beginnings with birth and baptism, and thus is rooted in God's grace and mercy. In a sermon Donne said: "*God* wrapt mee up in his Covenant, and deriv'd mee from the *Christian* bloud, in my Mothers wombe, and *Christian* milke at my Nurses breast . . ."[14] Evelyn Simpson rightly says that the key to Donne's theology is the love and mercy of God. "Again and again in the sermons he loses himself in rapturous contemplation of the mercy of God."[15] Therefore the spiritual life is a rhythm of contrition and praise, contrition rooted in praise, praise rooted in contrition, in a never-ending spiral whereby through the grace of God the two contrapuntal notes become more completely one, echoing the *Gloria in Excelsis Deo*.[16]

During the Mitcham years, Donne wrote:

I dare not move my dimme eyes any way,
Despaire behind, and death before doth cast
Such terrour, and my febled flesh doth waste
By sinne in it, which it t'wards hell doth weigh . . .[17]

Here is the Prayer Book General Confession made personal. It is as if Donne were saying "there is no health in me." Here he may be thinking not of far distant sins of his youth, but rather of sins of the past still weighing him down, impinging upon his present health, such as, perhaps, his apostasy, the hurt he caused his mother, his lasciviousness, his rampant

INTRODUCTION

ambition, and his dragging Ann, his wife, into poverty with him. But the
next lines reflect Hooker's dictum that there can be no holy fear without
there being first an awareness of holy love.

> Only thou art above, and when towards thee
> By thy leave I can looke, I rise againe . . .   (ll.9–10)

Here he may have had in mind looking upon God on the cross, the Son of
God dying that sinners may know the divine love, feel the cleansing pain
of contrition, and be restored by divine forgiveness. The statement is
emphatic, with no qualifications: "I rise againe." I am forgiven, renewed.
And yet I do not rise from this broken world to life eternal, to the heaven
of heavens quite yet—not till I die. And so he wrote next:

> But our old subtle foe so tempteth me,
> That not one houre I can my selfe sustaine. . . .   (ll.11–12)

There is grace in this statement, grace in the realization of utter dependence upon God, grace in the realization that he can repent again and be
forgiven again if only he will love God and receive God's love, which is to
ask for forgiveness and be forgiven. The final couplet Rosten calls "the
key to Donne's religious writing as a whole."

> Thy Grace may wing me to prevent his art
> And thou like Adamant draw mine iron heart.   (ll.13–14)

That is, God's grace may bear me up and thus frustrate Satan's art, and
God like the lodestone, with a steadfast, attractive power draw me, as a
magnet drawing to itself a bit of iron, in this case drawing, wooing,
winning my cold, hard, stubborn heart. The "Adamant" is grace persistent,
ultimately irresistible, and yet in the context of actual life resisted by those
in Satan's power. The spiritual life is a lifelong struggle whose outcome is
decided, whose end is eternal bliss.

This mood of endless struggle is found not only in the writings of
Donne but also in the works of Herbert, whose great poem sequence is a
record of struggle, of resistance to grace and of yielding to grace. The
mood is there in Henry Vaughan's poems. His poem "Love-sick" is impressive with lines such as this, reminiscent of lines in Donne's *Holy
Sonnets:*

26

INTRODUCTION

So rise and run, as to out-run these skies,
These narrow skies (narrow to me) that barre,
So barre me in, that I am still at warre,
At constant warre with them. O come and rend,
Or bow the heavens! Lord bow them and descend,
And at thy presence make these mountains flow,
These mountains of cold ice in me! Thou art
Refining fire, O then refine my heart . . .

The command here is a sign of devotion, an acknowledgement of power-lessness to save oneself, of utter dependence upon God, and thus it is a recognition of God's grace as alone possessing power to save. The danger is, as Hooker taught, that of over-scrupulosity, "doubting not of God's mercie" but "notwithstanding scrupulous, and troubled with continuall feare, least defects in their own repentence bee a barre against them." (*Laws*, VI.6.17) Donne acknowledged the danger and named it despair. In "A Hymne to God the Father" he wrote, "I have a sinne of feare, that when I'have spunne / My last thred, I shall perish on the shore." Such fear was a part of that against which the faithful must struggle, not once, but on through all of life. The contrite human being must act, following the example of Mary, yielding to God's love, which is to yield to God's will.

Taken as a whole Donne's understanding of the Christian life of repentance and forgiveness, contrition and praise, was in the mainstream of Christian spirituality. It was not particularly exceptional or extreme, but on the whole well-balanced. Evelyn Simpson rightly says:

The conflict in Donne's soul . . . was of the same kind as that endured by Augustine and many others of the saints. It finds a parallel in St. Paul's words, "I delight in the law of God after the inward man; but I see another law in my members, warring against the law of my mind, and bringing me into captivity to the law of sin which is in my members"; and Donne could have repeated the Apostle's outburst, "O wretched man that I am! Who shall deliver me from the body of this death?"[18]

Having emphasized the continuities in Donne's spiritual journey, it is now necessary to speak of development on the journey. Judah Stampfer writes of "stages of unfolding" in Donne's life.[19] What he has in mind is "a process of inner baking" whereby there is a "gradual washing away of superficial excitements . . . in preparation for an utter engagement." Janel Mueller has another way of describing Donne's development. She likens

27

him to Augustine of Hippo whose writings Donne knew well and often quoted. Donne was like Augustine, being

a man of extraordinary sexual passion, ambition, self-consciousness, and verbal endowments, added to acute intelligence. Both were impelled to worldly experience and enjoyment beyond the impulsions of most men, and both adopted a Christian world-view that placed strong emphasis on the working of God's providence in the particulars of events and objects. . . .[20]

Mueller compares Augustine's *Confessions* to certain of Donne's divine poems and to his *Devotions*. Both men were seekers after truth, both were aware of the depths and reaches of their sin, both came to a deeper consciousness of God's grace and mercy, and both battled through life to claim the inheritance which was theirs as children of God.

There is no denying that there was development. As Judah Stampfer says, there was no violent conversion but rather an "unfolding," "a process of inner baking," not peaceful, as such language might imply, but rather worked out through a chaos of events, "flounderings, evasions, and periodic inactivity," eventually resulting in "a crystallization in a new being."[21]

One of the most helpful descriptions of Donne's spiritual development is provided by Robert Shaw, who traces the poet's spiritual journey by means of his poetry from "Satire Three," which he dates between 1594 and 1597, to the "Hymne to God the Father" and the "Hymne to God my God, in my sicknesse," dated 1623. Shaw's attention is fixed upon Donne's developing sense of vocation. That is to say, he traces Donne's spiritual development from the time when he had renounced allegiance to the Roman Catholic Church to expand "a humanist faith that truth can be determined by reason and embraced by an act of will," to the time when Donne was able to acknowledge the rightness of his priestly vocation and had reconciled the roles of poet and priest ("both their activities are directed to one end: the praise of God").[22] Shaw concludes:

The ease with which the poetic and priestly roles merge points up the degree to which Donne, once settled in his calling, was able to detach himself from his life and view it as an orderly whole. From the vantage point of his deathbed, all his life is seen as preparation for a religious death; in all that he has done or suffered, the mercy of God becomes apparent.[23]

Shaw located the crucial turning point in the poem Donne wrote "To Mr. Tilman after he had taken orders," where the poet states that the much scorned priesthood possesses joys which "passe speach." Shaw remarks on how unusual it is for Donne to be at a loss for words.

This surprising reticence signals a change in tone that overtakes Donne's religious poetry following his ordination. Now he writes with a public in view; one of his conscious motives is to edify an audience. But the adoption of a more public manner may indicate something more than a wish to speak to a broader range of readers, for the later poems show, I believe, some degree of liberation from the straitening egocentricity of the *Holy Sonnets*.[24]

The later poems, the sermons, the *Devotions*, all reflect Donne's continuing struggle, but the mood has changed. Shaw expresses this in part when speaking of the prominence of the doctrine of prevenient grace in the *Holy Sonnets*, with Donne assuming a passive posture for fear of taking initiative not in tune with the will of God, demanding that God act. In the later poems there is a softening of this doctrine of prevenient grace. Says Shaw: "It would be difficult to show that the later Donne holds a doctrine different in substance from the one implied in the *Holy Sonnets*; rather, he comes to view it with hope instead of fear."[25]

There is widespread agreement that Donne reached a stage in his unfolding, in which he knew the peace which comes when hope dominates fear. One need not accept Walton's word on this. A reading of the sermons and of the final poems is convincing enough. That is not to say that Donne altogether ceased seeking for truth or that he was free from all doubt. Faith involves seeking and doubting. There is, as we have seen, a degree of continuity from the Donne of the early satires to the Donne of "Deaths Duell," involving the persistence of seeking, the expression of remorse for past and present sin, the yearning for preferment and for financial security which that involved, and the need for acceptance. Evelyn Simpson has said that: "While Donne ... showed himself a sincere Christian, he can hardly be called a saint. Walton's biography gives us an exquisite portrait, but it omits the flaws in Donne's character, and the admixture of worldliness which we detect in his letters."[26] But history shows that all saints have flaws, for all are humans, far less than gods. And it is specifically the worldliness of Donne and the incarnational spirituality of the man, that many moderns find attractive, helping them to proceed upon their own erratic spiritual journeys in this world.

Judah Stampfer refers to the culmination of Donne's spiritual journey, the poet's will finally subdued to the divine will in God's manifest presence.

His God encountered at last, Donne rose to the epiphany in his last two hymns. Ever the gothic poet his flesh more subdued than ever, he stylizes the parts of his body, abstracts them into symbols; as he moves in skinny flashes toward earth, heaven, oblivion, God's spirit. His earlier comparisons with the world in "The Good-Morrow," "The Sunne Rising," are for rivalry and rejection. In "Hymne to God my God, in my sicknesse," he enacts its destiny in himself. Lying in bed, he hymns the earth, his body, preparing to become God's music, His new found instrument.[27]

One final point. Donne's spiritual journey leads more and more sincerely and deeply into the church. Hooker stated that we are in Christ "by our actual incorporation into that society which hath him for theire head and doth make together with him one body" (*Laws*, V.56.7). Donne shared with Hooker and the Caroline Divines a high view of the church, ordered by word and sacraments as administered by ordained ministers, instruments of God's grace and mercy. In a sermon preached at Heidelberg in 1619 Donne stated emphatically: "Natural men by passing often through the contemplation of nature have such a knowledge of God [that is, the outward evidence of the Book of Creatures]; but the knowledge which is to salvation, is by being in God's house, in the household of the Faithfull, in the Communion of Saints, and by having such a conversation in heaven in this life."[28] Thus, while his spiritual journey is profoundly personal, Donne's spirituality is ultimately corporate—the journey takes place in the company of the faithful, the company in which Word and Sacraments are found and the grace to persist on the journey received.

In such a conviction concerning the church, Donne was in the mainstream of Christian spirituality. The ultimate purpose of the Christian life for Donne was communion with God, in and through the communion of the faithful in the church as Christ's own body, of which Christ is the head.

With such conviction Donne revered the common worship of the people of God, the *Book of Common Prayer,* and the corporate ministry of word and sacraments. He wrote:

I believe in the Holy Ghost, but doe not find him, if I seek him only in private prayer; But in Ecclesia, when I goe to meet him in the Church, when I seeke him where hee hath promised to be found . . . in his Ordinances, and meanes of salvation in his Church, instantly the savour of the Myrrhe is exalted and multiplied upon me.[29]

The full knowledge of salvation through the church and its ministry of word and sacraments seemingly came slowly, gradually, and reached fruition as Donne lived into the ordained priesthood. He said, and must be taken seriously, "I date my life from my Ministry; for I received mercy, as I received the Ministry, as the Apostle speaks."[30]

* * *

In the following sections of this introduction we shall be considering selections from Donne's works according to their different kinds: poems, sermons, *Devotions,* and prayers. We shall be mindful of critical studies and refer to them as appropriate, but my chief concern is to explore poems, sermons, *Devotions,* and prayers as classics of Western spirituality, and thus as helps to those embarked upon spiritual journeys now.

III

The *Divine Poems:* A Meditative Sequence

Most of the attention given to Donne's *Divine Poems* has been concentrated on the *Holy Sonnets*. This is understandable when his poems are approached from a literary point of view. But for those concerned with Donne's spirituality it is important to view the entire landscape of the *Divine Poems* and to realize that the major segments—*La Corona*, the *Holy Sonnets*, *A Litany*, and the final Hymns—comprise a meditative sequence which can serve moderns as a means of fruitful devotion.

Meditative Style:
The Aim is Contrition, Repentance, and Newness of Life

Before reviewing the sequence in detail it is necessary to note the character of sixteenth/seventeenth century meditative style. Donne would have been familiar with Ignatius of Loyola's meditative method as found in the *Exercitia Spiritualia*. The method involved memory, reason, and will, and consisted of preparatory prayer, two preludes (the *compositio loci*, through the imagination seeing some situation or some place, and petition in accordance with the *compositio loci*), the meditation proper in three or five points, and the colloquy—a devotion aroused by the meditation. The memory is active in the preludes, reason in the meditation proper, and the will in the colloquy.

Helen Gardner has analyzed Donne's sonnets of 1613 in terms of the Ignatian method and concludes: "The influence of formal meditation lies behind the *Holy Sonnets*, not as a literary source, but as a way of thinking, a method of prayer."[1] Louis Martz has shown that Donne was influenced by more than the founder of the Society of Jesus, but also by Francis de Sales, who defined meditation as "an attentive thought iterated, or voluntarily intertained in the mynd, to excite the will to holy affections and resolutions."[2] In addition there was *The Arte of Divine Meditation* (1606), written by Donne's acquaintance, Joseph Hall. Hall, like Donne, was a poet as well as a priest. The *Arte* was well-known, having been reprinted in 1606 and 1607 and included in thirteen editions of Hall's *Opera* before his death in 1650.[3] It was Hall who wrote a preface to Donne's *Second Anniversary* and most likely one for the *First* as well. Hall, himself influenced by the *Scala Meditatoria* of Wessell Gansfort as found in Mombaer's *Rosetum* (1494), emphasized the understanding and the affections, with particular concern for the affections. He regarded the arousing of the affections "the very soul of meditation whereto all that is past serveth but as an instrument." In the first part of the meditation, according to Hall, we see (understanding involves sight); in the second part we taste, feel, and are affected by the sweetness or bitterness of our subject. Our passionate response is followed by contrition and results in confession. When thinking of Donne's *Holy Sonnets* it is helpful to ponder Hall's statement:

it is to be duly observed, how the mind is, by turns depressed and lifted up, being lifted up with out estate of Joy, it is cast down with complaint [contrition]; lifted up with Wishes, it is cast down with confession: which order doth best hold it in ure and just temper; and maketh it more feeling of comfort.[4]

After confession comes petition with the request that at God's hands that "which we acknowledge ourselves unable, and none but God able to perform," may come to pass.

The meditative style, as Donne knew it, was respectful of intellect but had as its end or purpose the modification of behavior, to which end poetry, devotions, sermons aimed at arousing the affections. And for this cause there was much consideration of Last Things, of death and judgment, the engendering of holy fear on the basis of an awareness of divine love and mercy, and the cultivation of contrition, defined by Richard Hooker as "a pensive and corrosive desire, that wee had done otherwyse, a desire which suffereth us to forslowe noe tyme, to feele noe quietnes within ourselves . . . till the light of Gods reconciled favour, shine in our darkened soule" (*Laws* VI.3.4).

Douglas Peterson has analysed the *Holy Sonnets* in relation to Richard Hooker's discussion of repentance in Book VI of his *Laws*,[5] and demonstrates, among other things, that these poems reflect the concern on the part of contemporary theology and piety to stimulate a fear of divine punishment for sin, a fear that cannot be beneficial without awareness of divine love. Thus the first six sonnets in the 1633 sequence are intended to arouse holy fear and the last six to make the penitent aware of that love, which in combination with holy fear leads to repentance and newness of life. According to Hooker, God works in the heart by faith to stimulate fear. Hooker then says, "Howbeit when faith hath wrought a feare of the event of sinne, yet repentance hereupon ensueth not, unlesse our beliefe conceive both the possibilitie and the meanes to avert evill. The possibilitie, in as much as God is mercifull . . ." (*Laws*, VI.3.2–3). Hooker had in mind here the penitential sequence of contrition, confession and satisfaction, which is at the very heart of sixteenth/seventeenth century liturgy and piety. The *Book of Common Prayer* as Donne knew it aimed at assisting the faithful to experience penitential renewal and to live by the rhythm of penitence and praise.

The poetry of contrition was concerned to aid people in achieving their deepest desires as the children of God. Hooker spoke to this, and it is as if he were speaking to Donne:

neyther can wee possibly forsake sin, unlesse wee first beginne againe, to love. What is love towards God, but a desire of union with God? And shall wee imagine a sinner converting himselfe to God, in whome there is noe desire of union with God presupposed? I therefore conclude, that feare worketh noe mans inclination to repentance, till somewhat else have wrought in us love alsoe (*Laws*, VI.3.3).

The problem is how to arouse holy fear in the context of holy love, thus avoiding despair and knowing the healing balm of God's forgiveness, rising up by the activity of the Holy Spirit to newness of life. The further problem is how to establish, on the basis of a realistic assessment of human nature, a habit of contrition and repentance which becomes as a heartbeat sustaining new life, realizing communion with God more and more fully. Hooker was well aware of the danger implicit in those who, fearing that they have not repented all, refuse divine forgiveness (*Laws*, VI.6.17)—a fact previously noted. Donne was "much concerned with the sin of diffidence, or its extremer form, despair"[6] and in his melancholy felt its impact. He knew that there was a resolution to the problem, but realizing the comfort of that resolution was something that came to him gradually.

One final preliminary consideration related to meditative style comes from Roger Rollin who argues that the *Holy Sonnets* "seem to have been written mainly for shock effect." That is, they are "intended to vex readers," and are "vexatious in part because they are sick poems in the service of preventative medicine, intended to instruct as well as to entertain."[7] In other words, they were written not only to express the poet's private feelings, but also to instruct readers in the way to go toward communion with God. Stanley Fish observed that George Herbert had a similar aim in *The Temple*. Herbert's method was that of catechesis, influenced by what we have been discussing as meditative style. His was catechesis not by rote but by means of platonic dialogue, and his goal was "the self-discovery of the respondant."[8] Says Fish:

What I am suggesting then is that Herbert's poetry is a strategy, and that as a strategy it shares with the catechistical practice of his parson a shape and a goal: the goal is the involvement of the reader in his own edification . . . and the shape is the bringing of the reader "by questions well ordered" to "that which he knows not."[9]

I propose that the *Divine Poems* of Donne be read as addressed to readers, with the intention of drawing them into a salvific process. That this involves the risk of despair cannot be denied. Furthermore, we must know "that, to be restored, our sickness must grow worse."[10] That is to say, we must realize the full extent of our sins, along with the full extent of God's mercy, if we are to enter fully into new life, into communion with God. Here we shall regard all of the *Divine Poems*, and not just the *Holy Sonnets*, as means towards sincere contrition and repentance. They were written with mind and heart, out of the poet's experience, to assist the faithful in the way of salvation. Let those concerned for literary/critical exactness now regard that which follows as a devotional reading, with a validity of its own.

The Shape of the Divine Poems

There is for the reader an overall shape to the *Divine Poems*, from beginning to end, with occasional poems scattered along the way, not disjunctive but not cohesively related to the main poems of the sequence. *La Corona* is primarily a meditation on Christ, presenting to the reader the subject matter for meditation, reminiscent of "The Sacrifice" in Herbert's *The Temple*. As there were liturgical roots for Herbert's poem so there were for *La Corona*, as, for instance, in the reflections of the *Horae* of the Blessed Virgin Mary found in the section entitled "Annunciation." In the liturgy angels descend with doctrine and ascend with prayer. Here the emphasis is on doctrine, that which David Tracy calls "focal meaning," the "event/gift/grace of Jesus Christ."[11] And yet the focal meaning is never presented without response; without, that is, personal involvement. The subject of meditation is always presented as already interpreted and is interpreted as received. And so the poet is in this poem from the beginning and invites the reader's participation, inviting the reader's identification with the poet's thoughts, which are the poet's prayers.

In the first of the seven sonnets comprising a crown of verse, there is a proper approach to the subject in adoration, prayer and praise, and there is the ego ("Weav'd in my low devout melancholie"). At once we are confronted by the element of paradox (a certain dissonance), Donne having declared, as Helen Gardner says, that melancholy is "not conducive to true devotion," but is its enemy.[12] Burton's *Anatomy of Melancholy* may be relevant here, but I propose (taking into account "low devout") the possibility that Donne meant something such as the Greek words *proskynein* and *latreuein* imply in the New Testament, which is to worship, to bow low, to abase one's self in the presence of the "All changing unchang'd Antient of dayes." All attention is focused on the revelation of "That All, which alwayes is All every where" revealed in human flesh, Jesus the Christ.

The miracle of the incarnation, the source of salvation, is celebrated in "Annuciation," "Nativitie," and "Temple." Images affective in their power to inspire wonder, occur as in the lines addressed to Mary:

> Ere by the spheares time was created, thou
> Wast in his minde, who is thy Sonne, and Brother,
> Whom thou conceiv'st, conceiv'd; yea thou art now
> Thy Makers maker, and thy Fathers mother . . .

This, which is reminiscent of the *Horae* of the Blessed Virgin Mary in the *Prymer*, brings to mind the "Figlia del tuo figlio" ("Daughter of thy Son"), in Canto 33 of Dante's *Paradiso* and "Dry Salvages IV" of Eliot's *Four Quartets*. Describing the indescribable, Donne writes, "Seest thou, my Soule, with thy faiths eyes," see the child, "Kisse him, and with him into Egypt goe . . ." That is to say, beyond the poet's address to himself, be there in this drama, which was and which is, as we remember in the present the events of the significant past.

The incarnation presumes the crucifixion/resurrection/ascension event. And the crucifixion/resurrection/ascension event presumes the incarnation. They interpret one another and together are the foundation of the church. In the sonnet called "Crucifying," the Christ, whom the poet declines to name, is depicted on the cross and the first, the focal prayer is uttered, rooted in scripture.[13] The Word gives the words:

Now thou art lifted up, draw mee to thee,
And at thy death giving such liberall dole,
Moyst, with one drop of thy blood, my dry soule.

Salvation, the poet declares in "Resurrection," is through Christ's sacrifice. As the last line of "Crucifying" calls to mind "At the round earths
imagin'd corners blow" with its "seal'd my pardon, with thy blood," so
"Resurrection" reminds one of "Death be not proud." "Ascension" provides a powerful conclusion, intended to arouse joy at Christ's victory,
which is our victory. Here is the impressive image of Christ as the ram
who broke the way, "batter'd heaven for mee," the ram who is at the same
time the "Mild lambe, which with thy blood, hast mark'd the path." He is
the light ("Bright torch"), an image Donne delights to use, "which shin'st,
that I the way may see." And then comes another prayer, inviting the
reader's participation:

Oh, with thine own blood quench thine owne just wrath,
And if thy holy Spirit, my Muse did raise,
Deigne at my hands this crowne of prayer and praise.

There can be no doubt that God is love, that we are sinful, that God's love
covers our sins with forgiveness, blotting them out, bringing new life, no
doubt that the Holy Spirit inspires our prayer and praise: angels descending with doctrine, angels ascending with "prayer and praise." At the beginning of the sequence, the reader is presented with the good news and is
encouraged to join in the meditation, culminating in prayer and praise.

The *Holy Sonnets*, and this is particularly true of the twelve in the
1633 sequence, represent the poet's response to the revelation of God in
Christ, the incarnate, the crucified, the resurrected, ascended Son of God.
The focus is on the Son, who in the last sonnet of *La Corona* is referred to
in the line "Joy at th'uprising of this Sunne, and Sonne," and in the first
sonnet of the 1633 sequence is present by reflection in the speaker: "I am
thy sonne, made with thy selfe to shine." The poet is baptized into Christ,
the Son, and is thus God's son, bought with Christ's blood, and in that
context "made with thy selfe to shine." Why doesn't he? Why don't we
mirror the sun and Son, the light of the world? Why do we betray ourselves, betraying the Spirit that indwells us? Why is evil able to control our
lives? Out of such questions comes the heartfelt prayer for grace. Theolo-
gically this is the prayer that the Spirit of sanctification, infused in us at
baptism, may become more effective in our lives, and that by means of

INTRODUCTION

grace (in the sacrament of Christ's body and blood) we may grow in grace and in favor with God.

The *Holy Sonnets* are meditations upon the revelation of God in Christ. As such they are deeply personal, impassioned, arousing holy fear in the context of holy love, at vital points connecting with the content of *La Corona*. In a sense they are "public demonstrations of spiritual malaise meant to be exemplary to disease prone readers," as Rollin says, but he has distorted the inner meaning. The *Holy Sonnets* represent the meditation of a vital, earthy, witty, utterly intent spiritual man who is convinced that his struggles are not unique but reflect something of the struggles of other persons. He thus writes in such a way as to enable not only himself on the way of sanctification, but others as well. So in the second sonnet, "Oh my blacke Soule" he anticipates the final judgment and his just condemnation but with the knowledge that he can repent and be cleansed of his sin in the blood of Christ. Hooker speaks of the *grace* of repentance, with the clear implication that repentance ends not in despair but in new life and is cause for rejoicing.

The third sonnet, "This is my playes last scene," confronts us with death and results in prayer for deliverance from eternal death. Donne prays, "Impute me righteous." The key to understanding here is that he has been made righteous by the imputation of Christ's merits. Why pray then to be made righteous? In part, the prayer is made to the end that the salvific imputation may be acknowledged and made the basis for day-to-day existence rather than be doubted. Sonnet 4 is another prayer for repentance: "Teach me how to repent; for that's as good as if thou' hadst seal'd my pardon, with thy blood." Indeed, Donne knows that what he prays for has been accomplished, the very prayer being proof of that. And so the poem ends in affirmation. The *Holy Sonnets*, even these poems dwelling on last things, on death and judgment, all point back to *La Corona* and toward the saving love of God in Christ.

Sonnet 5, "If poysonous mineralls," with its meditation on hell, has these powerful lines:

O God, Oh! of thine onely worthy blood,
And my teares, make a heavenly Leathean flood,
And drowne in it my sinnes blacke memorie.

God does, has done, and will do just that, through baptism (*baptismos*, drowning) and through the eucharist (Lancelot Andrewes spoke of Christ's body pierced upon the cross, "and forthwith there came out blood and water," the water of baptism, the blood of the eucharist, both washing our sins away).[14] Sonnet 6 pronounces death's doom. Sonnet 7 has us look at the crucifixion, but dwells on Christ's sacrifice as being for us—"he bore our punishment," and the final couplet points toward the incarnation and the wonder of God's love and mercy. The wonder builds in Sonnet 8 and reaches a climax in Sonnet 9, with its meditation on Christ on the cross, a meditation that is deeply personal. We are called to repent, yes, but always in the knowledge of divine mercy. Look to him:

> Teares in his eyes quench the amasing light,
> Blood fills his frownes, which from his pierc'd head fell,
> And can that tongue adjudge thee unto hell,
> Which pray'd forgivenesse for his foes fierce spight?

The question is put to the poet, but also to the reader, and the anticipated answer is given forcefully, "No, no."

We have referred to Sonnet 10, "Batter my heart," perhaps the best known of Donne's religious poems. It expresses the frustration of the penitent soul and is itself a fervent confession of sin, an expression of sincere contrition, an admission that he is totally reliant upon God. The poet protests that divine power expressed in sacrificial love, in humility (*tapeinos*), in kindness, is powerless to effect salvation in terms of human righteousness—or so it seems in his experience, given the persistence of his sins. He rails at God, somewhat as Luther did. But that is not all there is to this poem. It vividly displays the spiritual problem, for in spite of his plea, in spite of the contrition expressed in and through that plea, he continues to sin. The answer, the cure, is in acceptance of God as God is—God the Father who knocks, God the Spirit who breathes, God the Son who shines—and in adoration, with contrition, to live in the knowledge of God's love day by day. On another level, the poet is suggesting that it is through knocking, breathing, shining, that God overcomes us, if we admit the divine love into our hearts. In humility is the greatest power.

This surely does not express the full meaning of this poem, but it represents the poem as to some degree "curative medicine." It is followed in Sonnet 11 by a "wholesome meditation," a poem of adoration for what God (as-God-is) has done: chosen me, made me co-heir to his glory. Christ is, as Sonnet 12 declares, the "Lambe, whose death, with life the world hath blest." God is all love. Law and letter kill. Striving to do that which shall merit God's blessing will fail. Grace, revealed in the Spirit's working within and around us, draws us into the covenant which is the Son's with the Father.

The sonnets added in 1635 are in line with the 1633 sequence, as are those from the Westmorland manuscript. Space prevents reviewing them here. They are followed by *A Litanie*. Again, connections can be found. Sonnet 12 of the 1633 sequence refers to the "knottie Trinitie" (l.3) and *A Litanie* like the Great Litany of the *Book of Common Prayer*, opens in poems one through four with invocations of the Trinity, Father, Son, and Holy Ghost. And "your drossie clay" in "Ascension" of *La Corona* connects with "My heart is by dejection, clay" at the beginning of *A Litanie* (l.5) "Hee . . . gives mee his deaths conquest" in Sonnet 12 is echoed in the prayer that "I may rise up from death, before I'am dead" in "The Father" of *A Litanie* (l.9). And while "dejection" is specifically named, on the whole the emphasis is not one of despair. There is a note of command, "Father of Heaven . . . come / And re-create mee," but Gardner finds *A Litanie* to possess the quality of "sobriety"[15]—rare in Donne's poetry, more often found in his sermons and letters. Sanders speaks of balance, and of "a self-scrutiny at once sober and energetic."[16]

The stanzas that compose *A Litanie* may be considered meditations with prayers. We find in stanzas 1–4, fervent requests to the Son, "O be thou nail'd unto my heart, / . . . let it be . . . / Drown'd in thy blood" (ll.14, 17–18), to the Holy Ghost, "Double'in my heart thy flame" (l.24), and to the Trinity, "power, love, knowledge . . . / Of these let all mee elemented bee" (ll.33, 35). Here are prayers for that communion with God that makes "me new," binding me to God that I may live and live eternally, rising from death, before I am dead. Here is prayer that the divided, tormented soul may be one as the divine Trinity is one.

Stanzas 5 through 14 imitate the Roman Litany (see Cranmer's 1549 Litany), presenting for our meditation and prayers the communion of saints, from Mary and the angels to virgins and church fathers. Each is worthy of attention such as cannot be given here. Stanzas 15 through 22 (which resemble the tenor of Donne's letter of September, 1608, to Goodyer)[17] are prayers of deliverance. The verses are reminiscent of Herbert's "Church Porch," containing as they do homely wisdom for the faithful penitent. Number 16 is representative, but it should be noted that as we proceed toward the end there is more power of devotion evident. Number 20 speaks of Christ's "gallant humblenesse" (l.176) and urges upon the Christian a like humility. Stanza 21 is personal, dealing with internal well-being, praying for deliverance from that which makes us "ruinous." Stanza 22 concerns the corporate and external, praying for deliverance from that which betrays Christ's body, the church, and that which assaults and hurts mankind. Stanzas 23 through 28 are supplications, although they are sometimes more like deprecations with the prayer that the Lord may "heare us, when wee pray" (l.216). Stanza 23 is an impas-

40

sioned prayer that God may hear us as we pray or else "We know not what to say" (l.204). Stanza 24 is a prayer for deliverance from "intermitting aguish Pietie" (l.209) such as Donne had noted in his *Holy Sonnets*, to "evenesse" in devotions and in life. Stanzas 25 through 27 are prayers against dangers such as the poet and his readers know well. Stanza 28 provides the conclusion:

> O lamb of God, which took'st our sinne
> Which could not stick to thee,
> O let it not returne to us againe,
> But Patient and Physition being free,
> As sinne is nothing, let it no where be.

There is still anxiety, but it is qualified by a quiet confidence.

There follow Occasional Poems. "The Crosse," "Resurrection," and "Upon the Annunciation and Passion," present again for our meditation the focal meaning, the "event/gift/grace of Jesus Christ." The first is a defense against Puritan critics of the cross and the sign of the cross and proves how important for Donne the cross was as a symbol of great power. "Resurrection" is a curious piece, with its alchemical figures,[18] but has value not only in emphasizing the importance of the resurrection in general, but also for its final line, suggesting that Christ's risen body is the principle of life, the *anima mundi*. "Upon the Annunciation and Passion" is linked to *La Corona*, having been written at the same time. The incidental joining in 1608 of the Feast of the Annunciation with Good Friday provides fruitful meditation whose lesson is in the lines:

> This Church, by letting these dayes joyne, hath shown
> Death and conception in mankinde is one:
> Or' twas in him the same humility,
> That he would be a man, and leave to be. . .   (ll.33–36)

"Goodfriday, 1613. Riding Westward" continues the meditation on Christ's passion, but now in a different context. The poem is deeply personal, more so than the last three, reminding us of the *Holy Sonnets*, but here, in the end, there is a sense of resolution, such as was lacking in the earlier poems. This is a meditation on-the-way, written some eighteen months before Donne's ordination. He is riding westward on Good Friday and his mind keeps remembering the crucifixion, although his body seems to resist, going westward, away from the east and the cross. He does not want to see Christ on the cross; he who sees God must die. But he is

41

powerless to flee for long. His soul resists the body's flight, turns to view the awful sight, and is conscious of being viewed by the One upon the cross:

> . . . thou look'st towards mee,
> O Saviour, as thou hang'st upon the tree;
> I turne my backe to thee, but to receive
> Corrections, till thy mercies bid thee leave. (ll.35–38)

The speaker is God's image who shall come to himself when that now damaged image is restored. As Judah Stampfer says, "His true self is God, all else is rust and deformity. Let their identity be renewed, and he will turn, God's face to meet the face of God in ultimate godly intimacy."[19]

Perhaps it was then, on that journey, that Donne reached a stage along the way when he could say "yes" to Morton and the King. He was ordained in 1615 and sometime after 1618 wrote "To Mr. Tilman after he had taken orders." This poem is rightly considered as a turning point in Donne's sense of vocation, for here he extolls the ordained ministry ("What function is so noble, as to bee / Embassadour to God and destinie?"), interpreting it largely in terms of the minister as the preacher of God's word (ministers are "As Angels out of clouds") and concludes, significantly, I think, by speaking of heaven and earth meeting in the ordained:

> In whom must meet Gods graces, mens offences,
> And so the heavens which beget all things here,
> And th'earth our mother, which these things doth beare,
> Both these in thee, are in thy Calling knit,
> And make thee now a blest Hermaphrodite. (ll.50–54)

Indeed they have met and meet in Donne and the meeting, vexed as it is, is to be regarded as a priceless asset, for Donne the preacher will reach people in large part because he has lived his earthly life to the full and knows its joys and its sorrows, its benefits and its dangers.

Finally we come to the Hymns where the resolution of Donne's struggle is most apparent. In "A Hymne to Christ, at the Authors last going into Germany," dated 1619, Donne is prepared to surrender all—all his possessions, all his loves, in return for God's love and mercy, the forgiveness of his sins. Donne knows that his former loves were not evil in themselves. They may have been "fainter beames," but they were of divine origin and reflect God's love. However, that they may be more fully what they are in essence they must be surrendered, refined in the fire of divine love, and returned renewed to the now responsible self. In the third stanza Donne is seen struggling again. He protests that God will not act to obliterate those loves that stand in the way of the poet's more fully loving God, as he ought. The resolution comes in the realization that God's love is expressed in and through God's insistence that Donne act responsibly. Here is a momentous theological and spiritual discovery. Donne must freely love, as far as he can, in the knowledge that God rejoices in his imperfect love and perfects it. This knowledge brings peace but it does not prevent him, as he ends the poem, from praying for death, whereby his divorce from this world may be complete and God's love be for him all in all.

The "Hymne to God my God, in my sicknesse" was most likely written in 1623,[20] at the time of Donne's serious illness, out of which came the *Devotions*. There on his sickbed he contemplates death and views his experience as the tuning of the instrument whereby he shall be made God's music, to sing in the choir of saints forever. Significantly he finds calvary and paradise, Christ's cross and Adam's tree, Christ and Adam, meeting in him in his sickness, and prays:

> As the first *Adams* sweat surrounds my face,
> May the last *Adams* blood my soule embrace.

And he has assurance that it does. There is peace in the final stanza. Incidentally, the reader might care to note the final lines of *A Litanie*, especially "Patient and Physition being free," in relation to this hymn.

"A Hymne to God the Father" is dated from the same period of acute illness. It is a confession and a witness. In it Donne asks forgiveness for his own sins, for sins he caused others to commit, for sins shunned but "wallow'd in," and for the last sin, the sin of despair—that in the end he will be condemned and not be saved. He prays for assurance (there is the old sense of demand here, now softened) that at his death God's "Sunne / Shall shine as it shines now, and heretofore" (ll.15–16). This is the Sun / Son who shines in mercy, forgiving now, and thus giving assurance of forgiveness at the Last Judgment: "having done that, Thou hast done, / I have no more." (ll.17–18) The pun here is intended. Shaw helpfully explains Donne's conviction concerning the significance of biblical names. In scripture "the name is interpreted as a testimony to God's power as manifested in his calling of a particular individual."[21] In the "Hymne to God the Father," Donne's use of his own name is intended to signify a like calling and deliverance. But then there is the plain and simple explanation.

43

INTRODUCTION

Donne has come to full awareness that what's done is done: Christ died for his salvation: the light of this Sun shines upon him. Shaw concludes:

It is by removing the obscurities of sin that the true self, God's image, becomes visible. Creation and teleology, who we are and where we are going, are inseparably bound together: this we are to accept through faith on earth and know as truth in heaven. It may appear presumptuous for Donne to bid God, "sweare by thy selfe." But in fact it is nothing of the kind, for scripture informs us that this is the way God enters into covenants with his people.[22]

Donne knew that God has already sworn thus. He "simply wishes to remain within the light that he knows and has known."

At the conclusion of a meditation, according to Hall's *Arte*, there is first an expression of confidence in gaining that for which the devout penitent prays and then thanksgiving and recommendation "of ourselves to God: wherein the soul doth cheerfully give up itself, and repose wholly upon her Maker and Redeemer; committing herself to him, in all her ways . . ."[23] "Love (III)" represents such a conclusion for Herbert. Donne's final hymns represent such a conclusion for Donne—and for us.

This sense of resolution, not without further struggle, finds profound expression in the sermons, to which we now turn.

IV

Sermons

Donne as Preacher

As is clear from Donne's poem "To Mr. Tilman after he had taken orders," the poet's most prominent definition of a priest is related to the priest in the pulpit.

> *Maries* prerogative was to beare Christ, so
> 'Tis preachers to convey him, for they doe
> As Angels out of clouds, from Pulpits speake;
> And blesse the poore beneath, the lame, the weake.

Horton Davies cites a passage from Donne's sermon on 1 Corinthians 9:16, in which the preacher expresses his strong conviction:

Who but my selfe can conceive the sweetnesse of that salutation, when the Spirit of God says to me in a morning, Go forth today and preach, and preach consolation, preach peace, preach mercy. And spare my people, spare that people whom I have redeemed with my precious Blood . . . What a Coronation is our taking of Orders, by which God makes us a Royall Priesthood? And what an inthronization is comming up into a Pulpit, where God invests his servants with his Ordinance, as with a Cloud, and then presses that Cloud with a *Vae si non*, woe be unto thee, if thou doe not preach, and then enables him to preach peace, mercy, consolation, to the whole Congregation.[1]

From its beginning in 1549, the *Book of Common Prayer* emphasized word and sacraments, and Donne took sacraments seriously, but his calling was such that in practice the pulpit was his home and preaching his clearest vocation. Indeed, as a court preacher, as Reader at Lincoln's Inn, as Dean of St. Paul's, it was expected that he would concentrate on preaching.

INTRODUCTION

In a sermon on Ezekiel 33:32, preached at Whitehall in 1619, in which he began by citing 1 Corinthians 9:16, Donne speaks of the minister as prophet, *"Tuba,"* a trumpet. The emphasis is on the declaration of God's love and mercy, but the minister first sounds an alarm. "To them [the people] thou shalt be a *Tuba*, a Trumpet. Thy preaching shall awaken them and so bring them to some sense of their sins."[2] But then the preacher "shall become *Carmen musicum,* a musical and harmonious charmer, to settle and compose the soul again in a reposed confidence, and in a delight in God."[3] To this end the minister

... shall not present the messages of God rudely, barbarously, extemporally; but with such meditation and preparation as appertains to so great an employment, from such a King as God, to such a State as his Church ... And then ... he shall have a pleasant voice, that is, to preach first sincerely (for a preaching to serve turns and humors, cannot, at least should not please any), but then it is to preach acceptably, seasonably, with a spiritual delight, to a discreet and rectified congregation, that by way of such holy delight, they may receive the more profit.[4]

Indeed, Donne did not preach "rudely, barbarously, extemporally."[5] He labored long and hard on his sermons, collecting and organizing the materials he would use. As we had occasion to note, his sermons grew out of his personal devotions, his meditations on the texts presented to him by the Prayer Book Lectionary. Sometimes his sermons, such as "Deaths Duell," were written out in full before they were delivered, but normally he preached from outlines and notes, which were subsequently revised and then written out for publication. As to his manner, we know of his great reputation, we have the testimony of elegists such as Daniel Darnelly, and we have the statement made by Walton:

A Preacher in earnest; weeping sometimes for his Auditory, sometimes with them: always preaching to himself, like an Angel from a cloud, but in none; carrying some, as St. *Paul* was, to heaven in holy raptures, and enticing others by a sacred Art and Courtship to amend their lives; here picturing a vice so as to make it ugly to those that practised it; and a virtue so, as to make it be beloved even by those that lov'd it not; and all this with a most particular grace and an unexpressible addition of comeliness.[6]

It is impossible now to recapture the reality of Donne preaching, or the total context in which he preached and his auditors watched and listened.

46

We have only the sermons as they appeared in print and must be content with them.

Donne's sermons were part of a liturgical whole, normally involving Morning Prayer, Litany, and Ante-Communion. The liturgical context was different when the sermon was in the evening or in some place such as Paul's Cross. But normally there were lessons, canticles, psalms, confession and absolution, prayers, the eucharist—whole or abbreviated—and, as occasion required, baptism. Carrithers helpfully discusses the liturgical context, emphasizing that "Prayer Book worship particularizes and insists on the *communal* quality of the *mutual* involvement in the waking world."

The Anglican liturgy is "the people's work," in the language of the people. It engages a congregation understood as a local element of the body of Christ in closely communal acts of worship in response to, or dialogue or union with, the priest. No single point about external influence on Donne's preaching is more important.[7]

Donne seems to have been profoundly aware of his setting and of the people before him as participants in the liturgical action. For instance, in one sermon Donne said:

You may remember that I proposed to exercise your devotions and religious meditations in these *exercises*, with words that might present to you first the several persons in the Trinity, and the benefits which we *receive, in receiving* God *in* those distant notions of Father, Son, and Holy Ghost; and then with other words which might *present* those sins, and the danger of those sins which are most particularly opposed against those several persons.[8]

Carrithers states, "He will *exercise* and *present*, thereby making the sermon a form of drama akin to masque, wherein cast and audience may share or exchange roles. His listeners have joined him previously in Prayer Book actions of affirming belief in the Trinity and confessing sins. He will propose, oppose, and receive with his auditors in a kind of contest."[9] And as to his texts, they will have heard them read, as Hooker said, as a part of the congregation's praise, that which is done "to" God,[10] as part of the story, which is their story. We might also consider a point made by H. R. McAdoo,[11] that the pulpit (with the congregation) takes the place of the confessional, people being brought to repentance, receiving God's forgiveness, preparing to lead a new life, in the midst of the preached Word, which provides both means and context. Thus sermon after sermon inculcates holy fear in the knowledge of holy love, to build up the people of God as agents of the divine love in the world.

Finally, it should be noted that the sermon in Prayer Book worship provides the congregation with an opportunity to enter more deeply into the salvific story rehearsed doxologically in lessons, canticles, and psalms, summed up christologically in creed, inspiring the responses of penitence, praise and renewed commitment. Something of this is reflected in the sermon on Ezekiel 33:32 where in a famous passage Donne summarizes the gospel and the preacher's vocation, saying that preachers as trumpets

. . . are *musicum carmen,* a love-song . . . in proposing the love of God to man, wherein he loved him so, as that he gave his only begotten Son for him. God made this whole world in such an uniformity, such a correspondency, such a concinnity of parts, as that it was an Instrument, perfectly in tune: one may say, the trebles, the highest strings were disordered first; the best understandings, Angels and Men, put this instrument out of tune. God rectified all again, by putting in a new string, *semen mulieris,* the seed of woman, the *Messias:* And only by sounding that string in your ears, become we musicum *carmen,* true musick, true harmony, true peace to you.[12]

Donne goes on to say that if the preacher emphasizes reprobation, the God of wrath creating humanity in order to damn his creation, there is no music, "no harmony, no peace in such preaching. But if we take this instrument, when Gods hand tuned it the second time, in the promise of a *Messias,* an offer of the love and mercy of God to all that receive it in him; then we are truly *musicum carmen,* as a love-song."[13]

Thomas Bilney, writing long before Donne, spoke of the late-medieval preacher saying to his congregation, "Behold thou hast lain rotting in thine own lusts, by the space of these sixty years, even as a beast in his own dung, and wilt thou presume in one year to go forward toward heaven, and that in thine age, as much as thou wentest backward from heaven toward hell in sixty years?" Donne would have denounced such preaching, as did Bilney—there was no music in it, no hope, only despair. "Is this the preaching of repentance in the name of Jesus?" asked Bilney, "or rather to tread down Christ with Antichrist's doctrine? For what other thing did he speak in effect, than that Christ died in vain for thee?"[14] Donne was in agreement with Hooker who in 1581 at Paul's Cross preached that God's primary will was that "all mankind should be saved."[15] Not reprobation but rather God's love and mercy came first, last and always. The Puritans attacked Hooker for his teaching at Paul's Cross; they frowned on Donne's seemingly Arminian doctrine. But this conviction concerning divine love dominated his preaching, preaching aimed not at condemning people but at bringing them to repentance that they might be renewed by God's forgiveness. The preacher is meant to be *musicum carmen*.

The Sermon as Meditation

Sermons in Donne's time tended, as W. Fraser Mitchell has suggested, to be in one of three forms, one form patterned after an oration model used by many Roman Catholic preachers. Another form was a reflection of Calvinist explication of a scriptural text, with application. A third form, that used by Donne, was Ramist, with the opening of a text, division of the same into parts, extended treatment of each part, and then a summary, with application of the teaching in the sermon.[16] According to Blench, the English Reformers generally adhered to a method he identifies as "modern," the sermon being divided into exordium, division of the text into three tropes, and amplification of the members of the division.[17]

Here we are concerned with the sermon as a form of public meditation. Barbara Lewalski discusses what she calls "Protestant discourses on meditation," with their equation of meditation with sermon, their insistence on "application to self" of that which is preached and meditated upon, and their wide choice of subject matter presented for meditation.[18] Indeed the preaching of Donne, and others I prefer to call Anglo-Catholic rather than Protestant, was generally composed of preparation (the presentation of a biblical text and prayer), the explication and exposition of the text (which could be in specified divisions), together with proofs, and the application of both text and exposition to the lives of those in the congregation, with intent to arouse the affections and promote some modification in behavior. It is evident that we have here the structure of meditation as, for instance, provided by Hall in his *Arte*.[19]

Lewalski points out that Donne himself considered his sermons to be meditations, constantly referring "to the ideas he is developing as 'meditation.' "[20] For instance, "We cannot take into our Meditation, a better Rule, then that of the Stoic . . . There is no such unhappiness to a sinner, as to be happy."[21] Or again, "But this is not the object of our speculation, the subject of our meditation now."[22] Donne emphasizes the importance of application, urging people themselves to apply what they learn through their meditations. "You are this quorum [the assembly of the Elect], if you preach over the sermons which you hear, to your owne souls in your meditation."[23] Further, Donne speaks of his sermons arising out of his own meditations upon the scriptures, such as the psalms of the Old Testament and the letters of Paul in the New Testament, "as a hearty entertainer offers to others, the meat which he loves best himself, soe doe I oftenest present to God's people, in these congregations, the meditations which I feed upon at home, in these two Scriptures."[24]

Donne's sermons as a whole reflect the influence of the meditative style on him as a man and as a preacher. This influence is a source of much energy in the sermons. But relatively few sermons strictly speaking, qualify as public meditations. One that does so qualify, which is included in this book, is "Deaths Duell." Walter Davis demonstrates that Donne's last sermon is divided in accordance with the divisions of his *Devotions Upon Emergent Occasions:* meditation, expostulation, and prayer, or memory, understanding, and will. In the first part of the sermon Donne seeks "to draw forth from his audience's experience a full sense that life is a living dying from which a powerful God continually saves." The first part inspires terror. In the second part we are confronted by the understanding of deliverance from death, but here "the understanding enters in to show the limits of our understanding, to show us that any death can be a comfort known to God but not to man." Davis continues:

The third part of the sermon, deliverance by the death of the Son in mercy, falls into the long tradition of meditation on the Passion of Christ . . . and its motive is to activate our wills, in fact to make us weep . . . He faces the congregation directly . . . activating the will by making demands on it and acting like a spiritual director . . . He starts with composition of place, inviting the congregation to make its time and place Christ's time and place . . . . He proceeds to a consideration of each of the acts of Christ, then to the presumed acts of the members of the congregation, and then moves to an emotional response. By the end of these "steps," he suggests colloquy: "There wee leave you in that *blessed dependency,* to *hang* upon *him* that *hangs* upon the *Crosse,* there *bath* in his *teares,* there *suck* at his *woundes,* and *lye downe in peace* in his grave."[25]

Donne's attention is fixed upon the salvific story as applied to the daily life—and death—of the Christian. Davis has noted the importance of the typological interpretation of scripture in Donne's sermons,[26] and Mueller indicates the importance to Donne of the literal sense of scripture, as contrasted to the spiritual sense—moral, allegorical, anagogical, and tropological.[27] In his sermon on John 1:8, also included in this book, Donne said: "though it be ever lawfull, and often times very usefull, for the raising and exaltation of our devotion, and to present the plenty, and abundance of the holy Ghost in the Scriptures . . . to induce the *diverse senses* that the Scriptures do admit, yet this may not be admitted if there may be danger thereby, to neglect or weaken the *literal sense* it selfe."[28] And yet, as Mueller says:

Throughout the sermons his practice is to give little more than preliminary attention to the literal sense understood as the historical or factual content of a text; the emphasis is overwhelmingly on what the multiple senses term the moral sense—the applicability of the text to the state of a man's soul and what he ought to do.[29]

Donne's sermons should be read with this in view: His attention was on his congregation (and himself as one with them in the battles of life), and on the salvific story as a means of grace, powerful to change lives. He shared Hooker's teleological view; Hooker argued that what matters in the eucharist, for instance, is not the change of the elements but that for which the eucharist was provided, the changing of people, for which the elements are moral instruments to effect such change.[30] Thus, like the eucharist and as a vital part of the liturgy, the sermon is a means of grace, no less.

Some Sermons

The sermons in this book were chosen in part because they emphasize in various ways all that we have been considering, chiefly repentance and forgiveness, the descent of angels with doctrine, the ascent of angels with prayer, with Christ as the focal meaning of all, the light that illumines all.

Donne's sermon on John 1:8, here called "Christ the Light," was his first sermon as Dean, given at St. Paul's Cathedral on Christmas Day, 1621. Here Christ is presented as essential light. What is that light? "It is the working of Christ by his Spirit in his Church, in the infusion of faith and grace, for belief and manners." Along the way Donne discusses the place of natural light and the light of reason in the "rectified" Christian's apprehension of essential light. This he does meditating upon the various meanings of light. In one meditation he urges the use of the light of reason (understanding) in considering the events of Jesus' life and making application of them to oneself. The aim is that we should walk in light, having our conversation in heaven, and to this end Donne exhorts us to repentance: "Offer up thy sin thyself; bring it to the top of thy memory and thy conscience, that he [the priest] finding it there may sacrifice for thee. Tune the instrument, and it is the fitter for his hand." This he says in the sure knowledge of God's mercy and with a firm faith. The penitent soul

INTRODUCTION

rests upon the assurance that in and through Christ, the essential light, he has died to sin, been buried with Christ in baptism, and "hath had his resurrection from sin, his ascension to holy purposes of amendment of life, and his judgement, that is 'peace of conscience,' sealed unto him . . ."

In the sermon on 1 Corinthians 13:12 ("For now we see through a glass darkly, but then face to face; now I know in part, but then I shall know, even as I am known"), preached on Easter Day in 1628, Donne is again concerned with light, but this time in relation to the beatific vision. It is a sermon imbued with profound hope. We know God by the light of nature and as Christians by the light of grace, but both lights are partial, faith itself being darkness by comparison with the vision of God which shall be ours in heaven. Donne concludes with a statement of considerable importance for his spirituality and ours, citing St. Augustine as saying "that man does not love God, that loves not himself."

The sermon on 1 Corinthians 16:22 ("If any man love not the Lord Jesus Christ, let him be anathema, maranatha") intensifies the focus on Christ and is noteworthy for three things. In the first part, relying on St. John Damascene, Donne explains in considerable detail the two natures of Christ, the divine and the human. His theological exposition is not, however, designed to any merely academic end, but is rather pastoral, aimed toward the Christian's expression of love toward the Lord, Christ, Jesus, God and Man in one person, lest in loving not he become accursed. In the second part of the sermon there is an eloquent, extended exhortation implicitly involving the understanding that spirituality at its heart is a matter of loving, loving the Lord, Christ, Jesus, God and Man made One. The third part is of interest for the care with which Donne treats the conclusion of his text: "Let him be anathema, maranatha." He concludes: "It is not only a censorious speech . . . it is a shame for them . . . it is a judiciary speech. . . . I, says the Apostle, take away none of his mercy when he comes, but I will have nothing to do with them, till he comes." Divine mercy is emphasized to the end and in spite of other possible interpretations of the text.

Donne's sermon on Psalm 63:7, called here "In the Shadow of Thy Wings," is addressed to the afflicted. At the outset he describes a familiar condition:

how many children, and servants, and wives suffer under the anger, and moroseness, and peevishness, and jealousy of foolish masters, and parents, and husbands, though they must not say so? David and Solomon have cried out that all this world is vanity and levity; and God knows all is weight, and burden, and heaviness, and oppressed; and if there were not a weight of future glory to counterpose it, we shall all sink into nothing.

Thus present affliction is to be regarded seriously, but with remembrance of God's past actions. God has "been my help," he "has not left me to myself . . . he has helped me." Indeed, God loved you before you were created, "that you loving him, he might continue his love to you." A further sign of God's regard is in his dependence upon us. Donne speaks out in what constitutes an interesting essay on the relation between God's power and human responsibility. "He has been my help, but he has left something for me to do with him and by his help." Furthermore, our present affliction is to be regarded in relation to future joy. The sermon ends with a strong affirmation of the joy that is ours under the shadow of God's wings:

That soul that is dissected and anatomized to God, in a sincere confession, washed in the tears of true contrition, embalmed in the blood of reconciliation, the blood of Christ Jesus, can assign no reason, can give no just answer to that interrogatory, "Why art thou cast down O my soul? . . ." No man is so little as that he can be lost under these wings; no man so great that they cannot reach to him.

Donne's beautifully constructed sermon on Luke 23:23, entitled here "Prayer and the Divine Mercy," is a sermon on prayer and on the spirit of prayer as illuminated by Christ's example. Donne understands prayer as speech addressed toward God, but in the broadest sense. "It may be mental, for we may think prayers. It may be vocal, for we may speak prayers. It may be actual, for we do prayer." But not just any thought or speech or deed is prayer. It must be addressed toward God and must be both to good effect and be "of things which are good." Reminiscent of Herbert's definition of prayer as "Gods breath returning to its birth," Donne speaks of prayer as God's working within "the rectified man" who is the temple of the Holy Spirit "when he prays." He says, "it is the Holy Ghost itself that prays; and what can be denied where the asker gives?" Prayer is, furthermore, "an act of our reason, and therefore must be reasonable. For only reasonable things can pray; for the beasts and the ravens are not said to pray for food, but 'to cry.' " And then there is the specific prayer of Christ on the cross, "Father, forgive them, for they know not what they do," which indicates the spirit of prayer. The emphasis is on forgiveness and reconciliation, and on a Father who forgives.

INTRODUCTION

There is another sermon included here which deals with prayer. Delivered at St. Paul's, most likely sometime between November, 1621, and the end of 1622, it consists of a detailed exposition of Psalm 90:14, "O satisfy us early with thy mercy, that we may rejoice and be glad all our days." Its significance for the student of spirituality consists partly in the way Donne relates prayer and praise: "Prayer and praise is the same thing," he says, pointing out that what is in his translation a prayer ("O satisfy us early with thy mercy"), is in the Septuagint an utterance of praise ("Thou hast satisfied us"). He explains:

God's house in this world is called the house of prayer, but in heaven it is the house of praise: no surprisal with any new necessities here, but one even, incessant, and everlasting tenor of thanksgiving. And it is a blessed incohation of that state here, here to be continually exercised in the commemoration of God's former goodness towards us.

Prayer, then, properly arises out of the memory of God's mercies, and remembrance informs our prayers. The last part of the sermon concerns what the prayer of Psalm 90:14 produces and "it is joy, and continual joy, 'That we may rejoice and be glad all our days.' "

Sometime before the middle of 1623, possibly at St. Paul's, Donne preached a series of sermons on the thirty-second psalm, most probably during the penitential seasons of Advent and Lent. The one included here and entitled "The Grace of Repentance," is on Psalm 32:5. It is especially noteworthy, concerning as it does confession, with very practical advice for making a "good confession." Potter and Simpson suggest that it be read alongside Canto IX of Dante's *Purgatorio* and T. S. Eliot's *Ash Wednesday*. In the sermon Donne stresses the necessity of confessing one's sins, not in general but in particular and points to two dangers, the one being that of an obdurate conscience which will not acknowledge sins and the other being that of an over-tender conscience which exaggerates or otherwise falsifies sins and refuses divine forgiveness. Donne also emphasizes God's mercy, God who seeks us out even in our sin, to love and to forgive us. That seeking-out normally takes place in the context of the church's regular observances, wherein (in the church Donne serves) people are not dragged to private confession, "but be led to it with that sweetness, with which our church proceeds in appointing sick persons, if they feel their consciences troubled with any weighty matter, to make a special confession and to receive absolution at the hands of thy priest." Indeed, God gently leads us to and by the grace of repentance. There is a passage which calls to mind "Batter my heart, three person'd God":

INTRODUCTION

Here enters the fulness of his mercy . . . well expressed at our door in that . . . "Behold, I stand at the door and knock"; for first he comes; here is no mention of our calling of him before; he comes of himself; and then he suffers not us to be in ignorance of his coming . . . he appears not like lightning that passes away as soon as it is seen, that no man can read by it nor work by it . . . but he stands at the door and expects us all day, not only with a patience but with a hunger to effect his purpose upon us . . .

"Deaths Duell" was delivered at Whitehall, at the beginning of Lent, 1630, in the presence of King Charles I, and has long been considered to be Donne's own funeral oration. Its importance to spirituality is three-fold: 1. It provides an excellent example of the interdependence of holy fear and holy love, for it depicts death in sober, realistic, disturbing tones, and yet affirms that that which is apparent in death is not the final word. That final word rests with God, to whom belongs "the issues of death." 2. It is strongly christological, focusing upon Christ and his passion in a meditation toward the end of the sermon which is Donne's most vivid portrayal of the death in which rests all hope. 3. The sermon moves from intellect to affections. It is designed to move the congregation (and the reader) from complacency to repentance to conformity in this life with Christ's exemplary life and death. In his meditation, Donne goes through the events of Christ's last days and hours and seeks for ways that Christians may live in conformity with these events. For instance, concerning the Last Supper:

Take in the whole day from the hour that Christ received the Passover upon Thursday, unto the hour in which he died the next day. Make this present day that day in your devotion, and consider what he did, and remember what you have done. Before he instituted and celebrated the Sacrament . . . he proceeded to that act of humility, to wash his disciples' feet . . . In your preparation to the holy and blessed Sacrament, have you with a sincere humility sought a reconciliation with all the world, even with those that have been averse from it, and refused that reconciliation from you? If so, and not else, you have spent that first part of his last day in conformity with him.

That is the end of Christian spirituality: to live in conformity with Christ.

V

Devotions

In the winter of 1623 John Donne became ill. Evelyn Simpson has spoken of a "violent fever, which ran its course in about three weeks."[1] Bald speaks of the fever as "relapsing fever," an illness "sudden in its onset," which "reaches a crisis in from five to seven days. In spite of insomnia and prostration, the sufferer remains in full possession of his faculties, and, if he passes the crisis, is so weakened that convalesence is slow. The principal danger at this period is the possibility of a relapse, a fact which gives the fever its name."[2] In the midst of this experience Donne meditated. During his convalesence he wrote to Sir Robert Ker, "I have used this leisure to put the Meditations, had in my sickness, into some such order as may minister some holy delight."[3] In brief, Donne uses the experiences of his own illness and recovery to meditate upon his soul's condition and to pray. As Gerard Cox says, "By employing the method of figural interpretation, Donne could treat his recovery from sickness as a return to a state of grace that would in turn look forward to eternal life. The literal fact of his illness occasions a meditative examination of his condition that serves to motivate his appropriate desire for his salvation."[4]

The three-part division of the *Devotions* (Meditation, Expostulation, and Prayer) has been compared to the division of Ignatius of Loyola's *Spiritual Exercises*—prelude, meditation and colloquy, or the Ignatian emphasis on the three powers of the mind, memory, understanding, and will. But Anthony Raspa is surely correct in pointing out that "Donne's tripartite structure, for which we may mistakenly find a parallel in formal seventeenth-century methods of devotion, is original with him. He devised it because he needed such an argumentative structure to satisfy the dialectical cast of his mind." Raspa further points to the purpose of the *Devotions* as forcing the readers to make use of their memories, thus probing the eternal and engaging the understanding in order to reach a "deep comprehension of spiritual things." This comprehension leads "to the exercise of the will for love." He concludes that Donne, using this method of probing inspiration (comprehension), and love, "fulfilled the criterion of Donne's contemporary, Bishop Hall," who wrote: "Divine Meditation is nothing else but a bending of the mind upon some spiritual object, through divers forms of discourse, until our thoughts come to an issue."[5]

The Course of the Devotions

Cox pointed out that the *Devotions*, as an extended course of meditations on his soul's health, follows the course of repentance and is reminiscent of Richard Hooker's description of repentance in Book VI of the *Laws*.[6] The key is found in Donne's Prayer I:

Enable me by thy *grace* to look forward to mine end, and to look backward too, to the considerations of thy mercies afforded me from the beginning; that so by that practise of considering thy mercy, in my beginning in this world, when thou plantedst me in the *Christian Church*, and thy mercy in the beginning in the other world, when thou writest me in the *Book of life*, in my *Election*, I may come to a holy consideration of thy *mercy* in the beginning of all my actions here . . .[7]

The eye of faith being open to behold the mercy of God, Donne moves to the stimulation of holy fear. The physician arrives: "I see he *fears*, and I fear him: I overtake him, I overrun him in his fear, and I go the faster . . ."[8] In Prayer VI Donne says:

O most mighty God and merciful God, the God of all true *sorrow*, and true *joy* too, and of all hope too, as thou hast given me a *Repentance*, not to be repented of, so give me, O *Lord*, a *fear*, of which I may not be *afraid*.[9]

In accordance with Hooker's teaching, the holy fear required in true repentance is grounded in God's mercy. God is not the God of reprobation but of goodness and love. So in Prayer VIII we find:

O eternal and most gracious God, who though thou have reserved thy treasure of perfect joy, and perfect glory, to be given by thine own hands then, when by seeing thee, as thou art in thyself, and knowing thee, as we are known, we shall possess in an instant, and possess for ever, all that can any way conduce to our happiness . . .[10]

Donne enumerated the blessings that come from God, referring to *Nature*, *Industry*, and *Friends*, ending: "Of all these thy *instruments* have I received thy blessing, O God, but bless thy name most for the greatest . . . in the preaching of thy Gospel." He prays that now, in his distress, God may be his *Physician*.[11]

With faith, love, and fear pervading his very being, Donne confesses his sin in the presence of the persons of the Trinity, meeting to decide what is to be done "with this leperous soul."

I offer not to counsel them [the physicians], who meet in consultation for my *body* now, but I open my infirmities, I anatomize my *body* to them. So I do my *soul* to thee, O my *God*, in an humble confession, That there is no *vein* in me, that is not full of the blood of thy *Son*, whom I have crucified, and crucified againe, by multiplying many, and often repeating the same sinns . . .[12]

Such confession is done in the light of God's mercy—the very essence of the Holy Trinity—Donne acknowledging, "if you take this confession into a *consultation*, my case is not so desperate, my destruction is not decreed."[13] Sincere repentance assures forgiveness. But how sincere, how thorough is this confession of Donne's?

The poet/priest is convinced that his soul is still holding back for there are sins cloaked and hidden, not yet confessed. He meditates upon Last Things, identified by Hooker as "the resurrection of the dead, the judgment of the world to come, and the endless misery of sinners."[14] He fixes his attention on death in general and his own death in particular. He hears the church bells tolling for someone a short time ago alive, but now dead, and he thinks of himself in relation to that dead person and to all humanity:

No Man is an *Island*, entire of itself, every man is a piece of the *Continent*, a part of the *main*; if a clod be washed away by the *sea*, *Europe* is the less, as well as if a *Promontory* were, as well as if a *Manor* of thy *friends*, or of *thine own* were; Any Mans *death* diminishes *me*, because I am involved in Mankind; And therefore never send to know for whom the bell tolls; It tolls for thee.[15]

This contemplation of death and with it the other Last Things, does not drive Donne to despair, but to the divine love. The voice that says "that *I must die now*, is not the voice of a *Judge*, that speaks by way of *condemnation*, but of a *Physicion*, that presents health in that . . ."[16] Indeed, with this serious confrontation with death—his own death—Donne realizes that the cure of the body and of the soul is at hand. As the body is purged so the soul is purged through the working of the Holy Spirit within. And here, again, we find expression of contrition. In Prayer XX Donne confesses:

I am come by thy goodness, to the use of thine ordinary means for my *body*, to wash away those *peccant humors*, that endangered it. I have, O *Lord*, a *River* in my *body*, but a *Sea* in my *soul*, and a *Sea* swollen into the depth of a *Deluge*, above the *Sea*. Thou hast raised up certain *hills in me* heretofore, by which I might have stood safe, from these *inundations of sin*.

Donne speaks of natural faculties, education, the church with its word and sacraments as such hills. God has conducted him to the summit of these hills,

but this *Deluge*, this *inundation*, is got above all my *Hills;* and I have sinned and sinned, and multiplied *sinn* to *sinn*, after all these thy assistances against *sinn*, and where is there *water* enough to wash away this *Deluge?* There is a red *Sea*, greater than this *Ocean;* and there is a *little spring*, through which this *Ocean*, may pour itself into that red *Sea*. Let the *Spirit* of true *contrition*, and *sorrow* pass all my *sinns* through these *eyes*, into the wounds of thy *Son*, and I shall be clean, and my *soul* so much better purged than my *body*, as it is ordained for a *better*, and a *longer* life.[17]

The purging of the soul begins with confession, proceeds to *mundare*, which is the cleansing and purifying of the conscience by detestation of sins,[18] and ends with *succidere*, or the cutting down and weeding out of what remains that is unjustly obtained; this is restitution.[19] At the end there is recognition of the danger of relapse, physically and spiritually.[20]

The Devotions in the Twentieth Century

D. W. Harding, who provides another modern interpretation of the *Devotions*, points to the relevance in the twentieth century of this work of Donne's, writing:

The emotional need for the ordinary attentions of physicians, friends and servants which Donne felt so poignantly, can be seen as a facet of a much more general need for acceptance and love, with a dread of worthlessness that would reach its nadir for him in a sense of separation from God.[21]

This fundamental need is universal in time and space.

For the reader of selections from the *Devotions*, as found here, there is much to create a sense of distance, an awareness of the pastness of the past. For one thing the way in which the physicians go about treating Donne's fever, the bleeding to rid the body of noxious humors, seems crude if not barbaric. But the matters named by Harding are timeless: the threat of worthlessness now combined with a dread of meaninglessness, the need for acceptance and love even as we are, contrite but still fallible, and the need for what Hooker identified as communion or participation with God and with one another in God, which is to be seen in relation to the damage that strident independence, individualization and privatization do to persons and society now. Donne affirmed "No *Man* is an *Island,* entire of itself . . . I am involved in *Mankind,*" and Hooker his contemporary wrote, "God hath created nothing simply for itself: but each thing in all things, and of every thing each part in other have such interest, that in the whole world nothing is found whereunto any thing created can say, 'I need thee not.' "[22] The way to saving communion and community is by means of repentance, from contrition to confession, with absolution, eventuating in new life, involving restitution to others of what we have taken from them. This is the way to a sense of worth, assurance, acceptance, and love. The *Devotions* provide another means, alongside the *Divine Poems,* and the sermons, whereby the saving experience is extended by Donne to the reader then and now.

VI

Prayer and Prayers

Lancelot Andrewes, whose *Preces Privatae* has commended him as a profound man of prayer, defined prayer in his catechetical lectures given at Cambridge in the 1580s, as "the interpreter of our mind" and went on to say, "the operation of our hope is prayer; we go to God by prayers of our minds, not by the paces of our feet." Here this Caroline divine was thinking not only of public prayer, but of "inward meditation of the heart" and also family prayer. Prayer is *clavis dici, sera noctis,* "the key to open the day," and the "bar to shut in the night."[1] Prayer is thus more than prayers. It is, as John Macquarrie has said, "a fundamental style of thinking, passionate and compassionate, responsible and thankful."[2]

Donne's understanding of prayer was just as broad as that of Andrewes and Macquarrie. We have noted how, in a sermon on Luke 23:23, Donne said that prayer "may be mental, for we may think prayer. It may be vocal, for we may speak prayers. It may be actual, for we do prayer." But Donne also had something quite specific in mind when considering the nature of prayer. This is best expressed in a particular prayer, which begins:

O Eternal God, who art not only first and last, but in whom, first and last is all one, who art not only Mercy, and all Justice, but in whom Mercy and Justice is all one; who in the height of thy Justice, wouldest not spare thine own, and only most innocent Son; and yet in the depth of thy Mercy, would'st not have the wretched'st liver come to destruction; Behold us, O God, here gathered together in thy fear, according to thine ordinance, and in confidence of thy promise, that when two or three are gathered together in thy name, thou wilt be in the midst of them, and grant their petitions. We confess, O God, that we are not worthy so much as to confess; less to be heard, least to be pardoned our manifold sins. . . .[3]

Confession here involves remorse for such sensuality as betrays the Holy Spirit within, as well as for vanities, licentiousness, and the like "distempers." He says, much as he will say some years later in his sermon on Ezekiel 33:32, "These distempers, thou only, O God, who art true, and perfect harmony, canst tune, and rectify, and set in order again. Do so then, O most Merciful Father . . ." The prayer concludes with the affirmation that with this repentance new life begins. For all of the abundance of the divine mercies, thanks is given.

The prayer of contrition issues in the prayer of thanksgiving, in the knowledge of God's merciful forgiveness, displayed in heartrending clarity on the cross. Donne prayed, toward the end of his sickness in 1624, "receive the *sacrifice* of my humble thanks, that thou hast not only afforded me the ability to rise out of this *bed* of *weariness* and *discomfort*, but hast also made this *bodily* rising, by thy *grace*, an *earnest* of a *second resurrection* from *sinn*, and of a *third*, the everlasting glory."[4] He wrote of joy as characterizing the fulness of the Christian life. Thus he said, in his sermon on Psalm 63:7:

the true joy of a good soul in this world is the very joy of Heaven; and we go thither, not that being without joy, we might have joy infused into us, but that as Christ says, *Our joy might be full*, perfected, sealed with an everlastingness; for as he promises, *That no man shall take our joy from us*, so neither shall Death it self take it away, not so much as interrupt it . . .[5]

And thus prayer, for Donne, is intimately related not only to contrition but to thanksgiving, joy, and praise.

In his sermon on Psalm 90:14, Donne speaks of prayer and praise as amplified in the Lord's Prayer:

As that Prayer consists of seven petitions, and seven is infinite, so by being at first begun with glory and acknowledgement of his reigning in heaven, and then shut up in the same manner, with acclamations of power and glory, it is made a circle of praise, and a circle is infinite too, The Prayer, and the Praise is equally infinite. Infinitely poor and needy man, that ever needst infinite things to pray for; Infinitely rich and abundant man, that ever hast infinite blessings to praise God for.[6]

Lancelot Andrewes speaks of petitionary prayers in the context of the Lord's Prayer. Such prayer is commanded by God: "it is required as a part of God's service."[7] But it is important to observe the proper order. We pray first for God's kingdom, then for the working of God's righteousness, the doing of God's will, and only then for our daily bread.[8] Donne taught that petitions set in the context of praise are purified, strengthened, and perfected. He ends his sermon on Psalm 90:14 with these words:

Return to God, with a joyfull thankfulness that he hath placed you in a Church, which withholds nothing from you, that is necessary to salvation . . . And which obtrudes nothing to you, that is not necessary to salvation . . . Maintain and hold up this holy alacrity, this religious cheerfulness; For inordinate sadness is a great degree and evidence of unthankfulness, and the departing from Joy in this world, is a departing with one piece of our Evidence, for the Joyes of the world to come.[9]

In this edition there are prayers from the *Essays in Divinity* and there are prayers from the *Devotions*, both in the section containing selections from the *Devotions* and in the section of prayers. In addition, of course, the *Divine Poems* are prayers and there are prayers in the sermons. Indeed, throughout this introduction we have been concerned with prayer, if by prayer we mean the communion (communication) of John Donne with his God.

Here, in conclusion, it is important to acknowledge that Donne lived his life in communion with God, a communion marked by struggle and strife, but ultimately with a growing sense of peace and rest. That communion, it must be stressed, involved others. It developed in the context of the church with its word and sacraments: the means of grace. We have noted how in a sermon,[10] Donne confessed his need for public prayer, his inability always to pray in secret as he ought. Hooker identified corporate prayer as superior to private, the latter being rooted in the former.[11] As such, prayer involves communion with God but also with others in God. Donne was very much aware of the roots of human love in divine love, the divine inspiring the human, the human providing an avenue toward (and from) divine love.

There is something of this awareness in the *Holy Sonnet*, "Since she whome I lovd." In 1617, as Donne was growing into his priestly life, his wife, Ann, died. As he says in this poem, "my good is dead." In his grief he turned more fully toward God. "Wholy in heavenly things my mind is sett." Indeed, Ann in her life and death led him toward heaven. "Here the admyring her my mind did whett / To seeke thee God; so streames do shew the head." And thus he prays, entering into communion with God. She, as it were, was an angel descending with doctrine; Donne's spirit in

63

its grief and gratitude was an angel ascending with prayer. His love for Ann caused him now to seek the source and root of love, which is in God, whose infinite love was made known on the cross of Christ. But he cannot rest there: "though I have found thee, and thou my thirst hath fed, / A holy thirsty dropsy melts mee yett." The thirst persists. He yearns for her, for that known, deeply felt love, a holy love to him, sprung out of the root of love. There is in the last lines an expression of awe and adoration for the God who seeks the errant man still, who as a jealous lover offers all his love and desires all of Donne's love in return. The jealousy is "tender" but nevertheless real, and the implicit further prayer is that Donne may yield to receive that infinite love wholly, and wholly love God in return. All that is required here, that which is in a sense truly provided in the last hymns, is faith, realized in surrender. Prayer, for Donne, supremely concerns communion with God, involving communion with others, others who feed him, leading him toward the eternal love from whom all true loves flow.

VII

The Texts

Poems

In this edition, the text for the poems is based on that of Sir Herbert Grierson. I have used his edition of 1912, amended in 1929.[1] Helen Gardner built on Grierson's edition and I have checked all texts with those in Gardner's edition of 1952, amended in 1978.[2] Furthermore, I have adopted Dame Helen's order of the poems, being convinced by her detailed argument (pp. xxxvii ff.). And I have considered John T. Shawcross's editorial decisions as contained in both text and notes.[3] Where I have made a decision to follow Gardner or Shawcross in preference to Grierson I have made note of the fact.

In this edition an attempt has been made to retain the spelling and punctuation of the original, but the long ∫ has been silently changed to s; i/j and u/v have been distinguished according to modern practice. Such a conservative approach to the poems is warranted when consideration is given to the particular genre.

Finally, it should be noted that I have chosen only those poems that arguably belong in a Classics of Western Spirituality volume dedicated to the spirituality of John Donne. Thus the poems reprinted here constitute a selection, not all of the *Divine Poems* as found in the editions of Grierson, Gardner, and Shawcross. Shawcross said of his text of Donne's poetry that "like others before it," it is "eclectic and somewhat subjectively based."[4] The same can be said here both of the selection of texts and of the texts themselves.

Sermons

The basic text for the eight sermons in this edition is that of Potter and Simpson.[5] All students of John Donne owe a major debt to George R.

INTRODUCTION

Potter and Evelyn M. Simpson, who have produced a reliable critical text of all of the known sermons of Donne, along with helpful introductions and a magnificent index to the entire ten volumes. My hope is that those reading Donne's sermons for the first time in this edition will be lured to turn to the Potter-Simpson edition and keep on reading.

On the supposition that most readers of this volume will not be acquainted with original texts of seventeenth-century literature, I have seen fit to modernize spelling and punctuation. The results are bound to be problematic and the texts to a degree uneven. Such modernizing is at best dangerous. I have benefited by the work of such scholars as Edmund Fuller[6] and Theodore Gill[7] whose attempts at modernization proved invaluable. In addition, I have abbreviated most sermons. The omissions are indicated by the use of ellipses (. . .). I have attempted to do this with great care, but am aware of the damage such abbreviation is bound to cause. Such shortening of the texts has been done in the name of persuading readers to persist through the entire texts, not being bogged down by sometimes obtuse, sometimes perplexing passages (perplexing to twentieth-century readers, that is). For those who wish the complete texts there is the Potter-Simpson edition, widely available in libraries here and abroad.

The choice of sermons has, as indicated, been made on the basis of a presentation of the spirituality of John Donne. The selection is not intended to be representative of John Donne as preacher.

Devotions

The critical text for *Devotions Upon Emergent Occasions* is now that of Anthony Raspa.[8] We are very much in his debt for such an excellent, old spelling text, and for the critical apparatus he provides. Selections have been made from the *Devotions*, again on the basis of a presentation of Donne's spirituality. I urge that those who become involved in the selections here obtain Raspa's edition and read it carefully. Something of the rationale for the selections can be ascertained from the discussion in the introduction above.

The text has been modernized for this edition. I have benefited from the work done in the anonymously edited edition of the *Devotions* published by the University of Michigan Press.[9]

Prayers

The texts for the prayers printed in this edition have been provided by Helen Gardner in her edition of Donne's *Essays*[10] and by Raspa in his edition of the *Devotions*.[11] Some attempt has been made to modernize these texts and while I have benefited from the work of Herbert Umbach,[12] the modernization has been my effort to make the prayers more accessible to the twentieth-century reader.

The notes to sermons, devotions, and prayers are Donne's, from the margins of his texts, unless in brackets, in which case they are editorial additions.

In conclusion, this editor's fondest hopes will be realized as readers first encountering Donne's poetry and prose here turn to the critical texts cited and immerse themselves in the writings as Donne made them available to his posterity.

NOTES

I. A BRIEF LIFE

1. For most of the detail concerning Donne's life, I have relied upon the research of R. C. Bald as found in his *John Donne. A life* (New York: Oxford University Press, 1970). The interpretation is mine.
2. Bald, *John Donne*, p. 72.
3. Ibid., p. 155.
4. Ibid., p. 232.
5. "First Anniversary," ll.183–190.
6. Bald, *John Donne*, p. 326.
7. Ibid., p. 466.
8. Walton, *Lives*, p. 67, as quoted by Bald, p. 470.
9. The oration is reprinted in Bald, pp. 573–575.
10. Bald, *John Donne*, p. 498.

II. DONNE'S SPIRITUAL JOURNEY

1. Murray Rosten, *Soul of Wit: A Study of John Donne* (Oxford: At the Clarendon Press, 1974), p. 150.
2. See H. C. Porter, *Reformation and Reaction in Tudor England* (Cambridge: At the University Press, 1958), p. 393.
3. See John Booty, "Hooker and Anglicanism," *Studies in Richard Hooker*, ed. W. S. Hill (Cleveland and London: Case Western Reserve University Press, 1972), pp. 207–239.
4. Robert S. Jackson, *John Donne's Christian Vocation* (Evanston: Northwestern University Press, 1970), p. 175.
5. Ibid., p. 176.
6. T. S. Eliot, *Selected Prose*, ed. F. Kermode (New York: Harcourt Brace Jovanovich, 1975), p. 64.
7. Evelyn Simpson, *A Study of the Prose Works of John Donne*, 2nd ed. (Oxford: At the Clarendon Press, 1948), p. 6.
8. *Laws*, II.1.4. All references are to the Folger Library Edition of *The Works of Richard Hooker*, ed. W. Speed Hill (Cambridge: Belknap Press of Harvard University Press, 1977–).
9. See *The Divine Poems of John Donne*, ed. Helen Gardner, 2nd. ed. (Oxford: At the Clarendon Press, 1978), p. xliii, and Bald, *John Donne*, pp. 234–235.
10. Rosten, *Soul of Wit*, p. 154.
11. John Donne, *The Sermons of . . .*, ed. with Introduction and Critical Apparatus by George R. Potter and Evelyn M. Simpson, 10 vols. (Berkeley and Los Angeles: University of California Press, 1953–1962), 9:349.
12. *The Book of Common Prayer 1559: The Elizabethan Prayer Book*, ed. John E. Booty (Charlottesville, Va.: University Press of Virginia for the Folger Shakespeare Library, 1976), p. 50.
13. Ibid., p. 51.
14. Cited in Simpson, *Study*, p. 81.
15. Ibid., p. 90. See S. C. Scupholme, "Fraited with Salvation," "Anniversary Study of John Donne, 2," *Theology* 75 (1972), pp. 75–76.

16. *BCP, 1559,* p. 265.
17. "Thou hast made me, And shall thy worke decay?" *Holy Sonnet,* ll.5–8.
18. Simpson, *Study,* p. 86, citing Romans 7:22–24.
19. Judah Stampfer, *John Donne and the Metaphysical Gesture* (New York: Funk and Wagnalls, 1970), pp. 52–58.
20. John Donne, *Prebend Sermons,* ed. Janel M. Mueller (Cambridge: Harvard University Press, 1971), pp. 1–2.
21. Stampfer, *Metaphysical Gesture,* p. 57.
22. Robert B. Shaw, *The Call of God: The Theme of Vocation in the Poetry of Donne and Herbert* (Cambridge: Cowley Publications, 1981), pp. 37–38.
23. Ibid., pp. 65–66.
24. Ibid., p. 56.
25. Ibid., p. 57.
26. Simpson, *Study,* p. 40.
27. Stampfer, *Metaphysical Gesture,* p. 60.
28. Donne, *Sermons,* Potter and Simpson, 2:253.
29. Ibid., 5:250.
30. Ibid., 7:403.

III. THE DIVINE POEMS: A MEDITATIVE SEQUENCE

1. *The Divine Poems of John Donne,* ed. Helen Gardner, 2nd. ed. (Oxford: At the Clarendon Press, 1978), p. liv.
2. Louis Martz, *The Poetry of Meditation* (New Haven: Yale University Press, 1954), p. 15.
3. I rely here on my essay, "Joseph Hall, *The Arte of Divine Meditation,* and Anglican Spirituality," *The Roots of the Modern Christian Tradition,* ed. E. R. Elder (Kalamazoo, Mich.: Cistercian Publications, 1984), pp. 200–228.
4. Joseph Hall, *Works,* ed. Josiah Pratt (London, 1808), 7:51.
5. Douglas Peterson, *The English Lyric* (Princeton: Princeton University Press, 1967), pp. 330–348.
6. Gardner, *Divine Poems,* p. xliii.
7. Roger B. Rollin, " 'Fantastique Ague,' The Holy Sonnets and Religious Melancholy," *The Eagle and the Dove: Reassessing John Donne,* C. J. Summers, T.-L. Pebworth eds. (Columbia: University of Missouri Press, 1986), p. 131.
8. Stanley Fish, *The Living Temple* (Berkeley: University of California Press, 1978), p. 24.
9. Ibid., p. 27.
10. T. S. Eliot, *Four Quartets,* "East Coker IV," l. 156.
11. David Tracy, *Analogical Imagination* (New York: Crossroad, 1981), pp. 423–424.
12. Gardner, *Divine Poems,* p. 58.
13. John 12:32.
14. Lancelot Andrewes, Sermon on Zechariah 12:10; *Ninety-Six Sermons,* Library of Anglo-Catholic Theology (Oxford, 1841), 2:134.
15. Gardner, *Divine Poems,* p. xxiv.
16. Wilbur Sanders, *John Donne's Poetry* (Cambridge: At the University Press, 1971), p. 123.

NOTES

17. Gardner, *Divine Poems*, p. 88; *Letters*, pp. 48–52.
18. Ibid., p. 95.
19. Stampfer, *Metaphysical Gesture*, p. 283.
20. Gardner, *Divine Poems*, p. 135.
21. Shaw, *Call of God*, p. 61.
22. Ibid., p. 64.
23. Booty, "Joseph Hall," p. 214; Hall, *Works*, 7:70.

IV. SERMONS

1. Horton Davies, *Like Angels from a Cloud. The English Metaphysical Preachers, 1588–1645,* (San Marino: Huntington Library, 1986), p. 199; *Sermons*, Potter and Simpson eds., 7:133.
2. *Sermons*, Potter and Simpson eds., 2:167.
3. Ibid., pp. 166–167.
4. Ibid., p. 167.
5. See Bald, *John Donne*, p. 407.
6. Cited in ibid., p. 408. Walton *Lives*, p. 49.
7. Gale H. Carrithers, *Donne at Sermons* (Albany: State University of New York, 1972), p. 14.
8. *Sermons*, Potter and Simpson ed., 3:1–7. Carrithers' italics.
9. Carrithers, *Donne at Sermons*, pp. 17–18.
10. See Hooker, *Laws*, V.19.5.
11. See H. R. McAdoo, *The Structure of Caroline Moral Theology* (London: Longmans, Green and Co., 1949).
12. *Sermons*, Potter and Simpson ed., 2:170.
13. Ibid.
14. Thomas Bilney to Cuthbert Tunstal, Bishop of London, John Foxe, *Acts and Monuments*. G. Townsend editor. 3rd ed. (London, 1870), 4:640.
15. See Walton, *Lives* (London: Oxford University Press, 1973), p. 77, and John E. Booty, "Richard Hooker," *The Spirit of Anglicanism*, W. J. Wolf, ed. (Wilton, Ct.: Morehouse-Barlow, 1979), p. 4.
16. W. Fraser Mitchell, *English Pulpit Oratory from Andrewes to Tillotson* (New York: Russell and Russell, 1962), pp. 93–101.
17. J. W. Blench, *Preaching in England in the Late Fifteenth and Sixteenth Centuries* (New York: Barnes and Noble, 1964), pp. 102–103, 106–107.
18. Barbara Lewalski, *Donne's Anniversaries and the Poetry of Praise* (Princeton: Princeton University Press, 1973), p. 83.
19. See Booty, "Joseph Hall," p. 215.
20. See Lewalski, *Donne's Anniversaries*, pp. 90–91.
21. *Sermons*, Potter and Simpson eds., 1:168.
22. Ibid., 6:278.
23. Ibid., 6:347–348.
24. Ibid., 2:49.
25. Walter R. Davis, "Meditation, Typology, and the Structure of John Donne's Sermons," *The Eagle and The Dove*, Sumners and Pebworth eds., pp. 175–176.
26. Ibid., pp. 168–172.

27. Mueller, *Prebend Sermons*, p. 15.
28. *Sermons*, Potter and Simpson eds., 3:178–182.
29. Mueller, ibid., p. 17.
30. See Hooker, *Laws*, V.67.

V. DEVOTIONS
1. Simpson, *Study*, p. 243.
2. Bald, *John Donne*, p. 450.
3. Edmund Gosse, *The Life and Letters of John Donne* (London, 1899), 1:227.
4. Gerard Cox, III, "Donne's Devotions: A Meditative Sequence on Repentance," *Harvard Theological Review*, 66 (1973), p. 335.
5. John Donne, *Devotions Upon Emergent Occasions*, edited, with a commentary, by Anthony Raspa (New York: Oxford University Press, 1987), pp. xxxix–xl.
6. Cox, "Donne's Devotions," pp. 336–337.
7. *Devotions*, (1987), pp. 9–10. I have modernized the spelling.
8. Ibid., p. 29.
9. Ibid., p. 34.
10. Ibid., p. 44.
11. Ibid., p. 45.
12. Ibid., p. 48.
13. Ibid.
14. *Laws*, VI.3.2.
15. *Devotions* (1987), p. 87.
16. Ibid., p. 96.
17. Ibid., p. 109.
18. Ibid., pp. 110–115 (Devotion XXI).
19. Ibid., pp. 121–127 (Devotion XXIII).
20. Ibid., pp. 126–127.
21. D. W. Harding, "The Devotions Now," *John Donne: Essays in Celebration*, ed. H. G. Smith (London: Methuen, 1972), p. 402.
22. Hooker, *Works*, 7th Keble ed. (Oxford, 1888), 3:617.

VI. PRAYER AND PRAYERS
1. See my *Three Anglican Divines on Prayer: Jewel, Andrewes, and Hooker* (Cambridge: The Society of St. John the Evangelist, 1978), p. 15ff.
2. John Macquarrie, *Paths in Spirituality* (New York: Harper and Row, 1972), p. 30.
3. In John Donne, *Essays in Divinity*, ed. Evelyn Simpson (Oxford: At the Clarendon Press, 1952 [and 1965]), pp. 97–98.
4. *Devotions* (1987), p. 114.
5. *Sermons*, Potter and Simpson eds., 7:71.
6. Ibid., 5:271.
7. Andrewes, *Ninety-Six Sermons*, LACT, (Oxford, 1843), 5:331.
8. Ibid., p. 426.
9. *Sermons*, Potter and Simpson, eds., 5:294–295.
10. Ibid., 5:250.
11. Hooker, *Laws*, V.xxiv.2.

NOTES

VII. THE TEXTS

1. *The Poems of John Donne*, H. J. C. Grierson (London: Oxford University Press, 1912, etc.).
2. *The Divine Poems*, ed. with Intro. and Commentary, Helen Gardner, Second edition (Oxford: At the Clarendon Press, 1978).
3. *The Complete Poetry of John Donne*, with an Intro., Notes, and Variants, John T. Shawcross (Garden City, N.Y.: Doubleday and Co., Inc., Anchor Books, 1967).
4. Ibid., p. xxi.
5. *The Sermons of John Donne*, ed. with Intro. and Critical Apparatus, George R. Potter and Evelyn M. Simpson (Berkeley and Los Angeles: University of California Press, 1953–1962). 10 volumes.
6. *The Showing Forth of Christ: Sermons of John Donne*, selected and edited with an introduction, Edmund Fuller (New York, Evanston, and London: Harper and Row, 1964).
7. *The Sermons of John Donne*, selected and introduced, Theodore Gill (New York: Meridian Books, Living Age Books, 1958).
8. *Devotions Upon Emergent Occasions*, edited with commentary, Anthony Raspa (New York, Oxford: Oxford University Press, 1987. First published in 1975).
9. *Devotions Upon Emergent Occasions, Together with Death's Duel* (Ann Arbor: Ann Arbor Paperbacks, The University of Michigan Press, 1959, Fifth printing 1975).
10. *Essays in Divinity*, Evelyn M. Simpson ed. (Oxford: At the Clarendon Press, 1952; reprinted 1967).
11. See note #8, above.
12. Herbert H. Umbach, *The Prayers of John Donne* (New York: Bookman Associates, 1951).

Divine Poems

La Corona

1. *Deigne at my hands this crown of prayer and praise,*
Weav'd in my low devout melancholie,
Thou which of good, hast, yea art treasury,
All changing unchang'd Antient of dayes;
But doe not, with a vile crowne of fraile bayes,   5
Reward my muses white sincerity,
But what thy thorny crowne gain'd, that give mee,
A crowne of Glory, which doth flower alwayes;
The ends crowne our workes, but thou crown'st our ends,
For, at our end begins our endlesse rest,   10
The first last end, now zealously possest,
With a strong sober thirst, my soule attends.
'Tis time that heart and voice be lifted high,
Salvation to all that will is nigh.

Annunciation

2. *Salvation to all that will is nigh;*   15
That All, which alwayes is All every where,
Which cannot sinne, and yet all sinnes must beare,
Which cannot die, yet cannot chuse but die,
Loe, faithfull Virgin, yeelds himselfe to lye
In prison, in thy wombe; and though he there   20
Can take no sinne, nor thou give, yet he'will weare
Taken from thence, flesh, which deaths force may trie.
Ere by the spheares time was created, thou
Wast in his minde, who is thy Sonne, and Brother,
Whom thou conceiv'st, conceiv'd; yea thou art now   25
Thy Makers maker, and thy Fathers mother;
Thou'hast light in darke; and shutst in little roome,
Immensity cloysterd in thy deare wombe.

Nativitie

3. *Immensitie cloysterd in thy deare wombe,*
Now leaves his welbelov'd imprisonment,   30
There he hath made himselfe to his intent
Weake enough, now into our world to come;
But Oh, for thee, for him, hath th'inne no roome?
Yet lay him in this stall, and from the Orient,

75

Starres, and wisemen will travell to prevent 35
Th'effect of *Herods* jealous generall doome.
Seest thou, my Soule, with thy faiths eyes, how he
Which fils all place, yet none holds him, doth lye?
Was not his pity towards thee wondrous high,
That would have need to be pittied by thee? 40
Kisse him, and with him into Egypt goe,
With his kinde mother, who partakes thy woe.

Temple

4. *With his kinde mother who partakes thy woe,*
Joseph turne backe; see where your child doth sit,
Blowing, yea blowing out those sparks of wit, 45
Which himselfe on the Doctors did bestow;
The Word but lately could not speake, and loe,
It sodenly speakes wonders, whence comes it,
That all which was, and all which should be writ,
A shallow seeming child, should deeply know? 50
His Godhead was not soule to his manhood,
Nor had time mellowed him to this ripenesse,
But as for one which hath a long taske, 'tis good,
With the Sunne to beginne his businesse,
He in his ages morning thus began 55
By miracles exceeding power of man.

Crucifying

5. *By miracles exceeding power of man,*
Hee faith in some, envie in some begat,
For, what weake spirits admire, ambitious, hate;
In both affections many to him ran, 60
But Oh! the worst are most, they will and can,
Alas, and do, unto the immaculate,
Whose creature Fate is, now prescribe a Fate,
Measuring selfe-lifes infinity to'a span,
Nay to an inch. Loe, where condemned hee 65
Beares his owne crosse, with paine, yet by and by
When it beares him, he must beare more and die.
Now thou art lifted up, draw mee to thee,
And at thy death giving such liberall dole,
Moyst, with one drop of thy blood, my dry soule. 70

Resurrection

6. *Moyst with one drop of thy blood, my dry soule*
Shall (though she now be in extreme degree
Too stony hard, and yet too fleshly,) bee
Freed by that drop, from being starv'd, hard, or foule,
And life, by this death abled, shall controule   75
Death, whom thy death slue; nor shall to mee
Feare of first or last death, bring miserie,
If in thy little booke my name thou enroule,
Flesh in that long sleep is not putrified,
But made that there, of which, and for which 'twas;   80
Nor can by other meanes be glorified.
May then sinnes sleep, and deaths soone from me passe,
That wak't from both, I againe risen may
Salute the last, and everlasting day.

Ascention

7. *Salute the last and everlasting day,*   85
Joy at the uprising of this Sunne, and Sonne,
Yee whose just teares, or tribulation
Have purely washt, or burnt your drossie clay;
Behold the Highest, parting hence away,
Lightens the darke clouds, which hee treads upon,   90
Nor doth hee by ascending, show alone,
But first hee, and hee first enters the way.
O strong Ramme, which hast batter'd heaven for mee,
Mild Lambe, which with thy blood, hast mark'd the path;
Bright Torch, which shin'st, that I the way may see,   95
Oh, with thy owne blood quench thy owne just wrath,
And if thy holy Spirit, my Muse did raise,
Deigne at my hands this crowne of prayer and praise.

Holy Sonnets

1

As due by many titles I resigne
My selfe to thee, O God, first I was made
By thee, and for thee, and when I was decay'd
Thy blood bought that, the which before was thine;
I am thy sonne, made with thy selfe to shine,   5
Thy servant, whose paines thou hast still repaid,
Thy sheepe, thine Image, and, till I betray'd
My selfe, a temple of thy Spirit divine;
Why doth the devill then usurpe in mee?
Why doth he steale, nay ravish that's thy right?   10
Except thou rise and for thine owne worke fight,
Oh I shall soone despaire, when I doe see
That thou lov'st mankind well, yet wilt'not chuse me,
And Satan hates mee, yet is loth to lose mee.

2

Oh my blacke Soule! now thou art summoned
By sicknesse, deaths herald, and champion;
Thou art like a pilgrim, which abroad hath done
Treason, and durst not turne to whence hee is fled,
Or like a thiefe, which till deaths doome be read,   5
Wisheth himselfe delivered from prison;
But damn'd and hal'd to execution,
Wisheth that still he might be imprisoned.
Yet grace, if thou repent, thou canst not lacke;
But who shall give thee that grace to beginne?   10
Oh make thy selfe with holy mourning blacke,
And red with blushing, as thou art with sinne;
Or wash thee in Christs blood, which hath this might
That being red, it dyes red soules to white.

3

This is my playes last scene, here heavens appoint
My pilgrimmages last mile; and my race
Idly, yet quickly runne, hath this last pace,
My spans last inch, my minutes last point,

DIVINE POEMS

And gluttonous death, will instantly unjoynt   5
My body, and soule, and I shall sleepe a space,
But my'ever-waking part shall see that face,
Whose feare already shakes my every joynt:
Then, as my soule, to'heaven her first seate, takes flight,
And earth-borne body, in the earth shall dwell,   10
So, fall my sinnes, that all may have their right,
To where they'are bred, and would presse me, to hell.
Impute me righteous, thus purg'd of evill
For thus I leave the world, the flesh, the devill.

4

advances in astronomy

At the round earths imagin'd corners, blow
Your trumpets, Angells, and arise, arise
From death, you numberlesse infinities
Of soules, and to your scattred bodies goe,
All whom the flood did, and fire shall o'erthrow,   5
All whom warre, dearth, age, agues, tyrannies,
Despaire, law, chance, hath slaine, and you whose eyes,
Shall behold God, and never tast deaths woe.
But let them sleepe, Lord, and mee mourne a space,
For, if above all these, my sinnes abound,   10
'Tis late to aske abundance of thy grace,
When wee are there; here on this lowly ground,
Teach mee how to repent; for that's as good
As if thou'hadst seal'd my pardon, with thy blood.

5

If poysonous mineralls, and if that tree,
Whose fruit threw death on else immortall us,
If lecherous goats, if serpents envious
Cannot be damn'd; Alas; why should I bee?
Why should intent or reason, borne in mee,   5
Makes sinnes, else equall, in mee more heinous?
And mercy being easie, and glorious
To God; in his sterne wrath, why threatens hee?
But who am I, that dare dispute with thee
O God? Oh! of thine onely worthy blood,   10
And my teares, make a heavenly Lethean flood,
And drowne in it my sinnes blacke memorie;

79

That thou remember them, some claime as debt,
I thinke it mercy, if thou wilt forget.

6

Death be not proud, though some have called thee
Mighty and dreadfull, for, thou art not soe,
For, those, whom thou think'st, thou dost overthrow,
Die not, poore death, nor yet canst thou kill mee.
From rest and sleepe, which but thy pictures bee,   5
Much pleasure, then from thee, much more must flow,
And soonest our best men with thee doe goe,
Rest of their bones, and soules deliverie.
Thou art slave to Fate, Chance, kings, and desperate men,
And dost with poyson, warre, and sicknesse dwell,   10
And poppie, or charmes can make us sleepe as well,
And better then thy stroake; why swell'st thou then?
One short sleepe past, wee wake eternally,
And death shall be no more; death, thou shalt die.

7

Spit in my face you Jewes, and pierce my side,
Buffet, and scoffe, scourge, and crucifie mee,
For I have sinn'd, and sinn'd, and onely hee,
Who could do no iniquitie, hath dyed:
But by my death can not be satisfied   5
My sinnes, which passe the Jewes impiety:
They kill'd once an inglorious man, but I
Crucifie him daily, being now glorified.
Oh let mee then, his strange love still admire:
Kings pardon, but he bore our punishment.   10
And *Jacob* came cloth'd in vile harsh attire
But to supplant, and with gainfull intent:
God cloth'd himselfe in vile mans flesh, that so
Hee might be weake enough to suffer woe.

8

Why are wee by all creatures waited on?
Why doe the prodigall elements supply
Life and food to mee, being more pure than I,
Simple, and further from corruption?

Why brook'st thou, ignorant horse, subjection? 5
Why dost thou bull, and bore so seelily
Dissemble weaknesse, and by'one mans stroke die,
Whose whole kinde, you might swallow and feed upon?
Weaker I am, woe is mee, and worse then you,
You have not sinn'd, nor need be timorous. 10
But wonder at a greater wonder, for to us
Created nature doth these things subdue,
But their Creator, whom sin, nor nature tyed,
For us, his Creatures, and his foes, hath dyed.

9

What if this present were the worlds last night?
Marke in my heart, O Soule, where thou dost dwell,
The picture of Christ crucified, and tell
Whether that countenance can thee affright,
Teares in his eyes quench the amasing light, 5
Blood fills his frownes, which from his pierc'd head fell.
And can that tongue adjudge thee unto hell,
Which pray'd forgivenesse for his foes fierce spight?
No, no; but as in my idolatrie
I said to all my profane mistresses, 10
Beauty, of pitty, foulnesse onely is
A sign of rigour: so I say to thee,
To wicked spirits are horrid shapes assign'd,
This beauteous forme assures a pitious minde.

10

Batter my heart, three person'd God; for, you
As yet but knocke, breathe, shine, and seeke to mend;
That I may rise, and stand, o'erthrow mee,'and bend
Your force, to breake, blowe, burn and make me new.
I, like an usurpt towne, to'another due, 5
Labour to'admit you, but Oh, to no end,
Reason your viceroy in mee, mee should defend,
But is captiv'd, and proves weake or untrue.
Yet dearely'I love you,'and would be loved faine,
But am betroth'd unto your enemie: 10
Divorce mee,'untie, or breake that knot againe,
Take mee to you, imprison mee, for I

Except you'enthrall mee, never shall be free,
Nor ever chast, except you ravish mee.

11

Wilt thou love God, as he thee! then digest,
My Soule, this wholsome meditation,
How God the Spirit, by Angels waited on
In heaven, doth make his Temple in thy brest.
The Father having begot a Sonne most blest,   5
And still begetting, (for he ne'r begonne)
Hath deign'd to chuse thee by adoption,
Coheire to'his glory,'and Sabbaths endlesse rest.
And as a robb'd man, which by search doth finde
His stolne stuffe sold, must lose or buy'it againe: 10
The Sonne of glory came downe, and was slaine,
Us whom he'had made, and Satan stolne, to unbinde.
'Twas much, that man was made like God before,
But, that God should be made like man, much more.

12

Father, part of his double interest
Unto thy kingdome, thy Sonne gives to mee,
His joynture in the knottie Trinitie
Hee keepes, and gives to me his deaths conquest.
This Lambe, whose death, with life the world hath blest,   5
Was from the worlds beginning slaine, and he
Hath made two Wills, which with the Legacie
Of his and thy kingdome, doe thy Sonnes invest.
Yet such are thy laws, that men argue yet
Whether a man those statutes can fulfill;   10
None doth; but all-healing grace and spirit
Revive againe what law and letter kill.
Thy lawes abridgement, and thy last comand
Is all but love; Oh let this last Will stand!

13

Thou hast made me, And shall thy worke decay?
Repaire me now, for now mine end doth haste,
I runne to death, and death meets me as fast,
And all my pleasures are like yesterday;

I dare not move my dimme eyes any way,   5
Despaire behind, and death before doth cast
Such terrour, and my feeble flesh doth waste
By sinne in it, which it t'wards hell doth weigh;
Onely thou art above, and when towards thee
By thy leave I can looke, I rise againe;   10
But our old subtle foe so tempteth me,
That not one houre my selfe I can sustaine;
Thy Grace may wing me to prevent his art,
And thou like Adamant draw mine iron heart.

14

I am a little world made cunningly
Of Elements, and an Angelike spright,
But black sinne hath betraid to endlesse night
My worlds both parts, and (oh) both parts must die.
You which beyond that heaven which was most high   5
Have found new sphears, and of new lands can write,
Powre new seas in mine eyes, that so I might
Drowne my world with my weeping earnestly,
Or wash it, if it must be drown'd no more:
But oh it must be burnt! alas the fire   10
Of lust and envie have burnt it heretofore,
And made it fouler; Let their flames retire,
And burn me ô Lord, with a fiery zeale
Of thee and thy house, which doth in eating heale.

15

O might those sighes and teares returne againe
Into my breast and eyes, which I have spent,
That I might in this holy discontent
Mourne with some fruit, as I have mourn'd in vaine;
In mine Idolatry what showres of raine   5
Mine eyes did waste? what griefs my heart did rent?
That sufferance was my sinne; now I repent;
'Cause I did suffer I must suffer paine.
Th'hydroptique drunkard, and night-scouting thiefe,
The itchy Lecher, and selfe tickling proud   10
Have the remembrance of past joyes, for reliefe
Of comming ills. To (poore) me is allow'd

No ease; for, long, yet vehement griefe hath beene
Th'effect and cause, the punishment and sinne.

16

If faithfull soules be alike glorifi'd
As Angels, then my fathers soule doth see,
And adds this even to full felicitie,
That valiantly I hels wide mouth o'rstride:
But if our mindes to these soules be descry'd   5
By circumstances, and by signes that be
Apparent in us, not immediately,
How shall my mindes white truth by them be try'd?
They see idolatrous lovers weepe and mourne,
And vile blasphemous Conjurers to call   10
On Jesus name, and Pharisaicall
Dissemblers feigne devotion. Then turne
O pensive soule, to God, for he knowes best
Thy true griefe, for he put it in my breast.

17

Since she whom I lov'd hath payd her last debt
To Nature, and to hers, and my good is dead,
And her Soule early into heaven ravished,
Wholly on heavenly things my mind is sett.
Here the admyring her my mind did whett   5
To seeke thee God; so streames do shew their head;
But though I have found thee, and thou my thirst hast fed,
A holy thirsty dropsy melts mee yett.
But why should I begg more Love, when as thou
Dost wooe my soule for hers; offring all thine: 10
And dost not only feare least I allow
My Love to Saints and Angels things divine,
But in thy tender jealosy dost doubt
Least the World, Fleshe, yea Devill putt thee out.

18

Show me deare Christ, thy spouse, so bright and clear.
What! is it She, which on the other shore
Goes richly painted? or which rob'd and tore
Laments and mournes in Germany and here?
Sleepes she a thousand, then peepes up one yeare?   5

Is she selfe truth and errs? now new, now outwore?
Doth she, and did she, and shall she evermore
On one, on seaven, or on no hill appeare?
Dwells she with us, or like adventuring knights
First travaile we to seeke and then make Love?   10
Betray kind husband thy spouse to our sights,
And let myne amorous soule court thy mild Dove,
Who is most trew, and pleasing to thee, then
When she'is embrac'd and open to most men.

19

Oh, to vex me, contraryes meet in one:
Inconstancy unnaturally hath begott
A constant habit; that when I would not
I change in vowes, and in devotione.
As humorous is my contritione   5
As my prophane Love, and as soone forgott:
As ridlingly distemper'd, cold and hott,
As praying, as mute; as infinite, as none.
I durst not view heaven yesterday; and to day
In prayers, and flattering speaches I court God: 10
To morrow I quake with true feare of his rod.
So my devout fitts come and go away
Like a fantastique Ague: save that here
Those are my best dayes, when I shake with feare.

A Litanie.*

I
The Father

Father of Heaven, and him, by whom
It, and us for it, and all else, for us
   Thou madest, and govern'st ever, come
And re-create mee, now growne ruinous:
     My heart is by dejection, clay,   5
     And by selfe-murder, red.
From this red earth, O Father, purge away
All vicious tinctures, that new fashioned
I may rise up from death, before I'am dead.

II
The Sonne

   O Sonne of God, who seeing two things,   10
Sinne, and death crept in, which were never made,
   By bearing one, tryed'st with what stings
The other could thine heritage invade;
     O be thou nail'd unto my heart,
     And crucified againe,   15
Part not from it, though it from thee would part,
But let it be, by applying so thy paine,
Drown'd in thy blood, and in thy passion slaine.

III
The Holy Ghost

   O Holy Ghost, whose temple I
Am, but of mudde walls, and condensed dust,   20
   And being sacrilegiously
Halfe wasted with youths fires, of pride and lust,
     Must with new stormes be weatherbeat;
     Double in my heart thy flame,

---

* Donne, in his letter to Goodyer, 1609 or 1610, defined "Litany" as a "supplication" (that is, a
humble or earnest petition).

Which let devout sad teares intend; and let 25
(Though this glasse lanthorne, flesh, do suffer maime)
Fire, Sacrifice, Priest, Altar be the same.

IV
The Trinity

O Blessed glorious Trinity,
Bones to Philosophy, but milke to faith,
Which, as wise serpents, diversly 30
Most slipperinesse, yet most entanglings hath,
As you distinguish'd undistinct
By power, love, knowledge bee,
Give mee a such selfe different instinct
Of these; let all mee elemented bee, 35
Of power, to love, to know, you unnumbred three.

difficult diction

V
The Virgin Mary

For that faire blessed Mother-maid,
Whose flesh redeem'd us; That she-Cherubin,
Which unlock'd Paradise, and made
One claime for innocence, and disseiz'd sinne, 40
Whose wombe was a strange heav'n, for there
God cloath'd himselfe, and grew,
Our zealous thankes wee poure. As her deeds were
Our helpes, so are her prayers; nor can she sue
In vaine, who hath such titles unto you. 45

VI
The Angels

And since this life our nonage is,
And wee in Wardship to thine Angels be,
Native in heavens faire Palaces,
Where we shall be but denizen'd by thee,
As th'earth conceiving by the Sunne, 50
Yeelds faire diversitie,
Yet never knowes which course that light doth run,
So let mee study, that mine actions bee
Worthy their sight, though blinde in how they see.

JOHN DONNE

VII
The Patriarches
And let thy Patriarches Desire   55
(Those great Grandfathers of thy Church, which saw
  More in the cloud, then wee in fire,
Whom Nature clear'd more, then us Grace and Law,
    And now in Heaven still pray, that wee
      May use our new helpes right,)   60
Be satisfy'd, and fructifie in mee;
Let not my minde be blinder by more light
Nor Faith, by Reason added, lose her sight.

VIII
The Prophets
  The Eagle-sighted Prophets too,
Which were thy Churches Organs, and did sound   65
  That harmony, which made of two
One law, and did unite, but not confound;
    Those heavenly Poëts which did see
      Thy will, and it expresse
In rythmique feet, in common pray for mee,   70
That I by them excuse not my excesse
In seeking secrets, or Poëtiquenesse.

IX
The Apostles
  And thy illustrious Zodiacke
Of twelve Apostles, which ingirt this All,
  (From whom whosoever do not take   75
Their light, to darke deep pits, throw downe, and fall,)
    As through their prayers, thou'hast let mee know
      That their bookes are divine;
May they pray still, and be heard, that I goe
Th'old broad way in applying; O decline   80
Mee, when my comment would make thy word mine.

X
The Martyrs
  And since thou so desirously
Did'st long to die, that long before thou could'st,

And long since thou no more couldst dye,
Thou in thy scatter'd mystique body wouldst   85
   In Abel dye, and ever since
   In thine; let their blood come
To begge for us, a discreet patience
Of death, or of worse life: for Oh, to some
Not to be Martyrs, is a martyrdome.   90

XI
The Confessors

   Therefore with thee triumpheth there
A Virgin Squadron of white Confessors,
   Whose bloods betroth'd, not marryed were,
Tender'd, not taken by those Ravishers:
     They know, and pray, that wee may know,   95
     In every Christian
Hourly tempestuous persecutions grow;
Tentations martyr us alive; A man
Is to himselfe a Dioclesian.

XII
The Virgins

   The cold white snowie Nunnery,   100
Which, as thy mother, their high Abbesse, sent
   Their bodies backe againe to thee,
As thou hadst lent them, cleane and innocent,
     Though they have not obtain'd of thee,
     That or thy Church, or I,   105
Should keep, as they, our first integrity;
Divorce thou sinne in us, or bid it die,
And call chast widowhead Virginitie.

XIII
The Doctors

   Thy sacred Academie above
Of Doctors, whose paines have unclasp'd, and taught   110
   Both bookes of life to us (for love
To know thy Scriptures tells us, we are wrote
     In thy other booke) pray for us there
     That what they have misdone

Or mis-said, wee to that may not adhere; 115
Their zeale may be our sinne. Lord let us runne
Meane waies, and call them stars, but not the Sunne.

XIV

And whil'st this universall Quire,
That Church in triumph, this in warfare here,
    Warm'd with one all-partaking fire 120
Of love, that none be lost, which cost thee deare,
      Prayes ceaslesly,'and thou hearken too,
      (Since to be gratious
Our taske is treble, to pray, beare, and doe)
Heare this prayer Lord: O Lord deliver us 125
From trusting in those prayers, though powr'd out thus.

XV

From being anxious, or secure,
Dead clods of sadnesse, or light squibs of mirth,
    From thinking, that great courts immure
All, or no happinesse, or that this earth 130
      Is only for our prison fram'd,
      Or that thou art covetous
To them whom thou lovest, or that they are maim'd
From reaching this worlds sweet, who seek thee thus,
With all their might, Good Lord deliver us. 135

XVI

From needing danger, to bee good,
From owing thee yesterdaies teares to day,
    From trusting so much to thy blood,
That in that hope, wee wound our soule away,
      From bribing thee with Almes, to excuse 140
      Some sinne more burdenous,
From light affecting, in religion, newes,
From thinking us all soule, neglecting thus
Our mutuall duties, Lord deliver us.

XVII

From tempting Satan to tempt us, 145
By our connivence, or slack companie,

From measuring ill by vitious,
Neglecting to choake sins spawne, Vanitie,
From indiscreet humilitie,
Which might be scandalous,   150
And cast reproach on Christianitie,
From being spies, or to spies pervious,
From thirst, or scorne of fame, deliver us.

XVIII

Deliver us for thy descent
Into the Virgin, whose wombe was a place   155
Of middle kind; and thou being sent
To'ungratious us, staid'st at her full of grace;
And through thy poore birth, where first thou
Glorifiedst Povertie,
And yet soone after riches didst allow,   160
By accepting Kings gifts in the Epiphanie,
Deliver, and make us, to both waies free.

XIX

And through that bitter agonie,
Which is still the agonie of pious wits,
Disputing what distorted thee,   165
And interrupted evennesse, with fits;
And through thy free confession
Though thereby they were then
Made blind, so that thou might'st from them have gone,
Good Lord deliver us, and teach us when   170
Wee may not, and we may blinde unjust men.

XX

Through thy submitting all, to blowes
Thy face, thy clothes to spoile; thy fame to scorne,
All waies, which rage, or Justice knowes,
And by which thou could'st shew, that thou wast born;   175
And through thy gallant humblenesse
Which thou in death didst shew,
Dying before thy soule they could expresse,
Deliver us from death, by dying so,
To this world, ere this world doe bid us goe.   180

91

XXI

When senses, which thy souldiers are,
Wee arme against thee, and they fight for sinne,
   When want, sent but to tame, doth warre
And worke despaire a breach to enter in,
      When plenty, Gods image, and seale   185
      Makes us Idolatrous,
And love it, not him, whom it should reveale,
When wee are mov'd to seeme religious
Only to vent wit, Lord deliver us.

XXII

In Churches, when the'infirmitie   190
Of him which speakes, diminishes the Word,
   When Magistrates doe mis-apply
To us, as we judge, lay or ghostly sword,
      When plague, which is thine Angell, raignes,
      Or wars, thy Champions, swaie,   195
When Heresie, thy second deluge, gaines;
In th'houre of death, the'Eve of last judgement day,
Deliver us from the sinister way.

XXIII

Heare us, O heare us Lord; to thee
A sinner is more musique, when he prayes,   200
   Then spheares, or Angels praises bee,
In Panegyrique Allelujaes;
      Heare us, for till thou heare us, Lord
      We know not what to say;
Thine ear to'our sighes, teares, thoughts gives voice and word.
O Thou who Satan heard'st in Jobs sicke day,
Heare thy selfe now, for thou in us dost pray.

XXIV

That wee may change to evennesse
This intermitting aguish Pietie;
   That snatching cramps of wickednesse   210
And Apoplexies of fast sin, may die;
      That musique of thy promises,
      Not threats in Thunder may

Awaken us to our just offices;
What in thy booke, thou dost, or creatures say,   215
That we may heare, Lord heare us, when wee pray.

XXV

That our eares sicknesse wee may cure,
and rectifie those Labyrinths aright,
That wee, by harkning, not procure
Our praise, nor others dispraise so invite,   220
        That wee get not a slipperinesse
        And senslesly decline,
From hearing bold wits jeast at Kings excesse,
To'admit the like of majestie divine,
That we may locke our eares, Lord open thine.   225

XXVI

That living law, the Magistrate,
Which to give us, and make us physicke, doth
        Our vices often aggravate,
That Preachers taxing sinne, before her growth,
        That Satan, and invenom'd men   230
        Which well, if we starve, dine,
When they doe most accuse us, may see then
Us, to amendment, heare them; thee decline:
That we may open our eares, Lord lock thine.

XXVII

That learning, thine Ambassador,   235
From thine allegeance wee never tempt,
        That beauty, paradises flower
For physicke made, from poyson be exempt,
        That wit, borne apt high good to doe,
        By dwelling lazily   240
On Natures nothing, be not nothing too,
That our affections kill us not, nor dye,
Heare us, weake echoes, O thou eare, and cry.

XXVIII

Sonne of God heare us, and since thou
By taking our blood owest it us againe,   245

93

Gaine to thy self, or us allow;
And let not both us and thy selfe be slaine;
  O Lambe of God, which took'st our sinne
  Which could not stick to thee,
O let it not returne to us againe,   250
But Patient and Physition being free,
As sinne is nothing, let it no where be.

The Crosse

Since Christ embrac'd the Crosse it selfe, dare I
His image, th'image of his Crosse deny?
Would I have profit by the sacrifice,
And dare the chosen Altar to despise?
It bore all other sinnes, but is it fit   5
That it should beare the sinne of scorning it?
Who from the picture would avert his eye,
How would he flye his paines, who there did dye?
From mee, no Pulpit, nor misgrounded law,
Nor scandall taken, shall this Crosse withdraw,   10
It shall not, for it cannot; for, the losse
Of this Crosse, were to mee another Crosse;
Better were worse, for, no affliction,
No Crosse is so extreme, as to have none.
Who can blot out the Crosse, which th'instrument   15
Of God, dew'd on mee in the Sacrament?
Who can deny mee power, and liberty
To stretch mine armes, and mine owne Crosse to be?
Swimme, and at every stroake, thou art thy Crosse;
The Mast and yard make one, where seas do tosse;   20
Looke downe, thou spiest out Crosses in small things;
Looke up, thou seest birds rais'd on crossed wings;
All the Globes frame, and spheares, is nothing else
But the Meridians crossing Parallels.
Materiall Crosses then, good physicke bee,   25
But yet spirituall have chiefe dignity.
These for extracted chimique medicine serve,
And cure much better, and as well preserve;
Then are you your own physicke, or need none,
When Still'd, or purg'd by tribulation.   30
For when that Crosse ungrudg'd, unto you stickes,
Then are you to your selfe a Crucifixe.
As perchance, Carvers do not faces make,
But that away, which hid them there, do take:
Let Crosses, soe, take what hid Christ in thee,   35
And be his image, or not his, but hee.
But, as oft Alchimists doe coyners prove,

So may a selfe-dispising, get selfe-love,
And then as worst surfets, or best meates bee,
Soe is pride, issued from humility, 40
For, 'tis no child, but monster; therefore Crosse
Your joy in crosses, else, 'tis double losse.
And crosse thy senses, else, both they, and thou
Must perish soone, and to destruction bowe.
For if the'eye seeke good objects, and will take 45
No crosse from bad, wee cannot scape a snake.
So with harsh, hard, sowre, stinking, crosse the rest,
Make them indifferent; call nothing best.
But most the eye needs crossing, that can rome,
And move; To th'others th'objects must come home. 50
And crosse thy heart: for that in man alone
Points downewards, and hath palpitation.
Crosse those dejections, when it downeward tends,
And when it to forbidden heights pretends.
And as the braine through bony walls, doth vent 55
By sutures, which a Crosses forme present,
So when thy braine workes, ere thou utter it,
Crosse and correct concupiscence of witt.
Be covetous of Crosses, let none fall.
Crosse no man else, but crosse thy selfe in all. 60
Then doth the Crosse of Christ worke fruitfully
Within our hearts, when wee love harmlesly
That Crosses pictures much, and with more care
That Crosses children, which our Crosses are.

Resurrection, imperfect*

Sleep sleep old Sun, thou canst not have repast
As yet, the wound thou took'st on friday last;
Sleepe then, and rest; The world may beare thy stay,
A better Sun rose before thee to day,
Who, not content to'enlighten all that dwell   5
On the earths face, as thou, enlightned hell,
And made the darke fires languish in that vale,
As, at thy presence here, our fires grow pale.
Whose body having walk'd on earth, and now
Hasting to Heaven, would, that he might allow   10
Himselfe unto all stations, and fill all,
For these three daies become a minerall;
Hee was all gold when he lay downe, but rose
All tincture, and doth not alone dispose
Leaden and iron wills to good, but is   15
Of power to make even sinfull flesh like his.
Had one of those, whose credulous pietie
Thought, that a Soule one might discerne and see
Goe from a body,'at this sepulcher been,
And, issuing from the sheet, this body seen,   20
He would have justly thought this body a soule,
If not of any man, yet of the whole.
    Desunt cætera.

---

* The word "imperfect" indicates that the poem is incomplete, as does *Desunt cætera* at the end,
meaning "the rest is lacking."

Upon the Annunciation and Passion falling upon one day, 1608*

Tamely, fraile body, 'abstaine to day; to day
My soule eates twice, Christ hither and away.
She sees him man, so like God made in this,
That of them both a circle embleme is,
Whose first and last concurre; this doubtfull day   5
Of feast or fast, Christ came, and went away.
Shee sees him nothing twice at once, who'is all;
Shee sees a Cedar plant it selfe, and fall,
Her Maker put to making, and the head
Of life, at once, not yet alive, yet dead.   10
She sees at once the virgin mother stay
Reclus'd at home, Publique at Golgotha;
Sad and rejoyc'd shee's seen at once, and seen
At almost fiftie, and at scarce fifteene.
At once a Sonne is promis'd her, and gone,   15
Gabriell gives Christ to her, He her to John;
Not fully a mother, Shee's in Orbitie,
At once receiver and the legacie.
All this, and all betweene, this day hath showne,
Th'Abridgement of Christs story, which makes one   20
(As in plaine Maps, the furthest West is East)
Of the'Angels *Ave,*'and *Consummatum est.*
How well the Church, Gods Court of faculties
Deales, in some times, and seldome joyning these!
As by the selfe'fix'd Pole wee never doe   25
Direct our course, but the next starre thereto,
Which showes where the'other is, and which we say
(Because it strayes not farre) doth never stray;
So God by his Church, neerest to him, wee know,
And stand firme, if wee by her motion goe;   30
His Spirit, as his fiery Pillar doth
Leade, and his Church, as cloud; to one end both.
This Church, by letting these daies joyne, hath shown

---

* The feast of the Annunciation and Good Friday fell on March 25 in 1608.

Death and conception in mankinde is one;
Or'twas in him the same humility,   35
That he would be a man, and leave to be:
Or as creation he hath made, as God,
With the last judgement, but one period,
His imitating Spouse would joyne in one
Manhoods extremes: He shall come, he is gone: 40
Or as though one blood drop, which thence did fall,
Accepted, would have serv'd, he yet shed all;
So though the least of his paines, deeds, or words,
Would busie a life, she all this day affords;
This treasure then, in grosse, my Soule uplay,   45
And in my life retaile it every day.

Goodfriday, 1613. Riding Westward

Let mans Soule be a Spheare, and then, in this,
The intelligence that moves, devotion is,
And as the other Spheares, by being growne
Subject to forraigne motions, lose their owne,
And being by others hurried every day,   5
Scarce in a yeare their naturall forme obey:
Pleasure or businesse, so, our Soules admit
For their first mover, and are whirld by it.
Hence is't, that I am carryed towards the West
This day, when my Soules forme bends towards the East.   10
There I should see a Sunne, by rising set,
And by that setting endlesse day beget;
But that Christ on this Crosse, did rise and fall,
Sinne had eternally benighted all.
Yet dare I'almost be glad, I do not see   15
That spectacle of too much weight for mee.
Who sees Gods face, that is selfe life, must dye;
What a death were it then to see God dye?
It made his owne Lieutenant Nature shrinke,
It made his footstoole crack, and the Sunne winke.   20
Could I behold those hands which span the Poles,
And tune all spheares at once, peirc'd with those holes?
Could I behold that endlesse height which is
Zenith to us, and our Antipodes,
Humbled below us? or that blood which is   25
The seat of all our Soules, if not of his,
Made durt of dust, or that flesh which was worne
By God, for his apparell, rag'd, and torne?
If on these things I durst not looke, durst I
Upon his miserable mother cast mine eye,   30
Who was Gods partner here, and furnish'd thus
Halfe of that Sacrifice, which ransom'd us?
Though these things, as I ride, be from mine eye,
They'are present yet unto my memory,
For that looks towards them; and thou look'st towards mee,   35
O Saviour, as thou hang'st upon the tree;
I turne my backe to thee, but to receive

Corrections, till thy mercies bid thee leave.
O thinke mee worth thine anger, punish mee,
Burne off my rusts, and my deformity,   40
Restore thine Image, so much, by thy grace,
That thou may'st know mee, and I'll turne my face.

To Mr. Tilman after he had taken orders

Thou, whose diviner soule hath caus'd thee now
To put thy hand unto the holy Plough,
Making Lay-scornings of the Ministry,
Not an impediment, but victory;
What bringst thou home with thee? how is thy mind   5
Affected since the vintage? Dost thou finde
New thoughts and stirrings in thee? and as Steele
Toucht with a Loadstone, dost new motions feele?
Or, as a Ship after much paine and care,
For Iron and Cloth brings home rich Indian ware,   10
Hast thou thus traffiqu'd, but with farre more gaine
Of noble goods, and with lesse time and paine?
Thou art the same materials, as before,
Onely the stampe is changed; but no more.
And as new crowned Kings alter the face,   15
But not the monies substance, so hath grace
Chang'd onely Gods old Image by Creation,
To Christs new stampe, at this thy Coronation;
Or, as we paint Angels with wings, because
They beare Gods message, and proclaime his lawes,   20
Since thou must doe the like, and so must move,
Art thou new feather'd with cœlestiall love?
Deare, tell me where thy purchase lies, and shew
What thy advantage is above, below.
But if thy gainings doe surmount expression,   25
Why doth the foolish world scorne that profession,
Whose joyes passe speech? Why do they think unfit
That Gentry should joyne families with it?
As if their day were onely to be spent
In dressing, Mistressing and complement;   30
Alas poore joyes, but poorer men, whose trust
Seemes richly placed in sublimed dust;
(For, such are cloathes and beauty, which though gay,
Are, at the best, but of sublimed clay.)
Let then the world thy calling disrespect,   35
But goe thou on, and pitty their neglect.
What function is so noble, as to bee

Embassadour to God and destinie?
To open life, to give kingdomes to more
Than Kings give dignities; to keepe heavens doore? 40
Maries prerogative was to beare Christ, so
'Tis preachers to convey him, for they doe
As Angels out of clouds, from Pulpits speake;
And blesse the poore beneath, the lame, the weake.
If then th'Astronomers, whereas they spie 45
A new-found Starre, their Opticks magnifie,
How brave are those, who with their Engines, can
Bring man to heaven, and heaven againe to man?
These are thy titles and preheminences,
In whom must meet Gods graces, mens offences, 50
And so the heavens which beget all things here,
And the earth our mother, which these things doth beare,
Both these in thee, are in thy Calling knit,
And make thee now a blest Hermaphrodite.

A Hymne to Christ,
at the Authors last going into Germany*

In what torne ship soever I embarke,
That ship shall be my embleme of thy Arke;
What sea soever swallow mee, that flood
Shall be to mee an embleme of thy blood;
Though thou with clouds of anger do disguise   5
Thy face; yet through that maske I know those eyes,
    Which, though they turne away sometimes, they never will despise.

I sacrifice this Iland unto thee,
And all whom I lov'd there, and who lov'd mee;
When I have put our seas twixt them and mee,   10
Put thou thy sea betwixt my sinnes and thee.
As the trees sap doth seeke the root below
In winter, in my winter now I goe,
    Where none but thee, th'Eternall root of true Love I may know.

Nor thou nor thy religion dost controule,   15
The amorousnesse of an harmonious Soule,
But thou would'st have that love thy selfe: As thou
Art jealous, Lord, so I am jealous now,
Thou lov'st not, till from loving more, thou free
My soule: Who ever gives, takes libertie: 20
    O, if thou car'st not whom I love alas, thou lov'st not mee.

Seale then this bill of my Divorce to All,
On whom those fainter beames of love did fall;
Marry those loves, which in youth scatter'd bee
On Fame, Wit, Hopes (false mistresses) to thee.   25
Churches are best for Prayer, that have least light:
To see God only, I goe out of sight:
    And to scape stormy dayes, I chuse an Everlasting night.

---

* The title refers to Donne's journey to the continent with Lord Doncaster on May 12, 1619.

Hymne to God My God, in My Sicknesse

Since I am comming to that Holy roome,
    Where, with thy Quire of Saints for evermore,
I shall be made thy Musique; As I come
    I tune the Instrument here at the dore,
    And what I must doe then, thinke here before. 5

Whilst my Physitians by their love are growne
    Cosmographers, and I their Mapp, who lie
Flat on this bed, that by them may be showne
    That this is my South-west discoverie
    Per fretum febris, by these streights to die, 10

I joy, that in these straits, I see my West;
    For, though theire currants yeeld returne to none,
What shall my West hurt me? As West and East
    In all flatt Maps (and I am one) are one,
    So death doth touch the Resurrection. 15

Is the Pacifique Sea my home? Or are
    The Easterne riches? Is *Jerusalem?*
Anyan, and *Magellan*, and *Gibraltare*,
    All streights, and none but streights, are wayes to them,
    Whether where *Japhet* dwelt, or *Cham*, or *Sem*. 20

We thinke that *Paradise* and *Calvarie*,
    Christs Crosse, and *Adams* tree, stood in one place;
Looke Lord, and finde both *Adams* met in me;
    As the first *Adams* sweat surrounds my face,
    May the last *Adams* blood my soule embrace. 25

So, in his purple wrapp'd receive mee Lord,
    By these his thornes give me his other Crowne;
And as to others soules I preach'd thy word,
    Be this my Text, my Sermon to mine owne,
    Therefore that he may raise the Lord throws down. 30

A Hymne to God the Father

I

Wilt thou forgive that sinne where I begunne,
    Which is my sin, though it were done before?
Wilt thou forgive those sinnes through which I runne,
    And do run still: though still I do deplore?
      When thou hast done, thou hast not done,   5
          For, I have more.

II

Wilt thou forgive that sinne by which I'have wonne
    Others to sinne? and, made my sinne their doore?
Wilt thou forgive that sinne which I did shunne
    A yeare, or two: but wallow'd in, a score?   10
      When thou hast done, thou hast not done,
          For I have more.

III

I have a sinne of feare, that when I have spunne
    My last thred, I shall perish on the shore;
But sweare by thy selfe, that at my death thy sonne   15
    Shall shine as he shines now, and heretofore;
      And, having done that, Thou hast done,
          I have no more.

No more worries

NOTES

LA CORONA
4. *Antient of dayes;:* See Dan. 7.
5. *bayes,:* leaves.
10. *rest,:* "rest;" in Grierson, "rest," in Gardner.
24. *Brother,:* "Brother;" in Grierson, "*Brother*," in Gardner.
36. *Herods jealous generall doome.:* Matthew 2:13–16.
44. *where your child doth sit,:* Luke 2:27–46.
47. *The Word:* the Logos (John 1:14–18).
54. *the Sunne:* Donne frequently identifies "sun" with "Son."
64. *span,:* a limited space. See Psalm 39:6 and Proverbs 8:27.
68. *lifted up, draw:* John 12:32.
70. *dry:* spiritually dry.
75. *abled,:* enabled.
76. *slue,:* slew.
78. *booke:* Book of Life (Revelation 3:5).
91. *Nor doth hee by ascending,:* See Colossians 2:15.
93. *O strong Ramme,:* See Micah 2:13. It should also be noted that the ram is the sign of Aries and of the coming of spring, about the time of Easter.

HOLY SONNETS
Sonnets 1–12 were in the 1633 edition.

AS DUE BY MANY TITLES I RESIGNE
1. *titles:* legal rights.
3. *decay'd:* participant in Adam's fall.
4. *bought:* redeemed.
6. *still:* always.
9. *in:* "on" in Grierson, "in" in Gardner.

OH MY BLACKE SOULE!
NOW THOU ART SOMMONED
5. *deaths doome be read,:* the sentence on Judgment Day.
11. *blacke,:* indicating foulness.
12. *red,:* color of sin and contrition.
13. *Christs blood,:* See 1 John 1:7.

THIS IS MY PLAYES LAST SCENE,
HERE HEAVENS APPOINT
4. *My spans:* life-span's.
   last: "latest" in Grierson. I follow Gardner here. See *Divine Poems,* p. 67.
7. *ever-waking part:* soul.
   that face,: God's face on Judgment Day.
8. *Whose feare:* the fear of whom.
9. *seate,:* residence.

13. *Impute me righteous,:* See the doctrine of justification wherein the Christian is made righteous by imputation of Christ's merits.

AT THE ROUND EARTHS IMAGIN'D CORNERS, BLOW
1. *round earths imagin'd corners,:* See Revelation 7:1.
5. *fire:* See 2 Peter 3:10.
8. *never tast deaths woe.:* See Luke 9:27 and see 1 Corinthians 16:51.

IF POYSONOUS MINERALLS, AND IF THAT TREE
1. *tree,:* this is the tree of the knowledge of Good and Evil whose fruit Adam and Eve consumed, with dire results.
3. *goats,:* identified with Pan and Satan.
   serpents: identified with Satan.
10. *onely:* alone.
11. *Lethean flood,:* forgetful (from Lethe).
13. *claime as debt,:* See Jeremiah 31:34.

DEATH BE NOT PROUD, THOUGH SOME HAVE CALLED THEE
8. *deliverie.:* liberation.
12. *swell'st:* puffed up with pride.
14. *death, thou shalt die.:* See 1 Corinthians 15:26.

SPIT IN MY FACE YOU JEWES, AND PIERCE MY SIDE
3. *hee,:* Jesus.
5. *satisfied:* atoned for.
11. *Jacob:* See Genesis 26:6–29. "Jacob" is translated "one who supplants."

WHY ARE WEE BY ALL CREATURES WAITED ON?
2. *prodigall:* wasteful.
4. *Simple,:* simpler.
6. *bore:* boar.
   seelily: meekly, naively.
7. *Dissemble:* feign.
10. *timorous.:* fearful.
13. *tyed,:* restricted.

WHAT IF THIS PRESENT WERE THE WORLDS LAST NIGHT?
5. *amasing:* fearful, terrifying.
8. *spight?:* malice.
11–12. *Beauty, ... rigour.:* Shawcross suggests: "Beauty is only a sign of pity; foulness is only a sign of rigor. That is, beauty arises from tenderness or kindness of love (mercy); ugliness arises from severity, cruelty, or mercilessness" (*The Complete Poetry of John Donne*, p. 344).
14. *forme:* Christ crucified.

NOTES

BATTER MY HEART, THREE PERSON'D GOD; FOR, YOU
1. *three person'd God;:* Father, Son and Holy Spirit.
2. *knocke,:* See Revelation 3:20.
8. *untrue.:* unfaithful.
9. *faine,:* gladly, with joy.
11. *againe,:* the knot was first broken by Christ, his incarnation and crucifixion.
13. *Except:* unless.
    enthrall: enslave.

WILT THOU LOVE GOD, AS HE THEE! THEN DIGEST
4. *Temple:* See 1 Corinthians 3:16; 6:19.
6. *he:* the Son, who is outside time, eternal, without a beginning.
12. *unbinde.:* release from the bonds man made with Satan.

FATHER, PART OF HIS DOUBLE INTEREST
1. *double interest:* as a divine member of the Holy Trinity and as a human being.
3. *joynture:* joint tenancy or possession.
   knottie: difficult to explain.
4. *deaths conquest.:* the conquest of death.
5-6. *This ... slaine:* See Revelation 13:8.
7. *two Wills,:* the Old and New Testaments.
8. *doe thy Sonnes invest.:* grant rights to, offering opportunity for moral and spiritual growth.
12. *Revive ... kill.:* See 2 Corinthians 3:6.
14. *last Will:* See John 13:34.

Sonnets 13–16 were added in 1635.

THOU HAST MADE ME, AND SHALL THY WORKE DECAY?
8. *it t'wards hell doth weigh;:* See Isaiah 36:7.
11. *foe:* Satan.
13. *prevent:* frustrate.
14. *Adamant:* magnetic loadstone.
    iron: sinful.

I AM A LITTLE WORLD MADE CUNNINGLY
1. *little world:* a person was said to be a microcosm.
2. *Elements,:* earth, water, air, fire.
   spright,: spirit.
4. *parts,:* soul and body, the dwelling place of the "Angelike spright" (1 Cor. 6:19).
5. *You:* Christ.
7. *Powre:* pour.
9. *Drown'd no more::* See Genesis 9:11.
10. *burnt!:* See 2 Peter 3:10; the fire at the end of history.

109

13–14. *zeale . . . house,:* Psalm 69:9.

       eating heale.: partaking of the body and blood of Christ in the Eucharist.

O MIGHT THOSE SIGHES AND TEARES RETURNE AGAINE

  6. *rent:* tear apart.

  7. *sufferance:* suffering, tolerance of idolatry.

  9. *hydroptique:* thirsty.

    night-scouting: night-prowling.

IF FAITHFULL SOULES BE ALIKE GLORIFI'D

  3. *even:* to the extent of; see Revelation 22:18.

  5. *descry'd:* known; revealed.

  10. *Conjurers:* magicians.

  14. *griefe,:* suffering.

Sonnets 17–19 are from the Westmorland MS.

SINCE SHE WHOM I LOV'D HATH PAYD HER LAST DEBT

  1. *she:* Donne's wife.

  2. *hers,:* her nature as a mortal being.

  6. *head;:* source.

  8. *dropsy:* a disease characterized in part by intense thirst.

  13. *jealosy:* zealousness.

  14. *World, . . . Devill:* avarice, gluttony, vainglory.

SHOW ME DEARE CHRIST, THY SPOUSE, SO BRIGHT AND CLEAR

  1. *spouse,:* true church; see Matthew 25:1–13.

  2. *other shore:* European continent; referring to Roman Catholicism.

  4. *here?:* Lutheran Church in Germany and Calvinist Puritans in England.

  6. *selfe truth:* truth itself.

  8. *On one, . . . appeare?:* refers to Mount Moriah where Solomon built the Temple, the seven hills of Rome, and Calvin's Geneva, where there is "no hill."

  11. *Betray:* reveal.

  14. *open:* accessible.

OH, TO VEX ME, CONTRARYES MEET IN ONE

  5. *humorous:* changeable.

  11. *feare of his rod.:* See Job 9:34–5.

  13. *fantastique:* imaginary.

    Ague: fever involving paroxysms.

A LITANIE

  7. *red earth,:* "Adam"—made from red earth.

  12. *one,:* death, by crucifixion.

    tryed'st: proved.

NOTES

19. *temple:* See 1 Corinthians 6:19.
25. *intend;:* intensify.
26. *glasse lanthorne,:* flesh is a lantern through which the divine light shines, unless it be maimed by lust and pride.
29. *Bones to:* foundation of.
32. *distinguish'd undistinct:* the Holy Trinity.
34. *Give . . . instinct:* Give one an awareness of the Triune unity, and the distinct but related nature of power, love, knowledge, attributes of the Trinity—Father, Son and Holy Spirit.
40. *disseiz'd:* ousted.
45. *titles unto:* claims upon.
49. *denizen'd:* admitted to the rights of citizenship, although an alien.
53. *study,:* meditate; be intelligent.
55. *Patriarches Desire:* desire for the Kingdom of Heaven; see Hebrews 11:16.
57. *More . . . fire,:* God appears in a pillar of cloud by day and a pillar of fire by night (Exodus 13:21).
58. *clear'd:* enlightened.
64. *Eagle-sighted:* eagles were known to possess exceptional vision.
65–66. *sound/That harmony,:* foretold Christ as the mediator of the Old and New Covenants.
73. *Zodiacke:* circle.
74. *ingirt this all.:* encircle the universe; the apostles in legend were said to have gone to all parts of the world.
76. *throw downe,:* See Matthew 15:14.
80. *decline:* humble.
86. *Abel:* the first martyr (see Genesis 4:2–8) and type of Christ.
92. *white:* the liturgical color for virgins and confessors as contrasted to red for martyrs.
94. *Tender'd,:* offered.
98. *Tentations:* temptations.
99. *Dioclesian:* Roman Emperor (284–305) and persecutor of Christians.
101. *as:* like.
105. *That:* the nunnery.
 or thy Church,: the church of the time of the apostles, called by Eusebius a pure virgin.
111. *Both bookes:* the Books of Life in Revelation (see Revelation 13:8) and the scripture as a whole.
112. *wrote:* "wrought" in Gardner and Shawcross.
116–117. *Lord . . . Sunne.:* Let us take the middle way steering for the stars, but not taking them to be the chief light or sun.
124. *pray, beare, and doe:* pray to the Father, suffer with the Son, and engage in the fruits of the Spirit.
126. *powr'd:* poured.
127. *secure,:* careless.
133. *maim'd:* incapacitated.
142. *light affecting, in religion, newes,:* from lightly adopting novel beliefs and actions in religion.

147. *by vitious,:* by vices rather than by virtues.
152. *spies pervious,:* See Galatians 2:4; accessible to spies.
153. *thirst,:* pride of life.
164. *pious wits,:* theologians.
167–171. *And through ... men.:* See John 18:4–6.
178. *expresse,:* press out, extract.
193. *sword,:* See Ephesians 6:17.
194. *thine Angell,:* See 2 Samuel 24:15–16.
198. *sinister:* worse.
206. *Job's sicke day,:* See Job 2:4–7.
219–220. *That wee, by harkning, ... invite,:* "That by lending a ready ear, we do not procure flattery from others, nor invite them to speak against others" (Gardner, p. 91).
223. *excesse,:* excellency.
226–234. See Gardner, p. 91.
230. *invenom'd men:* those poisoned by Satan, the serpent.
231. *starve,:* die.
238. *For physicke:* for purgation of sin.
239–241. *That wit, ... nothing too,:* Reason is given us that we may know God. If it is content with the investigation of nature, which counts for nothing without its Creator, then reason is worthless as well.

THE CROSSE

2. *th'image:* as in the sign of the Cross in Baptism; see line 16.
20. *yard:* long spar which crosses the mast.
27. *extracted chimique medicine:* the spiritual crosses serve to counteract destructive humors.
30. *Still'd,:* both stopped and distilled (being purified).
31. *stickes,:* is impaled.
34–35. *take:/ Let:* 1635, etc., and Gardner have "take:," Grierson has "take;."
37. *prove,:* that is, attempting to turn base metal into gold coins.
41. *'tis:* pride.
   Crosse: cancel.
46. *snake.:* the devil or sin.
48. *indifferent; call:* Grierson has "indifferent all; call"; I prefer the 1633 reading, followed by Gardner.
50. *th'others:* Grierson has "th'other" but most manuscripts read "th'others" and the sense of this line seems to demand the plural. See Gardner, p. 93.
56. *sutures,:* seams.
63. *pictures:* types of Christ's cross.
   care: concern.

RESURRECTION, IMPERFECT

1. *repast:* recovered from.
9. *Whose body ...:* See Ephesians 4:9–10.
10. *allow,:* admit and reveal his identity.
12. *minerall;:* mine.

NOTES

22. *of the whole.:* God being all; the risen body of the Lord being the principle of all life. See 1 Corinthians 15:28.

UPON THE ANNUNCIATION AND PASSION FALLING UPON ONE DAY, 1608

1. *Tamely,:* submissively.
3. *She:* his soul.
4. *circle:* That Christ's life began and ended on that day provides a circle, an emblem of perfection and of God.
6. *feast or fast,:* The Annunciation is a feast day in the church calendar, Good Friday a fast day.
8. *Cedar:* symbol of the Godhead.
17. *Orbitie,:* bereavement.
21. *plaine Maps,:* on a flat map points at either end correspond.
22. *Ave . . . Consummatum est.:* See Luke 1:28 and John 19:30.
31. *fiery Pillar:* See Exodus 13:21.
33. *daies:* feasts.
38. *one period,:* one aim; the same point in time.
39. *Spouse:* Church.
45. *uplay,:* store up for distribution in the future; see Matthew 6:19–21.

GOODFRIDAY, 1613. RIDING WESTWARD

1–10. *Let mans Soule . . . the East.:* Gardner writes: "The soul is the moving principle, or 'forme' to the body; the intelligence, or Angel, which moves the sphere, is then its 'naturall forme'. Devotion is the intelligence or 'forme' of the soul" (p. 98). See the rest in Gardner, pp. 98–9.
11. *Sunne, by rising:* Christ was identified with the Sun, which directs the motions of all the other spheres.
12. *endlesse day:* the enlightenment brought by Christ.
17. *selfe life,:* life itself; see Exodus 33:20.
20. *footstoole:* See Isaiah 66:1.
22. *tune:* Grierson has "turne," but 1633 has "tune" and this seems to me to be in line with what Donne has written elsewhere, as in his sermon on Ezekiel 33:32.
27. *durt:* dirt made of dust by being moistened with blood.
32. *Halfe of that Sacrifice,:* God providing the other half.
34. *memory,:* in the back of the mind and this looks east toward the cross.

TO MR. TILMAN AFTER HE HAD TAKEN ORDERS

2. *Plough,:* See Luke 9:62.
6. *since the vintage?:* since reaching the harvest, deciding upon ordination.
8. *Loadstone,:* magnet.
13–18. *Thou art . . . Coronation;:* See Gardner (p. 101) for an alternative wording.
23. *purchase:* pursuit.

34. *sublimed:* refined.
38. *Embassadour to God:* See 2 Corinthians 5:20.
46. *Opticks:* telescopes.
47. *Engines,:* Grierson has "Engine"; I follow Gardner and Shawcross here; meaning devices, means of grace.
54. *Hermaphrodite.:* used here to mean the combination of opposites, as God's grace with human sin.

A HYMNE TO CHRIST, AT THE AUTHORS LAST GOING INTO GERMANY

2. *Arke,:* symbol of God's providence; see Exodus 13:21.
7. The last line in each stanza is two lines in Grierson.
10. *seas:* emblem of Christ's blood which joins one to another.
11. *sea:* Perhaps Noah's flood is implied here.
15. *controule,:* neither Christ nor religion stand in the way of love.
18. *jealous:* demanding devotion.
24. *scatter'd:* This is "scattered" in Grierson, but "scatter'd" in Gardner and Shawcross for the sake of metrical requirement.
28. *an Everlasting night.:* prayer for death and thus for final divorce from this world.

HYMNE TO GOD MY GOD, IN MY SICKNESSE

4. *Instrument:* the soul.
9. *South-west discoverie:* The South is hot (fever) and the West the place were the sun sets (death). He is to die of a raging (*fretum*) fever.
11. *straits,:* See Matthew 7:13–14.
18. *Anyan,:* the Bering Strait.
20. *Japhet ... Cham, or Sem.:* sons of Noah, who propagated the world, Europe, Africa, and Asia.
23. *Adams:* Adam and Christ.
24–25. *As the first ... embrace.:* See 1 Corinthians 15:45.
26–27. *So, in his purple ... Crowne,:* See Mark 15:17.
28–29. *And as the others ... owne,:* See 1 Corinthians 9:27.
30. *that he may raise the Lord throws down.:* See Job 22:29 and Psalm 146:8, in the Vulgate.

A HYMNE TO GOD THE FATHER

1. *that sinne:* original sin.
2. *is:* "was" in Grierson; see Psalm 51:5; this sin which was still is.
3. *those sinnes:* "that sinne;" in Grierson. I follow Gardner here.
5. *When thou hast done, thou hast not done,:* a pun on his own name.
7. *by which I'have wonne:* Grierson has "which I have wonne"; see Gardner, p. 110.
10. *wallow'd:* Grierson has "wallowed."
13–14. *spunne My last thred,:* lived my last moment.
14. *perish on the shore,:* rather than journey to heaven.

NOTES

15–16. *sweare . . . shines now,:* sonne is here a type of Divine mercy; see, for the ending of this poem, Genesis 15:12; 22:16; Hebrews 6:13–19.

17. *hast:* "haste" in Grierson; "hast" in Gardner.

18. *have:* "feare" in Grierson; "have" in Gardner and Shawcross; see Gardner, *Divine Poems,* p. 111.

Sermons

Christe the Light[1]

John 1:8. "He was not that light, but was sent to bear witness of that light."

... Now, though the words of this text ... are placed in the first part of the chapter, that which concerns Christ's divine nature, yet they belong and they have a respect to all three: To his divine nature, to his offices, and to his calling of his apostles. For, first, light denotes his divine nature; secondly, the testimony that is given of him by John Baptist (of whom the words of our text are spoken) declares him to be the Messias, and Messias (which signifies anointed) involves all his offices, for his three offices [prophet, priest, and king] are his three vocations; and thirdly, the application of this testimony, given by John Baptist here, by the apostles and their successors after, intimates or brings to our memory this their first vocation, in this chapter. So that the Gospel, and this text all the chapter. ... Therefore it is too large to go through at this time.[2]

Divisio

At this time we shall insist upon such branches as arise out of that consideration, what and who this light is; for we shall find it to be both a personal light (it is some body) and otherwise too a real light (it is some thing), therefore we inquire what this light is (what thing) and who this light is (what person) which John Baptist is denied to be. Hereafter we shall consider the testimony which is given of this light; in which part in due time we shall handle the person of the witness John Baptist, in whom we shall find many considerable and extraordinary circumstances; and then his citation and calling to this testimony; and thirdly, the testimony itself that

[1]. Preached at St. Paul's Cathedral, Christmas Day, 1621. *Sermons*, Potter and Simpson eds., 7:348–75.
[2]. In this sermon Donne is concerned with only the first part, the divine nature. The other parts were his concern in two other sermons, the first on St. John the Baptist Day, June 24, 1622, and the other a few months later. This sermon was the first that Donne preached at St. Paul's Cathedral, London.

he gave; and lastly, why any testimony was requisite to so evident a thing as light. But the first part, who and what this light is, belongs most properly to this day and will fill that portion of the day which is afforded us for this exercise. Proceed we therefore to that, John Baptist was not that light, who was, what was?

Part 1. *Quis lux*

Though most expositors, as well ancient as modern, agree with one general and unanimous consent that light in this verse is intended and meant of Christ, Christ is this light, yet in some precedent and subsequent passages in this chapter I see other senses have been admitted of this word, light, than perchance those places will bear; certainly other than those places need; particularly in the fourth verse ("In it was life, and that life was the light of men") there they understand "life" to be nothing but this natural life which we breath, and "light" to be only that natural light, natural reason, which distinguishes us men from other creatures. Now it is true that they may have a pretence for some ground of this interpretation in antiquity itself, for, so says Saint Cyril, "*Filius Dei Creativè illuminat,*" Christ doth enlighten us in creating us. And so some others of the Fathers and some of the Schools, understand by that light natural reason and that life, conservation in life. But this interpretation seems to me subject to both these dangers, that it goes so far and yet reaches not home. So far in wresting in divers senses into a word which needs but one and is of itself clear enough, that is "light," and yet reaches not home, for it reaches not to the essential light which is Christ Jesus, nor to the supernatural light, which is faith and grace, which seems to have been the evangelist's principal scope, to declare the coming of Christ (who is the essential light) and his purpose in coming, to raise and establish a Church, by faith and grace, which is the supernatural light. For as the Holy Ghost himself interprets life to be meant of Christ ("He that hath the Son hath life"),[3] so we may justly do of light too ("He that sees" the Son, the "Son of God hath light"). For light is never (to my remembrance) found in any place of the Scripture where it must necessarily signify the light of nature, natural reason; but wheresoever it is transferred from the natural to a figurative sense, it takes a higher signification than "that." Either it signifies essential light, Christ Jesus (which answers our first question, "*Quis lux,* who is this light," it is Christ, personally) or it signifies the supernatural light of faith and grace (which answers our second question, "*Quid lux,* what is this light," for it is

---

3. 1 John 5:12.

the working of Christ by his Spirit in his Church, in the infusion of faith and grace, for belief and manners). And therefore though it be ever lawful, and oftentimes very useful, for the raising and exaltation of our devotion, and to present the plenty and abundance of the Holy Ghost in the Scriptures, who satisfies us as with marrow and with fatness, to induce the diverse senses that the Scriptures do admit, yet this may not be admitted, if there may be danger thereby, to neglect or weaken the literal sense itself. For there is no necessity of that spiritual wantonness of finding more then necessary senses; for the more lights there are the more shadows are also cast by those many lights. And, as it is true in religious duties, so is it in interpretation of matters of religion, *necessarium et satis convertuntur*, when you have done that you ought to do in your calling, you have done enough. There are no such evangelical counsels as should raise works of supererogation, more then you are bound to do, so when you have the necessary sense, that is the meaning of the Holy Ghost in that place, you have senses enough, and not till then, though you have never so many and never so delightful.

Illa lux

Light, therefore, is in all this chapter fitliest understood of Christ, who is noted here with that distinctive article, "*Illa lux*, that light." For "*non sic dicitur lux, sicut lapis*,"[4] Christ is not so called "Light" as he is called a "Rock," or a "Cornerstone;" not by a metaphor, but truly and properly. It is true that the Apostles are said to be light, and that with an article "the light"; but yet with a limitation and restriction, "the light of the world,"[5] that is, set up to convey light to the world. It is true that John Baptist himself was called "light," and with large additions "*Lucerna ardens*, a burning, and a shining lamp,"[6] to denote both his own burning zeal and the communicating of this his light to others. It is true that "all the faithful" are said to be "light in the Lord;"[7] but all this is but to signify that they had been in darkness before; they had been beclouded but were now illustrated; they were light, but light by reflection, by illustration of a greater light. And in the first creation, ". . . The evening and the morning made the day, evening" before "morning, darkness" before "light," so in our regeneration, when we are made new creatures, the Spirit of God finds us in natural darkness, and by him we are made light in the Lord. But Christ

---

4. Augustine.
5. Matthew 5:[14].
6. John 5:[35].
7. Ephesians 5:[8].

himself, and he only, is "*Illa lux, vera lux,* that light, the true light." Not so opposed to those other lights as though the Apostles, or John Baptist, or the faithful, who are called lights, were false lights; but that they were weak lights. But Christ was *fons lucis,* the fountain of all light; light so, as nobody else was so; so, as that he was nothing but light. . . .

All other men, by occasion of this flesh, have dark clouds, yea nights, yea long and frozen winter nights of sin, and of the works of darkness. Christ was incapable of any such nights or any such clouds, any approaches toward sin; but yet Christ admitted some shadows, some such degrees of human infirmity, as by them, he was willing to show, that the nature of man, in the best perfection thereof, is not "*vera lux, tota lux,* true light, all light," which he declared in that "*Si possibile,*" and that "*Transeat calix,* If it be possible, let this cup pass;"[8] words to which himself was pleased to allow so much of a retraction and a correction, "*Veruntamen,* yet Father," whatsoever the sadness of my soul have made me say, "yet not my will but thine be done; not mine, but thine;" so that they were not altogether all one; human infirmity made some difference. So that no one man, not Christ (considered but as a man), was "*tota lux,* all light," no cloud. No not mankind, consider it collectively, can be light so as that there shall be no darkness. . . .

Nay not only no man (for so we may consider him in the whole course of his life), but no one act of the most perfect and religious man in the world, though that act employ but half a minute in the doing thereof can be "*vera lux,* true light," all light, so perfect light, as that it may serve another, or thyself, for a lantern to his or thy feet, or a light to his or thy steps, so that he or thou may think it enough to do so still. For another man may do so good works as it may justly work to thy shame and confusion, and to the aggravating of thy condemnation, that thou livest not as well as he, yet it would not perchance serve thy turn to live but so well; for "to whom God gives more, of him he requires more." . . .

[*Meditation on Natural Light*]

In all philosophy there is not so dark a thing as light. As the sun, which is *fons lucis naturalis,* the beginning of natural light, is the most evident thing to be seen and yet the hardest to be looked upon, so is natural light to our reason and understanding. Nothing clearer, for it is clearness itself, nothing darker, it is enwrapped in so many scruples. Nothing nearer, for it is

8. Matthew 26:39.

round about us, nothing more remote, for we know neither entrance nor limits of it. Nothing more easy, for a child discerns it, nothing more hard, for no man understands it. It is apprehensible by sense and not comprehensible by reason. If we wink, we cannot choose but see it; if we stare, we know it never the better. No man is yet got so near to the knowledge of the qualities of light as to know whether light itself be a quality or a substance. If then this natural light be so dark to our natural reason, if we shall offer to pierce so far into the light of this text, the essential light Christ Jesus (in his nature, or but in his offices), or the supernatural light of faith and grace (how far faith may be had and yet lost, and how far the free will of man may concur and cooperate with grace, and yet still remain nothing in itself), if we search farther into these points then the Scripture hath opened us a way, how shall we hope to unentangle or extricate ourselves? They had a precious composition for lamps amongst the ancients, reserved especially for tombs, which kept light for many hundreds of years; we have had in our age experience in some casual openings of ancient vaults of finding such lights as were kindled (as appeared by their inscription) fifteen or sixteen hundred years before; but as soon as that light comes to our light it vanishes.

So this eternal and this supernatural light, Christ and faith, enlightens, warms, purges, and does all the profitable offices of fire and light, if we keep it in the right sphere, in the proper place (that is, if we consist in points necessary to salvation and revealed in the Scripture) but when we bring this light to the common light of reason, to our inferences, and consequences, it may be in danger to vanish itself and perchance extinguish our reason too. We may search so far and reason so long of faith and grace as that we may lose not only them but even our reason too, and sooner become mad than good. Not that we are bound to believe anything against reason, that is to believe we know not why. It is but a slack opinion, it is not belief, that is not grounded upon reason.

He that should come to a heathen man, a mere natural man, uncatechized, uninstructed in the rudiments of the Christian religion, and should at first, without any preparation, present him first with this necessity: Thou shalt burn in fire and brimstone eternally except thou believe in a Trinity of persons, in an unity of one God, except thou believe the Incarnation of the second person of the Trinity, the Son of God, except thou believe that a virgin had a son and the same Son that God had, and that God was man too and being the immortal God yet died, he should be so far from working any spiritual cure upon this poor soul, as that he should rather bring Christian mysteries into scorn than him to a belief. For that man, if you proceed so (believe all or you burn in hell), would find an easy, an obvious way to escape all; that is, first not to believe in hell itself, and then nothing could bind him to believe the rest.

The reason therefore of man, must first be satisfied; but the way of such satisfaction must be this, to make him see, that this World, a frame of so much harmony, so much concinnity and conveniencey, and such a correspondence and subordination in the parts thereof, must necessarily have had a workman, for nothing can make itself: that no such workman would deliver over a frame and work of so much majesty to be governed by fortune, casually, but would still retain the administration thereof in his own hands: that if he do so, if he made the world and sustain it still by his watchful providence, there belongeth a worship and service to him for doing so: that therefore he hath certainly revealed to man what kind of worship and service shall be acceptable to him: that this manifestation of his will must be permanent, it must be written, there must be a Scripture, which is his Word and his Will: and that therefore from that Scripture, from that Word of God, all articles of our belief are to be drawn.

If then his reason confessing all this ask for further proof, how he shall know that these Scriptures accepted by the Christian Church are the true Scriptures, let him bring any other book which pretendeth to be the Word of God into comparison with these. It is true, we have not a demonstration; not such an evidence as that one and two are three, to prove these to be the Scriptures of God; God hath not proceeded in that manner to drive our reason into a pound and to force it by peremptory necessity to accept these for Scriptures, for then here had been no exercise of our will and our assent, if we could not have resisted. But yet these Scriptures have so orderly, so sweet, and so powerful a working upon the reason and the understanding, as if any third man, who were utterly dis-charged of all preconceptions and anticipations in matter of religion, one who were altogether neutral, disinterested, unconcerned in either part, nothing towards a Turk and as little toward a Christian, should hear a Christian plead for his Bible and a Turk for his Alcoran, and should weigh the evidence of both; the majesty of the style, the punctual accomplishment of the prophecies, the harmony and concurrence of the four evangelists, the consent and unanimity of the Christian Church ever since, and many other such reasons, he would be drawn to such an historical, such a gram-matical, such a logical belief of our Bible as to prefer it before any other that could be pretended to be the Word of God. He would believe it and he would know why he did so. For let no man think that God hath given him so much ease here as to save him by believing he knoweth not what, or why.

[*Essay on Natural Reason*]

Knowledge cannot save us, but we cannot be saved without knowledge; faith is not on this side knowledge but beyond it; we must necessarily come to knowledge first, though we must not stay at it when we are come thither. For a regenerate Christian being now a new creature hath also a new faculty of reason, and so believeth the mysteries of religion out of another reason then as a mere natural man he believed natural and moral things. He believeth them for their own sake by faith, though he take knowledge of them before by that common reason, and by those human arguments which work upon other men, in natural or moral things. Divers men may walk by the seaside and the same beams of the sun giving light to them all, one gathereth by the benefit of that light pebbles or speckled shells for curious vanity, and another gathers precious pearl or medicinal amber by the same light. So the common light of reason illumines us all; but one employs this light upon the searching of impertinent vanities, another by a better use of the same light finds out the mysteries of religion; and when he hath found them, loves them, not for the light's sake, but for the natural and true worth of the thing itself.

Some men by the benefit of this light of reason, have found out things profitable and useful to the whole world; as in particular printing by which the learning of the whole world is communicable to one another, and our minds and our inventions, our wits and compositions may trade and have commerce together, and we may participate of one another's understandings, as well of our clothes, and wines, and oils, and other merchandise . . . All the ways, both of wisdom and of craft lie open to this light, this light of natural reason: But when they have gone all these ways by the benefit of this light, they have got no further then to have walked by a tempestuous sea, and to have gathered pebbles and speckled cockle shells . . .

But, if thou canst take this light of reason that is in thee, this poor snuff that is almost out in thee, thy faint and dim knowledge of God that riseth out of this light of nature, if thou canst in those embers, those cold ashes, find out one small coal and wilt take the pains to kneel down and blow that coal with thy devout prayers, and light thee a little candle (a desire to read that book which they call the Scriptures, and the Gospel, and the Word of God); if with that little candle thou canst creep humbly into low and poor places; if thou canst find thy Savior in a manger, and in his swathing clouts, in his humiliation, and bless God for that beginning; if thou canst find him flying into Egypt and find in thyself a disposition to accompany him in a persecution, in a banishment, if not a bodily banishment, a local banishment, yet a real, a spiritual banishment, a banishment from those sins, and that sinful conversation which thou hast loved more then thy parents, or country, or thine own body, which perchance thou hast consumed and destroyed with that sin; if thou canst find him contenting and containing himself at home in his father's house and not breaking out, no not about the work of our salvation till the due time was come when it was to be done; and if according to that example thou canst contain thyself in that station and vocation in which God hath planted thee, and not, through a hasty and precipitate zeal, break out to an imaginary and intempestive, and unseasonable reformation either in civil or ecclesiastical business, which belong not to thee; if with this little poor light, these first degrees of knowledge and faith, thou canst follow him into the garden and gather up some of the drops of his precious blood and sweat which he shed for thy soul; if thou canst follow him to Jerusalem and pick up some of those tears which he shed upon that city and upon thy soul; if after all this thou canst turn this little light inward and canst thereby discern where thy diseases and thy wounds and thy corruptions are, and canst apply those tears, and blood and balm to them . . . thou shalt never envy the luster and glory of the great lights of worldly men, which are great by the infirmity of others . . . Thou shalt see that thou by thy small light hath gathered pearl and amber, and they by their great lights nothing but shells and pebbles; they have determined the light of nature, upon the book of nature, this world, and thou hast carried the light of nature higher, thy natural reason and even human arguments have brought thee to read the Scriptures, and to that love God hath set to the seal of faith. Their light shall set at noon . . . and thy light shall grow up from a fair hope to a modest assurance . . . Reason is that first and primogenial light, and goes no farther in a natural man; but in a man regenerate by faith, that light does all that reason did and more; and all his moral, civil, and domestic and indifferent actions (though they be never done without reason), yet their principal scope and mark is the glory of God, and though they seem but moral, or civil, or domestic, yet they have a deeper tincture, a heavenly nature, a relation to God in them.

[*Transition*]

The light in our text, then, is essentially and personally Christ himself. From him flows the supernatural light of faith and grace, here also intended. And because this light of faith and grace flowing from that fountain of light, Christ Jesus, works upon the light of nature and reason, it may conduce to the raising of your devotions if we do (without any long insisting upon the several parts thereof) present to you some of those many and divers lights which are in this world, and admit an application to this light in our text, the essential light, Christ Jesus, and the supernatural light, faith and grace.

[*The first couple:*] Lux essentiae *and* lux gloriae

Of these lights we shall consider some few couples; and the first pair, "*Lux Essentiae*" and "*Lux Gloriae*," the light of the essence of God and the light of the glory of his Saints. And though the first of these be that essential light by which we shall see God face to face, as he is, and the effluence and emanation of beams from the face of God, which make that place heaven, of which light it is said, "That God who only hath immortality, dwells in *luce inaccessibili*,"[9] in the light that none can attain to, yet by the light of faith and grace in sanctification we may come to such a participation of that light of essence, or such a relection of it in this world, that it shall be true of us which was said of those Ephesians, "You were once darkness, but now are light in the Lord:"[10] he does not say "enlightened," nor "lightsome," but light itself, light essentially, for our conversation is in heaven.[11] And as God says of Jerusalem, and his blessings here in this world, "*Calceavi te Ianthino*, I have shod thee with badgers skin" . . .[12] (which the ancients take for some precious stuff), that is, I have enabled thee to tread upon all the most estimable things of this world . . . so the "precious promises of Christ, make us partakers of the divine nature,"[13] and the light of faith makes us the same "Spirit with the Lord."[14] And this is our participation of the light of essence in this life. The next is the light of glory.

This is that glorification which we shall have at the last day of which glory we consider a great part to be in that denudation, that manifestation of all to all; as, in this world, a great part of our inglorious servitude is in those disguises, and palliations, those colors and pretences of public good with which men of power and authority apparel their oppressions of the poor; in this are we the more miserable, that we cannot see their ends, that there is none of this denudation, this laying open of ourselves to one another, which shall accompany that state of glory, where we shall see one another's bodies and souls, actions and thoughts. And therefore, as if this place were now that tribunal of Christ Jesus, and this that day of judge-

---

9. 1 Timothy 6:16.
10. Ephesians 5:8.
11. Philippians 3:20.
12. Ezekiel 16:10.
13. 2 Peter 1:4.
14. 1 Corinthians 6:17.

ment and denudation, we must be here, as we shall be there, content to stand naked before him; content that there be a discovery, a revealing, a manifestation of all our sins, wrought upon us, at least to our own consciences, though not to the congregation. If we will have glory, we must have this denudation.

We must not be glad when our sins scape the preacher. We must not say (as though there were a comfort in that), though he have hit such a man's adultery, and another's ambition, and another's extortion, yet, for all his diligence, he hath missed my sin; for if thou wouldest fain have it missed, thou wouldest fain hold it still. And then, why camest thou hither? What camest thou for to church, or to the sacrament? Why doest thou delude God with this complemental visit, to come to his house, if thou bring not with thee a disposition to his honor and his service? Camest thou only to try whether God knew thy sin and could tell thee of it by the preacher? Alas, he knows it infallibly; and, if he take no knowledge of his knowing it, to thy conscience, by the words of the preacher, thy state is the more desperate.

God sends us to preach forgiveness of sins; where we find no sin we have no commission to execute. How shall we find your sins? In the old sacrifices of the law the priest did not fetch the sacrifice from the herd, but he received it from him that brought it, and so sacrificed it for him. Do thou therefore prevent the preacher? Accuse thyself before he accuse thee; offer up thy sin thyself; bring it to the top of thy memory and thy conscience, that he finding it there may sacrifice for thee. Tune the instrument, and it is the fitter for his hand. Remember thou thine own sins, first, and then every word that falls from the preacher's lips shall be a drop of the dew of heaven, dram of the "balm of Gilead," a portion of the blood of thy Savior, to wash away that sin, so presented by thee to be so sacrificed by him. . . .

This then is our first couple of these lights. By our conversation in heaven here (that is, a watchfulness that we fall not into sin) we have *"lucem essentiae,"* possession and fruition of heaven, and of the light of God's presence; and then, if we do, by infirmity, fall into sin, yet by this denudation of our souls, this manifestation of our sins to God by confession, and to that purpose a gladness when we hear our sins spoken of by the preacher, we have *"lumen gloriae,"* and inchoation of our glorified estate; and then another couple of these lights, which we propose to be considered, is *"lumen fidei,"* and *"lumen naturae,"* the light of faith and the light of nature.

[*The second couple:*] Lux fidei *and* Lux naturae

Of these two lights, faith and grace, first, and then nature and reason, we said something before, but never so much because contentious spirits have cast such clouds upon both these lights that some have said, nature doth all alone, and other, that nature hath nothing to do at all, but all is grace. We decline wranglings that tend not to edification; we say only to our present purpose (which is the operation of these several couples of lights) that by this light of faith, to him that hath it, all that is involved in prophecies is clear and evident, as in a history already done; and all that is wrapped up in promises is his own already in performance. That man needs not go so high for his assurance of a Messias and Redeemer, as to the first promise made to him in Adam;[15] nor for the limitation of the stock and race from whence this Messias should come, so far as to the renewing of this promise in Abraham;[16] nor for the description of this Messias, who he should be and of whom he should be born, as to Isaiah;[17] nor to Micah for the place;[18] nor for the time when he should accomplish all this, so far as to Daniel;[19] no, nor so far as to the evangelists themselves for the history and the evidence that all this that was done in his behalf by the Messias was done 1600 years since. But he hath a whole Bible and an abundant library in his own heart, and there by this light of faith (which is not only a knowing, but an applying, an appropriating of all to thy benefit) he hath a better knowledge then all this, then either prophetical or evangelical, for though both these be irrefragable and infallible proofs of a Messias . . . yet both these might but concern others: this light of faith brings him home to thee.

How sure so ever I be that the world shall never perish by water, yet I may be drowned; and how sure so ever that the "Lamb of God hath taken away the sins of the world," I may perish without I have this applicatory faith. And as he needs not look back to Isaiah, nor Abraham, nor Adam, for the Messias, so neither needs he to look forward. He needs not stay in expectation of the Angels' trumpets to awaken the dead; he is not put to his "*usquequo Domine*, How long, Lord, wilt thou defer our restitution?" but he hath already "died the death of the righteous;" which is to die to sin; he hath already had his burial by being buried with Christ in Baptism; he hath

---

15. Genesis 3:15.
16. Genesis 12:3.
17. Isaiah 7:14.
18. Micah 5:2.
19. Daniel 9:24.

had his resurrection from sin, his ascension to holy purposes of amendment of life, and his judgement, that is, "peace of conscience," sealed unto him, and so by this light of applying faith, he hath already apprehended an eternal possession of God's eternal kingdom. And the other light in this second couple is "*Lux naturae,*" the light of nature.

This, though a fainter light, directs us to the other, nature to faith: and as by the quantity in the light of the moon we know the position and distance of the sun, how far or how near the sun is to her, so by the working of the light of nature in us we may discern (by the measure and virtue and heat of that) how near to the other greater light, the light of faith, we stand. If we find our natural faculties rectified so as that that free will which we have in moral and civil actions be bent upon the external duties of religion (as ever natural man may, out of the use of that free will, come to church, hear the Word preached, and believe it to be true), we may be sure the other greater light is about us. If we be cold in them, in actuating, in exalting, in using our natural faculties so far, we shall be deprived of all light; we shall not see the invisible God in visible things, which Saint Paul makes so inexusable,[20] so unpardonable a thing; we shall not see the hand of God in all our worldly crosses, nor the seal of God in all our worldly blessings; we shall not see the face of God in his house, his presence here in the church, nor the mind of God in his Gospel, that his gracious purposes upon mankind extend so particularly, or reach so far, as to include us.

I shall hear in the Scripture his "*Venite omnes,* come all," and yet I shall think that his eye was not upon me, that his eye did not beckon me and I shall hear the "*Deus vult omnes salvos,* that God would save all," and yet I shall find some perverse reason in myself, why it is not likely that God will save me. I am commanded "*scrutari Scripturas,* to search the Scriptures;" now that is not to be able to repeat any history of the Bible without book, it is not to ruffle a Bible, and upon any word to turn to the chapter and to the verse; but this is "*exquisita scrutatio,*" the true searching of the Scriptures, to find all the histories to be examples to me, all the prophecies to induce a Savior for me, all the Gospel to apply Christ Jesus to me.

Turn over all the folds and plaits of thine own heart and find there the infirmities and waverings of thine own faith, and an ability to say, "Lord I believe, help mine unbelief," and then, though thou have no Bible in thy hand, or though thou stand in a dark corner, nay though thou canst not

---

20. Romans 1:20.

read a letter, thou hast searched that Scripture, thou hast turned to Mark 9. ver. 24. Turn thine ear to God, and hear him turning to thee, and saying to thy soul, "I will marry thee to myself forever." And thou hast searched the Scripture and turned to Hos. 2. ver. 19. Turn to thine own history, thine own life, and if thou canst read there that thou hast endeavored to turn thine ignorance into knowledge and thy knowledge into practice, if thou find thyself to be an example of that rule of Christ's, "If you know these things, blessed are you if you do them," then thou hast searched that Scripture and turned to Jo. 13. ver. 17. This is "*scrutari Scripturas,* to search the Scriptures," not as though thou wouldest make a concordance, but an application; as thou wouldest search a wardrobe not to make an inventory of it, but to find in it something fit for thy wearing.

John Baptist was not the light, he was not Christ, but "he bore witness of him." The light of faith, in the highest exaltation that can be had in the elect, here, is not that very "beatifical vision" which we shall have in heaven, but it bears witness to that light. The light of nature in the highest exaltation is not faith, but it bears witness of it. The lights of faith and of nature are subordinate John Baptists: faith bears me witness that I have Christ, and the light of nature, that is the exalting of my natural faculties towards religious uses, bears me witness that I have faith. Only that man whose conscience testifies to himself, and whose actions testify to the world that he does what he can, can believe himself, or be believed by others, that he hath the true light of faith.

And therefore, as the Apostle saith, "Quench not the Spirit;"[21] I say too, "Quench not the light of nature," suffer not that light to go out; study your natural faculties; husband and improve them, and love the outward acts of religion, though an hypocrit and though a natural man may do them. Certainly he that loves not the militant church, hath but a faint faith in his interest in the triumphant. He that cares not though the material church fall, I am afraid is falling from the spiritual. For can a man be sure to have his money, or his plate, if his house be burnt? or to preserve his faith, if the outward exercises of religion fail? He that undervalues outward things in the religious service of God, though he begin at ceremonial and ritual things, will come quickly to call sacraments but outward things, and sermons and public prayers but outward things, in contempt. . . . The bell that calls me to church does not catechize me, nor preach to me, yet I observe the sound of that bell, because it brings me to him that does those offices to me. The light of nature is far from being enough; but, as a candle may

---

21. 1 Thessalonians 5:19.

131

kindle a torch, so into the faculties of nature, well employed, God infuses faith. And this is our second couple of light, the subordination of the light of nature, and the light of faith.

[*The third couple:*] Lux aeternum corporum *and* Lux incensionum

And a third pair of lights of attestation, that bear witness to the light of our text, is "*Lux aeternorum corporum*," that light which the sun and moon, and those glorious bodies give from heaven, and "*Lux incensionum*," that light which those things that are naturally combustible and apt to take fire, do give upon earth; both these bear witness of this light, that is, admit an application to it. For, in the first of these, the glorious lights of heaven, we must take nothing for stars that are not stars; nor make astrological and fixed conclusions out of meteors that are but transitory; they may be comets, and blazing stars, and so portend much mischief, but they are none of those "*aeterna corpora*," they are not fixed stars, not stars of heaven. So it is in the Christian Church (which is the proper sphere in which the light of our text; that light, the essential light Christ Jesus moves by that supernatural light of faith and grace, which is truly the intelligence of that sphere, the Christian Church). As in the heavens the stars were created at once, with one "*Fiat*," and then being so made, stars do not beget new stars, so the Christian doctrine necessary to salvation was delivered at once, that is, entirely in one sphere, in the body of the Scriptures. And then, as stars do not beget stars, articles of faith do not beget articles of faith. . . . "Other foundation can no man lay then Christ;"[22] not only no better, but no other; what other things soever are added by men, enter not into the nature and condition of a foundation. . . .

Now for the consideration of the other light of this third couple, which is "*Lux incensionum*," the light of things which take and give light here upon earth, if we reduce it to application and practise, and contract it to one instance, it will appear that the devotion and zeal of him that is best affected, is, for the most part, in the disposition of a torch, or a knife, ordained to take fire and to give light. If it have never been lightened, it does not easily take light, but it must be bruised and beaten first; if it have been lighted and put out, though it cannot take fire of itself, yet it does easily conceive fire if it be presented within any convenient distance. Such also is the soul of man towards the fires of the zeal of God's glory, and

---

22. 1 Corinthians 3:11.

compassion of other's misery. If there be any that never took this fire, that was never affected with either of these, the glory of God, the miseries of other men, can I hope to kindle him? It must be God's work to bruise and beat him with his rod of affliction, before he will take fire. . . .

But for you who have taken this fire before, that have been enlightened in both sacraments, and in the preaching of the word; in the means and in some measure of practise of holiness heretofore, if in supplying oil to your lamps, which God by his ordinance had kindled in you, you have let this light go out by negligence or inconsideration, or that storms of worldly calamities have blown it out, do but now at this instant call to mind what sin of yesterday, or t'other day, or long ago, begun, and practised, and prevailed upon you, or what future sin, what purpose of doing a sin tonight, or tomorrow, possesses you; do but think seriously what sin or what cross hath blown out that light, that grace, which was formerly in you, before that sin or that cross invaded you, and turn your soul, which hath been enlightened before, towards this fire which God's Spirit blows this minute, and you will conceive new fire, new zeal, new compassion.

As this "*Lux incensionum*" kindles easily when it hath been kindled before, so the soul accustomed to the presence of God in holy meditations, though it fall asleep in some dark corner, in some sin of infirmity awhile, yet, upon every holy occasion it takes fire again, and the meanest preacher in the church shall work more upon him than the four doctors of the church should be able to do, upon a person who had never been enlightened before, that is, never accustomed to the presence of God in his private meditations or in his outward acts of religion. And this is our third couple of lights that bears witness, that is, admit an application to the light of our text; and then the fourth and last couple which we consider is "*Lux depuratarum mixtionum*," the light and lustre of precious stones, and then "*Lux repercussionum*," the light of repercussion and reflection, when one body, though it have no light in itself, casts light upon other bodies.

[*The fourth couple:*] Lux depuratarum mixtionum *and* Lux repercussionum

In the application of the first of these lights, "*Depuratarum mixtionum*, precious stones," we shall only apply their making and their value. Precious stones are first drops of the dew from heaven, and then refined by the sun of heaven. When by long lying they have exhaled and evaporated and breathed out all their gross matter, and received another concoction from the sun, then they become precious in the eye and estimation of men: so those actions of ours that shall be precious or acceptable in the eye of

God, must at first have been conceived from heaven, from the Word of God, and then receive another concoction by a holy deliberation, before we bring those actions to execution, lest we may have mistaken the root thereof. Actions precious or acceptable in God's eye must be holy purposes in their beginning and then done in season; the dove must lay the egg and hatch the bird; the Holy Ghost must infuse the purpose and sit upon it and overshadow it and mature and ripen it, if it shall be precious in God's eye.

The reformation of abuses in state or church is a holy purpose, there is that drop of the dew of heaven in it; but if it be unseasonably attempted and have not a farther concoction then the first motions of our own zeal, it becomes ineffectual. Stones precious in the estimation of men begin with the dew of heaven and proceed with the sun of heaven. Actions precious in the acceptation of God are purposes conceived by his Spirit and executed in his time to his glory, not conceived out of ambition nor executed out of sedition. And this is the application of this "*Lux depuratarum mixtionum,*" of precious stones, out of their making. We proposed another out of their valuation, which is this, that whereas a pearl or diamond of such a bigness, of so many carats, is so much worth, one that is twice as big is ten times as much worth. So, though God vouchsafe to value every good work thou dost, yet as they grow greater he shall multiply his estimation of them infinitely. When he hath prized at a high rate the chastity and continency of thy youth, if thou add to this a moderation in thy middle age from ambition, and in thy latter age from covetousness and indevotion, there shall be no price in God's treasure (not the last drop of the blood of his Son) too dear for thee, no room, no state in his kingdom (not a joint tenancy with his only Son) too glorious for thee. This is one light in this couple, the luster of precious stones; the other the last is "*Lux repercussionum,*" the light of repercussion, of reflection.

This is when God's light cast upon us reflecteth upon other men too, from us; when God doth not only accept our works for ourselves, but employs those works of ours upon other men. And here is a true and a divine supererogation, which the devil (as he doth all God's actions, which fall into his compass) did mischievously counterfeit in the Roman Church, when he induced their doctrine of supererogation, that a man might do so much more then he was bound to do for God, as that that superplusage might save whom he would; and that if he did not direct them in his intention upon any particular person, the bishop of Rome was general administrator to all men and might bestow them where he would. But here is a true supererogation, not from man or his merit, but from God; when our good works shall not only profit us that do them, but others that see them done; and when we by this light of "repercussion," of "reflection," shall be made *"specula divinae gloriae, quae accipiunt et reddunt,"*[23] such looking glasses as receive God's face upon ourselves and cast it upon others by a holy life and exemplary conversation.

Conclusio

To end all, we have no warmth in ourselves; it is true, but Christ came even in winter: we have no light in ourselves; it is true, but he came even in the night. And now I appeal to your own consciences and I ask you all (not as a judge but as an assistant to your consciences and *amicus curiae*), whether any man have made as good use of this light as he might have done. Is there any man that in the compassing of his sin hath not met this light by the way, "Thou shouldest not do this"?[24] Any man that hath not only as Balaam did met this light as an angel (that is, met heavenly inspirations to avert him), but that hath not heard as Balaam did, his own ass; that is, those reasons that use to carry him, or those very worldly respects that use to carry him, dispute against that sin and tell him not only that there is more soul and more heaven, and more salvation, but more body and more health, more honor and more reputation, more cost and more money, more labor and more danger spent upon such a sin than would have carried him the right way.

Recapitulatio

"They that sleep, sleep in the night, and they that are drunk, are drunk in the night."[25] But to you the day star, the Sun of Righteousness, the Son of God is risen this day. The day is but a little longer now then at shortest; but a little it is. Be a little better now than when you came, and mend a little at every coming, and in less then seven year's apprenticeage, which your occupations cost you, you shall learn, not the mysteries of your twelve companies, but the mysteries of the twelve tribes, of the twelve apostles, of their twelve articles, whatsoever belongeth to the promise, to the performance, to the imitation of Christ Jesus.

He who is *"Lux una,"* light and light alone, and *"Lux tota,"* light and all light, shall also, by that light which he sheddeth from himself upon all his, the light of grace, give you all these attestations, all these witnesses of that his light. He shall give you *"Lucem essentiae"* (really and essentially to be incorporated into him, to be made partakers of his divine nature, and

---

23. Tertullian.
24. Numbers 22:22.
25. 1 Thessalonians 5:7.

the same Spirit with the Lord, by a conversation in heaven, here), and "*lucem gloriae*" (a gladness to give him glory in a denudation of your souls and your sins, by humble confession to him and a gladness to receive a denudation and manifestation of yourselves to yourselves by his messenger, in his medicinal and musical increpations, and a gladness to receive an inchoation of future glory, in the remission of those sins). He shall give you "*lucem fidei*" (faithful and unremoveable possession of future things in the present, and make your hereafter now, in the fruition of God), and "*lucem naturae*" (a love of the outward beauty of his house and outward testimonies of this love, in inclining your natural faculties to religious duties). He shall give you "*lucem aeternorum corporum*" (a love to walk in the light of the stars of heaven, that never change, a love so perfect in the fundamental articles of religion, without impertinent additions), and "*lucem incensionum*" (an aptness to take holy fire by what hand, or tongue, or pen soever it be presented unto you, according to God's ordinance, though that light have formerly been suffered to go out in you). He shall give to you "*lucem depuratarum mixtionum*" (the luster of precious stones made of the dew of heaven and by the heat of heaven, that is, actions intended at first, and produced at last, for his glory; and every day multiply their value in the sight of God, because thou shalt every day grow up from grace to grace), and "*lucem repercussionum*" (he shall make you able to reflect and cast this light upon others, to his glory and their establishment).

Lighten our darkness, we beseech thee, O Lord, with all these lights; that in thy light we may see light; that in this essential light, which is Christ, and in this supernatural light, which is grace, we may see all these, and all other beams of light, which may bring us to thee, and him, and that blessed Spirit which proceeds from both. Amen.

Now in a Glass,
Then Face to Face[1]

1 Corinthians 13:12. "For now we see through a glass darkly, but then face to face; now I know in part, but then I shall know, even as also I am known."

These two terms in our text, *"Nunc"* and *"Tunc,"* "Now" and "Then," "Now in a glass, Then face to face," Now in part, Then in perfection, these two secular terms, of which one designs the whole age of this world from the creation to the dissolution thereof (for, all that is comprehended in this word, "Now"), and the other designs the everlastingness of the next world (for that incomprehensibleness is comprehended in the other word, "Then"), these two words that design two such ages, are now met in one day; in this day in which we celebrate all resurrections in the root, in the resurrection of our Lord and Savior Christ Jesus, blessed forever. For the first term, "Now" ("Now in a glass, now in part") is intended most especially of that very act which we do now at this present, that is, of the ministry of the Gospel, of declaring God in his Ordinance, of preaching his Word. "Now," in this ministry of his Gospel, "we see in a glass, we know in part," and then the "Then," the time of "seeing face to face" and "knowing as we are known," is intended of that time which we celebrate this day, the day of resurrection, the day of judgment, the day of the actual possession of the next life. So that this day this whole Scripture is fulfilled in your ears; for now (now in this preaching) you have some sight, and then (then when that day comes, which, in the first root thereof, we celebrate this day) you shall have a perfect sight of all. "Now we see through a glass," etc.

---

[1]. Preached at St. Paul's, Easter Day, 1628. *Sermons*, Potter and Simpson eds., 8:219–36.

JOHN DONNE

Divisio

That therefore you may better know him when you come to see him face to face, then, by having seen him in a glass now, and that your seeing him now in his Ordinance, may prepare you to see him then in his essence, proceed we thus in the handling of these words. First, that there is nothing brought into comparison, into consideration, nothing put into balance, but the sight of God, the knowledge of God. It is not called a better sight nor a better knowledge, but there is no other sight, no other knowledge proposed, or mentioned, or intimated, or imagined but this. All other sight is blindness, all other knowledge is ignorance. And then we shall see how there is a twofold sight of God, and a twofold knowledge of God proposed to us here; a sight and a knowledge here in this life, and another manner of sight and another manner of knowledge in the life to come. For here we see God *in speculo*, "in a glass," that is by reflection, and here we know God *in ænigmate*, says our text, "darkly" (so we translate it), that is, by obscure representations, and therefore it is called a "knowledge but in part." But in heaven our sight is "face to face," and our knowledge is "to know, as we are known."

For our sight of God here, our theater, the place where we sit and see him, is the whole world, the whole house and frame of nature, and our medium, our "glass," is the Book of Creatures, and our light by which we see him, is the light of natural reason. And then, for our knowledge of God here, our place, our academy, our university is the Church, our medium is the Ordinance of God in his Church, Preaching and Sacraments; and our light is the light of faith. This we shall find it to be, for our sight and for our knowledge of God here. But for our sight of God in heaven, our place, our sphere is heaven itself, our medium is the patefaction, the manifestation, the revelation of God himself, and our light is the light of glory. And then for our knowledge of God there, God himself is all, God himself is the place; we see Him, in Him; God is our medium, we see Him, by him; God is our light; not a light which is His, but a light which is He; not a light that flows from Him, no, nor a light which is in Him, but that light which is He himself. "Lighten our darkness, we beseech thee, O Lord, O Father of lights, that in thy light we may see light,"[2] that now we see this through this thy glass, thine Ordinance, and, by the good of this, hereafter "face to face."

2. [Psalm 36:9]

SERMONS

Part 1. *General considerations. Visio*

The sight is so much the noblest of the senses, as that it is all the senses. As the reasonable soul of man, when it enters, becomes all the soul of man, and he hath no longer a vegetative and a sensitive soul, but all is that one reasonable soul, so, says St. Augustine . . . all the senses are called seeing . . . Employ then this noblest sense upon the noblest object, see God, see God in everything, and then you need not take off your eyes from beauty, from riches, from honor, from anything . . .

When Christ took the blind man by the hand,[3] though he had then begun his cure upon him, yet he asked him if he saw ought. Something he was sure he saw, but it was a question whether it were to be called a sight, for he saw men but as trees. The natural man sees beauty, riches, and honor, but yet it is a question whether he sees them or no, because he sees them but as a snare. But he that sees God in them, sees them to be beams and evidences of that beauty, wealth, the honor, that is in God, that is God himself . . .

Scientia

The first act of the will is love, says the School,[4] for till the will love, till it would have something, it is not a will. But then . . . it is impossible to love anything till we know it:[5] First our understanding must present it as *verum*, as a known truth, and then our will embraces it as *bonum*, as good and worthy to be loved. Therefore the Philosopher[6] concludes easily as a thing that admits no contradiction, that naturally all men desire to know that they may love. . . . As St. Paul desires to know nothing else, so let no man pretend to know anything but Christ crucified;[7] that is, crucified for him, made his. In the eighth verse of this chapter [1 Cor. 13] he says, "Prophecy shall fail, and tongues shall fail, and knowledge shall vanish," but this knowledge of God in Christ made mine, being crucified for me, shall dwell with me forever. And so from this general consideration, all sight is blindness, all knowledge is ignorance, but of God, we pass to the particular consideration of that twofold sight and knowledge of God expressed in this text, "Now we see through a glass, etc."

---

3. Mark 8:23.
4. [School, that is theologians of the medieval universities, such as Thomas Aquinas.]
5. Augustine.
6. [The Philosopher, that is Aristotle.]
7. [1 Corinthians 2:2]

Part 2. *Particular considerations. Visio*

First then we consider (before we come to our knowledge of God) our sight of God in this world, and that is, says our Apostle, "*In speculo*, we see as in a glass." But how do we see in a glass? Truly that is not easily determined. The old writers in the optics said that when we see a thing in a glass we see not the thing itself, but a representation only. All the later men say, we do see the thing itself, but not by direct but by reflected beams. It is a useless labor for the present to reconcile them. This may well consist with both, that as that which we see in a glass assures us that such a thing there is (for we cannot see a dream in a glass, nor a fancy, nor a chimera), so this sight of God, which our Apostle says we have "in a glass," is enough to assure us that a God there is.

This glass is better than the water; the water gives a crookedness and false dimensions to things that it shows, as we see by an oar when we row a boat ... But in the glass which the Apostle intends, we may see God directly, that is, see directly that there is a God ... It is a true sight of God, though it be not a perfect sight which we have this way. This way, our theater where we sit to see God, is the whole frame of nature; our medium, our glass in which we see him, is the creature; and our light by which we see him is natural reason.

Theatrum Mundus

Aquinas calls this theater where we sit and see God, the whole world. And David compasses the world and finds God everywhere, and says at last, "Whither shall I fly from thy presence? If I ascend up into heaven, thou art there."[8] At Babel they thought to build to heaven, but did any men ever pretend to get above heaven, above the power of winds, or the impression of other malignant meteors. . . ; can any man get above the power of God? "If I take wings of the morning, and dwell in the uttermost parts of the sea, there thy right hand shall hold me, and lead me." If we sail to the waters above the firmament, it is so too. Nay, take a place which God never made, a place which grew out of our sins; that is hell; yet, "If we make our bed in hell, God is there too.," . . . In a word, whether we be in the Eastern parts of the world, from whom the truth of religion is passed, or in the Western, to which it is not yet come; whether we be in the darkness of ignorance or the darkness of the works of darkness, or darkness of oppression of spirit in sadness, the world is the theater that represents God, and everywhere every man may, nay must see him.

---

8. Psalm 139:8.

Medium, Creatura

The whole frame of the world is the theater and every creature the stage, the medium, the glass in which we may see God. . . . There is not so poor a creature but may be thy glass to see God in. The greatest flat glass that can be made cannot represent anything greater than it is. If every gnat that flies were an arch-angel, all that could but tell me, that there is a God, and the poorest worm that creeps tells me that. If I should ask the basilisk how camest thou by those killing eyes, he would tell me, thy God made me so. And if I should ask the slow-worm, how camest thou to be without eyes, he would tell me, thy God made me so. The cedar is no better a glass to see God in than the hysop upon the wall; all things that are, are equally removed from being nothing; and whatsoever hath any being is by that very being a glass in which we see God, who is the root and the fountain of all being. The whole frame of nature is the theater, the whole volume of creatures is the glass, and the light of reason is our light, which is another circumstance.

Lux rationis

Of those words (John 1:9), "That was the true light, that lighteth every man that commeth into the world," the slackest sense that they can admit gives light enough to see God by. If we spare St. Chrysostom's sense, that that light is the light of the Gospel and of grace, and that that light considered in itself, and without opposition in us "does enlighten," that is, would enlighten "every man," if that man did not wink at that light; if we forbear St. Augustine's sense, "that light enlightens every man," that is, every man that is enlightened is enlightened by that light; if we take but St. Cyril's sense, that this light is the light of natural reason which, without question, "enlightens every man that comes into the world," yet have we light enough to see God by that light, in the theater of nature and in the glass of creatures.

God affords no man the comfort, the false comfort of atheism. He will not allow a pretending atheist the power to flatter himself so far as seriously to think there is no God. He must pull out his own eyes and see no creature, before he can say he sees no God. He must be no man and quench his reasonable soul, before he can say to himself, there is no God. The difference between the reason of man and the instinct of the beast is this, that the beast does but know, but the man knows that he knows. The beastial atheist will pretend that he knows there is no God, but he cannot say that he knows that he knows it, for his knowledge will not stand the battery of an argument from another, nor of a ratiocination from himself. He dares not ask himself, Who is it that I pray to, in a sudden danger, if there be no God? Nay he dares not ask, Who is it that I swear by, in a sudden passion, if there be no God? Whom do I tremble at, and sweat under, at midnight, and whom do I curse by next morning, if there be no God? It is safely said in the School ... How weak soever those means which are ordained by God seem to be, and be indeed in themselves, yet they are strong enough to those ends and purposes for which God ordained them.

And so, for such a sight of God as we take the Apostle to intend here, which is to see that there is a God, the frame of nature, the whole world is our theater, the Book of Creatures is our medium, our glass, and natural reason is light enough. But then, for the other degree, the other notification of God, which is the knowing of God, though that also be first to be considered in this world, the means is of a higher nature than served for the sight of God; and yet, whilst we are in this world, it is but *in ænigmate*, in an obscure riddle, a representation, darkly, and in part, as we translate it.

Scientia Dei
As the glass which we spoke of before, was proposed to the sense, and so we might see God, that is see that there is a God, this *ænigma* that is spoken now, this dark similitude and comparison is proposed to our faith, and so far we know God, that is believe in God in this life, but by *ænigma*, by dark representations and allusions. Therefore says St. Augustine, that Moses saw God in that conversation which he had with him in the Mount, ... removed from all benefit and assistance of bodily senses (he needed not that glass, the help of the creature), and more then so, ... removed from all allusions, or similitudes, or presentations of God, which might bring God to the understanding and so to the belief. Moses knew God by a more immediate working then either sense, or understanding, or faith. Therefore says that father, "*Per speculum et ænigma*," by this which the Apostle calls a glass and this which he calls *ænigma*, a dark representation, "*intelliguntur omnia accomodata ad notificandum Deum*," he understands all things by which God hath notified himself to man: by the glass to his reason, by the *ænigma*, to his faith. And so, for this knowing of God by way of believing in him (as for seeing him, our theater was the world, the creature was our glass, and reason was our light), our academy to learn this knowledge is the Church, our medium is the Ordinance and Institution of Christ in his Church, and our light is the light of faith in the application of those Ordinances in that Church.

Academia, Ecclesia
This place then where we take our degrees in this knowledge of God, our academy, our university for that, is the Church. For, though, as there may

be some few examples given of men that have grown learned who never studied at university, so there may be some examples of men enlightened by God and yet not within that covenant which constitutes the Church, yet the ordinary place for degrees is the university and the ordinary place for illumination in the knowledge of God is the Church. Therefore did God, who ever intended to have his kingdom of heaven well peopled, so powerfully, so miraculously enlarge his way to it, the Church, that it prospered as a wood which no felling, no stubbing, could destroy. We find in the Acts of the Church five thousand martyrs executed in a day, and we find in the Acts of the Apostles five thousand brought to the Church by one sermon;[9] still our Christenings were equal to our burials at least.

Therefore when Christ says to the Church, "Fear not little flock,"[10] it was, . . . says Chrysologus, not because it should fall from great to little, but rise from little to great. Such care had Christ of the growth thereof, and then such care of the establishment and power thereof, as that the first time that ever he names the Church, he invests it with an assurance of perpetuity: "Upon this Rock will I build my Church, and the gates of hell shall not prevail against it."[11] Therein is denoted the strength and stability of the Church in itself, and then the power and authority of the Church upon others, in those often directions, *"Dic Ecclesiæ,"* complain to the Church and consult with the Church,[12] and then *"Audi Ecclesiam,"* hearken to the Church, be judged by the Church; hear not them that hear not the Church; and then *"Ejice de Ecclesia,"* let them that disobey the Church be cast out of the Church. In all which we are forbidden private conventicles, private spirits, private opinions, for, as St. Augustine says well . . . If a wall stand single, not joined to any other wall, he that makes a door through the wall and passes through that door, *"Adhuc foris est,"* for all this is without still; *"Nam domus non est,"* one wall makes not a house; one opinion makes not catholic doctrine, one man makes not a Church. For this knowledge of God, the Church is our academy; there we must be bred and there we may be bred all our lives and yet learn nothing. Therefore, as we must be there, so there we must use the means, and the means in the Church are the Ordinances, and institutions of the Church.

Medium, Institutio

The most powerful means is the Scripture, but the Scripture in the Church. Not that we are discouraged from reading the Scripture at home:

---

9. Acts 4:4.
10. Luke 12:3.
11. Matthew 16:18.
12. [Matthew 18:17]

God forbid we should think any Christian family to be out of the Church. At home the Holy Ghost is with thee in the reading of the Scriptures, but there he is with thee as a remembrancer ("The Holy Ghost shall bring to your remembrance whatsoever I have said unto you," says our Savior).[13] Here in the Church he is with thee as a Doctor to teach thee. First learn at Church and then meditate at home. Receive the seed by hearing the Scriptures interpreted here and water it by returning to those places at home. When Christ bids you "Search the Scriptures,"[14] he means you should go to them, who have a warrant to search, a warrant in their calling. To know which are Scriptures, to know what the Holy Ghost says in the Scriptures, apply thyself to the Church. Not that the Church is a judge above the Scriptures (for the power and the commission which the Church hath, it hath from the Scriptures), but the Church is a judge above thee, which are the Scriptures and what is the sense of the Holy Ghost in them.

So then thy means are the Scriptures. That is thy evidence. But then this evidence must be sealed to thee in the Sacraments and delivered to thee in preaching, and so sealed and delivered to thee in the presence of competent witnesses, the congregation. When St. Paul was carried up . . . in an ecstasy "into Paradise,"[15] that which he gained by this powerful way of teaching is not expressed in a *"Vidit,"* but an *"Audivit."* It is not said that he saw, but that he heard unspeakable things. The eye is the devil's door, before the ear, for, though he do enter at the ear by wanton discourse, yet he was at the eye before. We see before we talk dangerously. But the ear is the Holy Ghost's first door. He assists us with ritual and ceremonial things which we see in the Church, but ceremonies have their right use when their right use hath first been taught by preaching. Therefore to hearing does the Apostle apply faith. And, as the Church is our academy and our medium the Ordinances of the Church, so the light by which we see this, that is know God so as to make him our God, is faith; and that is our other consideration in this part.

Lumen, fides

Those heretics against whom St. Chrysostom and others of the fathers writ, the Anomæi, were inexcusable in this, that they said they were able to know God in this life as well as God knew himself. But in this more especially lay their impiety, that they said they were able to do all this by the light of nature, without faith. By the light of nature, in the theater of

---

13. John 14:26.
14. [John 5:39]
15. 2 Corinthians 12:4.

the world, by the medium of creatures, we see God. But to know God by believing not only Him but in Him is only in the academy of the Church, only through the medium of the Ordinances there, and only by the light of faith.

The School does ordinarily design four ways of knowing God, and they make the first of these four ways to be by faith; but then by faith they mean no more but an assent that there is a God; which is but that which in our former considerations we called the seeing of God, and which indeed needs not faith; for the light of nature will serve for that, to see God so. They make their second way contemplation, that is an union of God in this life, which is truly the same thing that we mean by faith, for we do not call an assent to the Gospel faith, but faith is the application of the Gospel to our selves; not an assent that Christ died, but an assurance that Christ died for all. Their third way of knowing God is by apparition, as when God appeared to the patriarchs and others in fire, in angels, or otherwise. And their fourth way is . . . by his clear manifestation of himself in heaven.

Their first way, by assenting only, and their third way of apparition, are weak and uncertain ways. The other two, present faith and future vision, are safe ways, but admit this difference, that that of future vision is *gratiæ consummantis,* such a knowledge of God as when it is once had can never be lost nor diminished, but knowledge by faith in this world is *gratiæ communis,* it is an effect and fruit of that grace which God shed upon the whole Communion of Saints, that is, upon all those who in this academy, the Church, do embrace the medium, that is, the Ordinances of the Church. And this knowledge of God, by this faith, may be diminished and increased, for it is but *in ænigma,* says our text, darkly, obscurely; clearly in respect of the natural man but yet obscurely in respect of that knowledge of God which we shall have in heaven; for, says the Apostle, "As long as we walk by faith, and not by sight, we are absent from the Lord."[16] Faith is a blessed presence, but compared with heavenly vision it is but an absence; though it create and constitute in us a possibility, a probability, a kind of certainty of salvation, yet that faith, which the best Church hath, is not so far beyond that sight of God which the natural man hath, as that sight of God which I shall have in heaven is above that faith which we have now in the highest exaltation. Therefore there belongs a consideration to that which is added by our Apostle here, that the knowledge which I have of God here (even by faith, through the ordinances of the Church) is but a knowledge in part. "Now I know in part."

---

16. 2 Corinthians 5:6.

JOHN DONNE

Ex parte

That which we call "in part," the Syriac translates "*modicum ex multis;*" though we know by faith, yet for all that faith, it is but a little of a great deal that we know yet, because though faith be good evidence, yet faith is but "the evidence of things not seen;"[17] and there is better evidence of them when they are seen. For, if we consider the object, we cannot believe so much of God, nor of our happiness in him, as we shall see then. For when it is said that the heart comprehends it not, certainly faith comprehends it not neither. And if we consider the manner, faith itself is but darkness in respect of the vision of God in heaven. For those words of the Prophet, "I will search Jerusalem with candles,"[18] are spoken of the times of the Christian Church and of the best men in the Christian Church; yet they shall be searched with candles, some darkness shall be found in them. To the Galatians well instructed and well established, the Apostle says, "Now, after ye have known God, or rather are known of God."[19] The best knowledge that we have of God here, even by faith, is rather that he knows us, than that we know him. And in this text it is in his own person that the Apostle puts the instance, "Now I (I, an Apostle, taught by Christ himself) know but in part." And therefore, as St. Augustine saith, "*Sunt quasi cunabula charitatis Dei, quibus diligimus proximum,*" the love which we bear to our neighbor is but as the infancy, but as the cradle of that love which we bear to God. So that sight of God which we have "*in speculo,* in the glass," that is in nature, is but "*cunabula fidei,*" but the infancy, but the cradle of that knowledge which we have in faith, and yet that knowledge which we have in faith is but "*cunabula visionis,*" the infancy and cradle of that knowledge which we shall have when we come to see God "face to face."

Faith is infinitely above nature, infinitely above works, even above those works which faith itself produces, as parents are to children and the tree to the fruit; but yet faith is as much below vision and seeing God face to face. And therefore, though we ascribe willingly to faith more then we can express, yet let no man think himself so infallibly safe, because he finds that he believes in God, as he shall be when he sees God. The faithfulest man in the Church must say, ... "Lord increase my faith."[20] He that is least in the kingdom of heaven shall never be put to that. All the world is but *speculum,* a glass in which we see God. The Church itself and that

---

17. Hebrews 11:1.
18. Zephaniah 1:12.
19. Galatians 4:9.
20. [Luke 17:5]

146

which the Ordinance of the Church begets in us, faith itself, is but *ænigma*, a dark representation of God to us, till we come to that state, "To see God face to face, and to know, as also we are known."

Cælum, Sphæra

Now as for the sight of God here, our theater was the world, our medium and glass was the creature, and our light was reason, and then for our knowledge of God here, our academy was the Church, our medium the Ordinances of the Church, and our light the light of faith. So we consider the same terms, first for the sight of God and then for the knowledge of God in the next life. First, the sphere, the place where we shall see him is heaven. He that asks me what heaven is means not to hear me, but to silence me; he knows I cannot tell him. When I meet him there, I shall be able to tell him, and then he will be as able to tell me; yet then we shall be but able to tell one another, this, this that we enjoy is heaven, but the tongues of angels, the tongues of glorified saints, shall not be able to express what that heaven is, for even in heaven our faculties shall be finite. Heaven is not a place that was created, for all place that was created shall be dissolved. God did not plant a Paradise for himself and remove to that, as he planted a Paradise for Adam and removed him to that. But God is still where he was before the world was made. And in that place, where there are more suns than there are stars in the firmament (for all the saints are suns), and more light in another sun, the sun of righteousness, the Son of Glory, the Son of God, than in all them in that illustration, that emanation, that effusion of beams of glory, which began not to shine 6,000 years ago, but 6,000 millions of millions before that, in those eternal, in those un-created heavens, shall we see God.

Medium, Revelatio sui

This is our sphere and that which we are fain to call our place; and then our medium, our way to see him is *patefactio sui*, God's laying himself open, his manifestation, his revelation, his evisceration, and embowelling of himself to us, there. Doth God never afford this patefaction, this manifes-tation of himself in his essence to any in this life? We cannot answer yea, nor no, without offending a great part in the School. So many affirm, so many deny, that God hath been seen in his essence in this life. There are that say that it is . . . little less than an article of faith that it has been done; and Aquinas denies it so absolutely as that his followers interpret him, *de absoluta potentia*, that God by his absolute power cannot make a man, remaining a mortal man, and under the definition of a mortal man, capable of seeing his essence; as we may truly say that God cannot make a beast, remaining in that nature, capable of grace or glory. . . . As it may be fairly argued that Christ suffered not the very torments of hell, because it is essential to the torments of hell to be eternal, they were not torments of hell if they received an end; so it is faily argued too that neither Adam in his ecstasy in Paradise, nor Moses in his conversation in the Mount, nor the other Apostle in the Transfiguration of Christ, nor St. Paul in his rapture to the third heavens, saw the essence of God, because he that is admitted to that sight of God, can never look off, nor lose that sight again. Only in heaven shall God proceed to this *patefaction,* this manifestation, this revelation of himself; and that by the light of glory.

Lux Gloriæ

The light of glory is such a light as that our Schoolmen dare not say confidently that every beam of it is not all of it. When some of them say that some souls see some things in God and others, others, because all have not the same measure of the light of glory, the rest cry down that opinion and say that as the essence of God is indivisible and he that sees any of it sees all of it, so is the light of glory communicated entirely to every blessed soul. God made light first, and three days after that light became a sun, a more glorious light. God gave me the light of nature when I quickened in my mother's womb by receiving a reasonable soul. And God gave me the light of faith when I quickened in my second mother's womb, the Church, by receiving my baptism. But in my third day, when my mortality shall put on immortality, he shall give me the light of glory, by which I shall see himself. To this light of glory the light of honor is but a glow-worm; the majesty itself but a twilight; the cherubims and seraphims are but candles; and that Gospel itself, which the Apostle calls the glorious Gospel, but a star of the least magnitude. And if I cannot tell what to call this light by which I shall see it, what shall I call that which I shall see by it, the essence of God himself? And yet there is something else than this sight of God intended in that which remains. I shall not only "see God face to face," but I shall "know" him (which, as you have seen all the way, is above sight) and "know him, even as also I am known."

Deus omnia solus

In this consideration, God alone is all. In all the former there was a place, and a means, and a light; here, for this perfect knowledge of God, God is all those. "Then," says the Apostle, "God shall be all in all."[21] . . . Says St.

---

21. 1 Corinthians 15:28.

Jerome, here God does all in all; but here he does all by instruments; even in the infusing of faith he works by the ministry of the Gospel; but there he shall be all in all, do all in all, immediately by himself; for Christ shall deliver up the kingdom to God, even the Father.[22] His kingdom is the administration of his Church by his Ordinances in the Church. At the resurrection there shall be an end of that kingdom; no more Church; no more working upon men by preaching, but God himself shall be all in all. "*Ministri quasi larvæ Dei*," says Luther. It may be somewhat too familiarly, too vulgarly said, but usefully, "The ministry of the Gospel is but as God's vizor," for by such a liberty the Apostle here calls it *ænigma*, a riddle, or (as Luther says too) God's picture; but in the resurrection God shall put off that vizor and turn away that picture and show us his own face. Therefore is it said, "That in heaven there is no temple, but God himself is the temple."[23] God is service, and music, and psalm, and sermon, and sacrament, and all *Erit vita de verbo sine verbo*. "We shall live upon the word and hear never a word;"[24] live upon him, who being the word, was made flesh, the eternal Son of God. *Hic non est omnia in omnibus, sed pars in singulis*. "Here God is not all in all; where he is at all in any man, that man is well."[25] *In Solomone sapientia*, says that father: it was well with Solomon, because God was wisdom with him, and patience in Job, and faith in Peter, and zeal in Paul but there was something in all these, which God was not. But in heaven he shall be so all in all . . . that every soul shall have every perfection in itself; and the perfection of these perfections shall be that their sight shall be "face to face," and their knowledge "as they are known."[26]

Facie ad faciem

Since St. Augustine calls it a debt, a double debt, a debt because she asked it, a debt because he promised it, to give even a woman, Paulina, satisfaction in that high point and mystery, "how we should see God face to face in heaven," it cannot be unfit in this congregation to ask and answer some short questions concerning that. Is it always a declaration of favor when God shows his face? No. "I will set my face against that soul, that eateth blood, and cut him off."[27] But when there is light joined with it, it is a declaration of favor. This was the blessing that God taught Moses for

---

22. [1 Corinthians 15:] Verse 24.
23. Revelation 21:22.
24. Augustine.
25. Jerome.
26. Idern.
27. Leviticus 17:10.

Aaron, to bless the people with, "The Lord make his face to shine upon thee, and be gracious to thee."[28] And there we shall "see him face to face," by the light of his countenance, which is the light of glory. What shall we see, by seeing him so, "face to face?" . . . We shall see whatsoever we can be the better for seeing.[29] First of all, all things that they believed here, they shall see there; and therefore . . . let us meditate upon no other things on earth then we would be glad to think on in heaven.[30] And this consideration would put many frivolous and many fond thoughts out of our mind, if men and women would love another but so, as that love might last in heaven.

This then we shall get concerning ourselves, by seeing God "face to face;" but what concerning God? Nothing but the sight of the humanity of Christ, which only is visible to the eye. So Theodoret, so some others have thought, but that answers not the *sicuti est*. And we know we shall see God (not only the body of Christ) as he is in his essence. Why? Did all that are said "to have seen God face to face" see his essence? No. In earth God assumed some material things to appear in and is said "to have been seen face to face" when he was seen in those assumed forms. But in heaven there is no material thing to be assumed, and if God be seen face to face there, he is seen in his essence. St. Augustine sums it up fully, upon these words, "*In lumine tuo*, In thy light we shall see light, *Te scilicet in te*," we shall see thee in thee; that is, says he, "face to face."[31]

Ut cognitus

And then, what is it "to know him, as we are known?" First, is that it which is intended here, "That we shall know God as we are known"? It is not expressed in the text so. It is only "that we shall know so;" not "that we shall know God so." But the frame and context of the place hath drawn that unanimous exposition from all that it is meant of our knowledge of God then. A comprehensive knowledge of God it cannot be. To comprehend is to know a thing as well as that thing can be known; and we can never know God so, but that he will know himself better. Our knowledge cannot be so dilated, nor God condensed and contracted so, as that we can know him that way, comprehensively. It cannot be such a knowledge of God as God hath of himself, nor as God hath of us; for God comprehends us and all this world and all the worlds that he could have made, and

---

28. Numbers 6:25.
29. Senon.
30. Jerome.
31. [Augustine] In Psalm 36:9.

himself. But it is, *nota similitudinis, non æqualitatis.* As God knows me, so I shall know God; but I shall not know God so as God knows me. It is not *quantum,* but *sicut;* not as much, but as truly; as the fire does as truly shine as the sun shines, though it shine not out so far, nor to so many purposes. So then I shall know God so as that there shall be nothing in me to hinder me from knowing God; which cannot be said of the nature of man, though regenerate, upon earth, no, nor of the nature of an angel in heaven, left to itself, till both have received a super-illustration from the light of glory.

And so it shall be a knowledge so like his knowledge, as it shall produce a love like his love, and we shall love him as he loves us. For, as St. Chrysostom and the rest of the fathers whom Oecumenius hath compacted interpret it, "*Cognoscam practicè, id est, accurendo.*" I shall know him, that is embrace him, adhere to him. *Qualis sine fine festivitas!*[32] What a Holy-day shall this be, which no working day shall ever follow! By knowing and loving the unchangeable, the immutable God, "*mutabimur in immutabili-tatem,*" we shall be changed into an unchangeableness, says that father that never said anything but extraordinarily. He says more, "*Dei præsentia si in inferno appareret.*"[33] If God could be seen and known in hell, hell in an instant would be heaven.

How many heavens are there in heaven? How is heaven multiplied to every soul in heaven, where infinite other happinesses are crowned with this, this sight and this knowledge of God there? And how shall all those heavens be renewed to us every day, "*qui non mirabimur hodiè,*"[34] that shall be as glad to see and to know God, millions of ages after every day's seeing and knowing, as the first hour of looking upon his face. And as this seeing and this knowing of God crowns all other joys and glories, even in heaven, so this very crown is crowned. There grows from this a higher glory, which is *participes erimus Divinæ naturæ*[35] (words, of which Luther says, that both testaments afford none equal to them), "That we shall be made partakers of the Divine nature"—immortal as the Father, righteous as the Son, and full of all comfort as the Holy Ghost.

Let me dismiss you with an easy request of St. Augustine. "*Fieri non potest ut seipsum non diligat, qui Deum diligit;* that man does not love God, that loves not himself." Do but love yourselves. "*Imo solus se diligere novit, qui Deum diligit;* only that man that loves God, hath the art of love to himself." Do but love yourselves. For if he love God, he would live

---

32. Augustine.
33. Idem.
34. Idem.
35. 1 Peter 1:4.

eternally with him, and if he desire that, and endeavor it earnestly, he does truly love himself, and not otherwise. And he loves himself, who by seeing God in the theater of the world, and in the glass of the creature, by the light of reason, and knowing God in the academy of the Church, by the Ordinances thereof, through the light of faith, endeavors to see God in heaven, by the manifestation of himself, through the light of glory, and to know God himself, in himself, and by himself as he is all in all; contemplatively by knowing as he is known, practically by loving as he is loved.

"Love the Lord, Love Christ, Love Jesus"[1]

1 Corinthians 16:22. "If any man love not the Lord Jesus Christ, let him be anathema, maranatha."

Christ is not defined, not designed by any name, by any word so often as that very word, "the Word, *sermo*, speech." In man there are three kinds of speech; *sermo innatus*, that inward speech, which the thought of man reflecting upon itself produces within (he thinks something); and then *sermo illatus*, a speech of inference, that speech which is occasioned in him by outward things, from which he draws conclusions, and determines; and lastly, *sermo prolatus*, that speech by which he manifests himself to other men. We consider also three kinds of speech in God; and Christ is all three. There is *sermo innatus*, his eternal, his natural word, which God produced out of himself, which is the generation of the second person in the Trinity; and then there is *sermo illatus*, his word occasioned by the fall of Adam, which is his decree of sending Christ as a redeemer; and there is also *sermo prolatus*, his speech of manifestation and application of Christ, which are his Scriptures. The first word is Christ, the second, the decree, is for Christ, the third, the Scripture is of Christ. Let the word be Christ, so he is God; let the word be for Christ, for his coming hither, so he is man; let the word be of Christ, so the Scriptures make this God and man ours. Now "if" in all these, if in any of these apprehensions, "any man love not the Lord Jesus Christ, let him be anthema, maranatha."

Divisio
By most of those who, from the perverseness of heretics, have taken occasion to prove the deity of Christ, this text hath been cited, and therefore I take it now, when in my course proposed I am to speak of the second person of the Trinity; but (as I said of the first person, the Father) not as in

---

[1]. Preached upon Trinity-Sunday. *Sermons,* Potter and Simpson eds., 3:292–312.

the School, but in the Church, not in a chair, but in a pulpit, not to a congregation that required proof in a thing doubted, but edification upon a foundation received; not as though any of us would dispute whether Jesus Christ were the Lord, but that all of us would join in that excommunication, "If any man love not the Lord Jesus Christ, let him be, etc." Let this then be the frame that this exercise shall stand upon. We have three parts: the person upon whom our religious worship is to be directed, "the Lord Jesus Christ"; and secondly we have the expression and the limitation of that worship, as far as it is expressed here, "love the Lord Jesus Christ"; and lastly, we have the imprecation upon them that do not, "If any man do not, let him be anathema, maranatha." In the first we have *verbum naturale, verbum innatum,* as he is the essential word, "the Lord," a name proper only to God; and then *verbum conceptum, verbum illatum,* God's decree upon consideration of man's misery, that Christ should be a redeemer, for to that intent he is *Christus,* anointed to that purpose; and lastly, *verbum prolatum, verbum manifestatum,* that this Christ becomes Jesus, that this decree is executed, that this person thus anointed for this office is become an actual Savior; so the Lord is made Christ and Christ is made Jesus. In the second part we shall find another argument for his deity, for there is such a love required towards the Lord Jesus Christ as pertains to God only. And lastly, we shall have the indeterminable and indispensable excommunication of them who though they pretend to "love the Lord" (God in an universal notion) yet do not "love the Lord Jesus Christ," God, in this apprehension of a Savior; and, "If any man love not, etc."

Dominus

First then, in the first branch of the first part, in that name of our Savior, "the Lord," we apprehend the eternal Word of God, the Son of God, the second person in the Trinity. For he is *persona producta,* begotten by another, and therefore cannot be the first; and he is *persona spirans,* a person out of whom, with the Father, another person, that is, the Holy Ghost proceeds, and therefore cannot be the last person, and there are but three, and so he is necessarily second. Shall we hope to comprehend this by reason? ... How small a thing were this mystery of heaven, if it could be shut in, in so narrow a piece of the earth, as thy heart?[2] ... Thou that knowest nothing of thine own begetting, or art ashamed to speak that little that thou doest know of it, wilt not thou be ashamed to offer to express the

2. Gregory of Nazianzus.

eternal generation of the Son of God?[3] It is true, *de modo*, how it was done, our reason cannot, but, *de facto*, that it was done, our reason may be satisfied. We believe nothing with a moral faith, till something have wrought upon our reason and vanquished that, and made it assent and subscribe. Our divine faith requires evidence too, and hath it abundantly; for, the works of God are not so good evidence to my reason as the Word of God is to my faith. The sun shining is not so good a proof that it is day, as the Word of God, the Scripture is, that that which is commanded there, is a duty. The root of our belief that Christ is God, is in the Scriptures, but we consider it spread into three brances: (1) the evident Word itself, that Christ is God; (2) the real declaration thereof in his manifold miracles; (3) the conclusions that arise to our understanding, thus illumined by the Scriptures, thus established by his miracles.

Ex Scripturis

In every mouth, in every pen of the Scriptures that delivers any truth, the Holy Ghost speaks, and therefore whatsoever is said by any there, is the testimony of the Holy Ghost, for the deity of Christ. And from the Father we have this testimony, that he is his Son, "This is my beloved Son,"[4] and this testimony that his Son is God, "Unto his Son he saith, Thy throne, O God, is for ever and ever."[5] The Holy Ghost testifies, and his Father, and himself; and his testimony is true, "I am Alpha and Omega, the beginning and the ending, saith the Lord, which is, which was, and which is to come, the Almighty."[6] He testifies with his Father; and then their angels and his apostles testify with him, "I Jesus have sent mine angels, to testify unto you these things in the Church, that I am the root and the offspring of David,"[7] not the offspring only, but the root too, and therefore was before David. God and his angels in heaven testify it, and visible angels upon earth, his apostles, "God hath purchased his Church, with his own blood," says St. Paul.[8] He who shed his blood for his Church, was God, and no false god, no mortal god, as the gods of the nations were, but, "This is the true God, and eternal life";[9] and then no small god, no particular god, as the gods of the nations were too, but "We look for the glorious appearing

---

3. Idem.
4. Matthew 3:17.
5. Hebrews 1:8.
6. Revelation 1:18.
7. Revelation 22:16.
8. Acts 20:28.
9. 1 John 5:20.

of our great God, our Savior Christ Jesus."[10] God, that is, God in all the persons, angels, that is angels in all their acceptation, angels of heaven, angels of the Church, angels excommunicate from both, the fallen angels, devils themselves, testify his Godhead, "Unclean spirits fell down before him, and cried, Thou art the Son of God."[11]

Miracula

This is the testimony of his Word. The testimony of his works, are his miracles. That his apostles did miracles in his name was a testimony of his deity. "His name, through faith in his name, hath made this man strong," says St. Peter at the raising of the cripple.[12] But that he did miracles in his own name, by his own power, is a nearer testimony. "Blessed be the Lord God of Israel," says David, . . . "Which doth his miracles alone,"[13] without deriving power from any other, or without using another instrument for his power. For . . . "Whosoever is able to change the course of nature, is the Lord of nature."[14] And he that is so, made it; and he that made it, that created it, is God. Nay, *plus est,* it is more to change the course of nature than to make it;[15] for in the creation there was no reluctation of the creature, for there was no creature, but to divert nature out of her settled course is a conquest upon a resisting adversary, and powerful in a prescription. The "*Recedat mare;* Let the sea go back," and the "*Sistat Sol;* Let the sun stand still," met with some kind of opposition in nature,[16] but in the "*Fiat mare,*" and "*Fial sol,*" let there be a sea, and a sun, God met with no opposition, no nature; he met with nothing.[17] And therefore . . . "Let us ask his miracles, and they will make us understand Christ; . . . if we understand them, that is, if we would understand them, they speak loud enough and plain enough."[18] In his miraculous birth of the Virgin, in his miraculous disputation with doctors at twelve years of age, in his fasting, in his invisibility, in his walking upon the sea, in his reassuming his body in the resurrection, Christ spoke in himself, in the language of miracles. So also had they a loud and plain voice in other men. In his miraculous curing the sick, raising the dead, dispossessing the devil, Christ spoke in other

---

10. Titus 2:3.
11. Mark 3:11.
12. Acts 3:16.
13. Psalm 72:18.
14. Epiphanius.
15. Tertullian.
16. [Exodus 14:21]
17. [Joshua 10:12]
18. Augustine.

men, in the language of miracles. And did so also, as in himself, and in other men, so in other things. In the miraculous change of water into wine, in the drying up of the fig tree, in feeding five thousand with five loaves, in shutting up the sun in darkness, and opening the graves of the dead to light, in bringing plenty of fish to the net, and in putting money into the mouth of a fish at the angle, Christ spoke in all these creatures, in the language of miracles. So the Scriptures testify of his deity, and so do his miracles, and so do those conclusions which arise from thence, though we consider but that one which is expressed in this part of the text, that he is "the Lord, if any love not the Lord, etc."

Dominus

We reason thus: God gives not his glory to others, and his glory is in his essential Name, and in his attributes; and to whomsoever he gives them, because they cannot be given from God, he who hath them is God. Of these none is so peculiar to him as the name of Jehovah. The name which for reverence the Jews forebore to sound and in the room thereof ever sounded, *Adonai*, and *Adonai* is *Dominus*, the name of this text, "the Lord." Christ by being the Lord thus, is Jehovah, and if Jehovah, God. . . . He is the Lord with the Father, as he was con-creator, his colleague in the creation. But for that dominion and lordship which he hath by his pur-chase, by his passion "*Calcavit solus*, He trod the wine-press alone."[19] Not only no man, but no person of the Trinity redeemed us, by suffering for us, but he. For the ordinary appellation of "Lord" in the New Testament (which is *kyrios*) it is but a name of civility, not only no name implying divine worship, but not implying any distinction of rank or degree among men. Mary Magdalene speaks of Christ and speaks to the gardner (as she thought) and both in one and the same word. It is *Kyrios, Dominus,* Lord to both. When she says, "They have taken away my Lord," meaning Christ, and when she says to the gardener, "Sir, if thou hast borne him hence," it is the same word too.[20] Here "the Lord" is God, and "no man can say that Jesus is the Lord but by the Holy Ghost."[21] All that was written in the Scriptures, all that was established by miracles, all that is deduced by reason, conduces to this, determines in this: "That every tongue should confess that Jesus Christ is the Lord,"[22] in which essential name, the name of his nature, he is first proposed as the object of our love.

---

19. [Isaiah 63:3].
20. John 20:15.
21. 1 Corinthians 12:3.
22. [Philippians 2:11].

JOHN DONNE

Christus

Now this Lord, Lord forever, is become that which he was not forever (otherwise than in a secondary consideration), that is, "Christ," which implies a person prepared and fitted and anointed to a peculiar office in this world. And can the Lord, the ever-living Lord, the Son of God, God himself, have any preferment, preferment by an office in this world? Was it a preferment to Dionysius, who was before in that height over men to become a school-master over boys? Were it a preferment to the King's son, to be made governor over a bee-hive, or over-seer over an ant-hill? And men, nay mankind is no more not that, not a bee-hive, not an ant-hill, compared to this person, who being "the Lord" would become "Christ." As he was "the Lord" we considered him as God, and that there is a God, natural reason can comprehend. As he is Christ, we consider him God and man, and such a person natural reason (not rooted in the Scriptures, not illustrated by the Scriptures) cannot comprehend. Man will much easilier believe "the Lord," that is God, than Christ, that is God and man in one person.

"Christ" then is the style, the title of his office. . . . "Christ" is not his name, but his addition. . . .²³ Christ signifies but anointed, and anointed is no more a name than appareled or shod is a name. So, as he was appareled in our flesh, and his apparel died red in his own blood, so as he was shod to tread the wine-press for us, so he was "Christ." That it is *nomen sacramenti,* as St. Augustine calls it, a mystery, is easily agreed to; for all the mysteries of all the religions in the world are but milk in respect of this bone, but catechisms in respect of this School-point, but alphabets in respect of this hard style, God and man in one person. That it is *nomen sacramenti,* as Augustine says, is easy; but that it is *nuncupatio potestatis,* as Lactantius calls it, is somewhat strange; that it is an office of power, a title of honor. For the Creator to become a creature, and the Lord of life the object of death, nay the seat of death in whom death did sojourn three days, can Lactantius call this a declaration of power? Is this *nuncupatio potestatis,* a title of honor? Beloved, he does, and he may; for it was so, for it was an anointing. *Christus* is *unctus;* and unction was the consecration of priests, "Thou shalt take the anointing oil, and pour it upon his head." . . .²⁴

There is a power above the priest, the regal power; not above the function of the priest, but above the person of the priest; but unction was the consecration of kings too. "Samuel saluted Saul with a kiss, and all the

---

23. Tertullian.
24. Exodus 29:7.

158

people shouted and said, 'God save the King;' " but, "Is it not," says Samuel, "because the Lord hath anointed thee to be captain over his inheritance?"[25] Kings were above priests; and in extraordinary cases God raised prophets above kings; for there is no ordinary power above them; but unction was the consecration of these prophets too. Elisha was anointed to be prophet in Elias' room, and such a prophet as should have use of the sword. "Him that scapes the sword of Hazael (Hazael was King of Syria) shall the sword of Jehu slay, and him that scapes the sword of Jehu (Jehu was King of Israel) shall the sword of Elisha slay."[26] In all these, in priests who were above the people, in kings who (in matter of government) were above the priests, in prophets who (in those limited cases expressed by God, and for that time wherein God gave them that extraordinary employment) were above kings, the unction imprinted their consecration, they were all "Christs," and in them all, thereby, was that *nuncupatio potestatis*, which Lactantius mentions. Unction, anointing was an addition and title of honor. Much more in our Christ who alone was all three: "A priest after the order of Melchizedek;"[27] "A king set upon the holy hill of Sion;"[28] and a prophet, "The Lord thy God will raise up a prophet, unto him shall ye hearken."[29] And besides all this three-fold unction, *humanitas uncta divinitate;* he had all the unctions that all the other had, and this which none other had. In him humanity was consecrated, anointed with the divinity itself.

So then, *unio unctio*, the hypostatical union of the godhead to the human nature, in his conception made him Christ;[30] for . . . then, in that union of the two natures "did God anoint him with the oil of gladness above his fellows."[31] There was an addition, something gained, something to be glad of; and to him, as he was God, "the Lord," so nothing could be added; if he were glad above his fellows, it was in that respect wherein he had fellows, and as God, as "the Lord," he had none; so that still, as he was made man he became this "Christ." In which his being made man, if we should not consider the last and principal purpose, which was to redeem man, if we leave out his part, yet it were object enough for our wonder, and subject enough for our praise and thanksgiving, to consider the dignity that the nature of man received in that union wherein this "Lord" was thus

25. 1 Samuel 10:1 and 24.
26. 1 Kings 19:16–17.
27. Psalm 110[:4].
28. Psalm 2:6.
29. Deuteronomy 18[:15].
30. Nazianzus; Cyril.
31. Psalm 45:7.

made this "Christ," for, the Godhead did not swallow up his manhood; but man, that nature remained still. The greater kingdom did not swallow up the less, but the less had that great addition which it had not before, and retained the dignities and privileges which it had before too. . . .[32]

"The name of Christ denotes one person, but not one nature." Neither is Christ so composed of those two natures as a man is composed of elements; for man is thereby made a third thing and is not now any of those elements. You cannot call man's body fire, or air, or earth, or water, though all four be in his composition. But Christ is so made of God and man as that he is man still, for all the glory of the deity, and God still for all the infirmity of the manhood . . . In this one Christ, both appear.[33] The Godhead bursts out, as the sun out of a cloud, and shines forth gloriously in miracles, even the raising of the dead, and the human nature is submitted to contempt and to torment, even to the admitting of death in his own bosom. . . . but still, both he that raises the dead, and he that dies himself, is one Christ; his is the glory of the miracles and the contempt and torment is his too.[34] This is that mysterious person who is *singularis,* and yet not *individuus; singularis,* there never was, never shall be any such, but we cannot call him individual, as every other particular man is, because . . . there is no genus or species of Christs.[35] It is not a name which so (as the name belongs to our Christ, that is, by being anointed with the divine nature) can be communicated to any other, as the name of man, may to every individual man. . . .

This person, this "Christ died for our sins," says St. Paul; but, says he, he died according to the Scriptures. . . .[36] The Apostle thought it a hard, a heavy, an incredible thing to say that this person, this Christ, this man and God, was dead. And therefore . . . that he might mollify the hardness of that saying . . . he adds this, Christ is dead, "according to the Scriptures." If the Scripture had not told us that Christ should die, and told us again that Christ did die, it were hard to conceive how this person, in whom the Godhead dwelt bodily, should be submitted to death. But therein principally is he *Christus,* as he was capable of dying. As he was *verbum naturale* and *innatum,* the natural and essential Word of God, he hath his first name in the text, he is "the Lord." As he is *verbum illatum*

---

32. Damasene.
33. Idem.
34. Idem.
35. Idem.
36. 1 Corinthians 15:3; Tertullian.

and *conceptum*, a person upon whom there is a decree and a commission that he shall be a person capable to redeem man by death, he hath this second name in the text, he is "Christ." As he is "the Lord," he cannot die; as he is "Christ" (under the decree) he cannot choose but die; but as he is Jesus, he is dead already, and that is his other, his third, his last name in this text, "If any man love not etc."

Jesus

We have inverted a little the order of these names or titles in the text, because the name of "Christ," is in the order of nature before the name of "Jesus," as the commission is before the execution of the commission. . . . Now we consider him as Jesus, a real, an actual Savior. And this was his name. The angel said to his mother, "Thou shalt call his name Jesus, for he shall save his people."[37] And we say to you, call upon this name Jesus, for he hath saved his people; for "now there is no condemnation to them that are in Christ Jesus."[38] As he was *verbum conceptum* and *illatum*, the word which the Trinity uttered among themselves, so he was decreed to come in that place, "the Lord of the vineyard" (that is, Almighty God seeing the misery of man to be otherwise irremediable), "The Lord of the vineyard said, what shall I do? I will send my beloved Son; it may be they will reverence him when they see him."[39] But did they reverence him when they saw him? This sending made him "Christ," a person whom, though the Son of God, they might see. They did see him; but then, says that Gospel, "they drew him out and killed him." And this he knew before he came, and yet came, and herein was Jesus, a real, an actual a zealous Savior, even of them that slew him. And in this (with piety and reverence) we may be bold to say that even the Son of God was *filius prodigus*, that poured out his blood even for his enemies; but rather in that acclamation of the prodigal child's father, "This my son was dead, and is alive again, he was lost, and is found."[40] For, but for this desire of our salvation, why should he who was "the Lord," be ambitious of . . . the name of Jesus, which was . . . no such name as was in any especial estimation among the Jews, for we see in Josephus divers men of that name, of no great honor, of no good conversation.[41] But because the name implies salvation, "Joshua," who had

---

37. Matthew 1:21.
38. Romans 8:1.
39. Luke 20:13.
40. [Luke 15:24]
41. Tertullian.

another name before . . . when he was prepared as a type of this Jesus, to be a Savior,[42] a deliver of the people . . . then he was canonized with that name of salvation and called Joshua, which is "Jesus."

The Lord then, the Son of God, had a *sitio* in heaven, as well as upon the Cross. He thirsted for our salvation there; and in the midst of the fellowship of the Father from whom he came, and of the Holy Ghost, who came from him and the Father, and all the angels, who came (by the lower way) from them all, he desired the conversation of man, for man's sake. He that was God, "the Lord," became "Christ," a man, and he that was "Christ," became "Jesus," no man, a dead man, to save man: to save man, all ways, in all his parts, and to save all men, in all parts of the world: to save his soul from hell, where he should have felt pains, and yet been dead then when we felt them; and seen horrid spectacles, and yet been in darkness and blindness then when we saw them; and suffered unsufferable torments, and yet have told over innumerable ages in suffering them: to save this soul from that hell, and to fill that capacity which it had, and give it a capacity which it hath not, to comprehend the joys and glory of heaven, this "Christ" became "Jesus."

To save this body from the condemnation of everlasting corruption, where the worms that we breed are our betters, because they have a life, where the dust of dead kings is blown into the street, and the dust of the street blown into the river, and the muddy river tumbled into the sea, and the sea remanded into all the veins and channels of the earth; to save this body from everlasting dissolution, dispersion, dissipation, and to make it in a glorious resurrection not only a temple of the Holy Ghost, but a companion of the Holy Ghost in the kingdom of heaven, this "Christ" became this "Jesus." To save this man, body and soul together, from the punishments due to his former sins, and to save him from falling into future sins by the assistance of his Word preached and his Sacraments administered in the Church, which he purchased by his blood, is this person, "the Lord," the "Christ," become this "Jesus," this Savior, to save so, all ways, in soul, in body, both; and also to save all men. For, to exclude others from that kingdom is a tyranny, an usurpation; and to exclude thy self, is a sinful, and a rebellious melancholy. But as melancholy in the body is the hardest humor to be purged, so is the melancholy in the soul, the distrust of thy salvation, too. Flashes of presumption a calamity will quench, but clouds of desperation calamities thicken upon us; but even in this inordinate dejection thou exaltest thy self above God and makest thy

42. Idem.

worst better than his best, thy sins larger than his mercy. Christ hath a Greek name and an Hebrew name; "Christ" in Greek, "Jesus" in Hebrew. He had commission to save all nations, and he hath saved all. Thou givest him another Hebrew name, and another Greek, when thou makest his name "Abbadon" and "Apollyon," a destroyer;[43] when thou wilt not apprehend him as a Savior and love him so; which is our second part, in our order proposed at first, "If any man love not, etc."

Part 2. [*Love the Lord*]

In the former part we found it to be one argument for the deity of Christ, that he was Jehovah, "the Lord;" we have another here, that this great branch, nay this very root of all divine worship due to God is required to be exhibited to this person, that is, love, "If any man love not, etc." If any man could see virtue with his eye he would be in love with her.[44] Christ Jesus hath been seen so: "*Quod vidimus,*" says the Apostle, "That which we have seen with our eyes, we preach to you,"[45] and therefore, "If any man love not, etc." If he love him not with that love which implies a confession that the Lord Jesus is God, that is, if he love him not with his whole heart, and all his power: "What doth the Lord thy God require of thee? To love him with all thy heart and all thy soul."[46] God forbids us not a love of the creature, proportionable to the good that that creature can do us: to love fire as it warms me, and meat as it feeds me, and a wife as she helps me; but because God does all this, in all these several instruments, God alone is centrically, radically, directly to be loved, and the creature with a love reflected and derived from him; and Christ to be loved with the love due to God himself. "He that loveth father or mother, son or daughter more than me, is not worthy of me,"[47] says Christ himself. If then we love him so, as we love God, entirely, we confess him to be the "Lord;" and if we love him so, as he hath loved us, we confess him to be "Christ Jesus." And we consider his love to us (for the present) in these two demonstrations of it, first "*Delexit in finem,*" as he loved, so he "loved to the end,"[48] and then "*Posuit animam,* Greater love there is not, than to die for one," and he did that.[49]

---

43. Revelation 9:11.
44. Cicero.
45. [1 John 1:1].
46. Deuteronomy 10:12.
47. Matthew 10:37.
48. [John 13:1].
49. [John 15:13].

JOHN DONNE

In finem

Our Savior Christ forsook not Peter when Peter forsook him: because he loved him, he loved him to the end. Love thou Christ to the end; to his end, and to thy end. *"Finem Domini vidistis,"* says St. James, "You have seen the end of the Lord;"[50] that is, says Augustine, to what end the Lord came. His way was contempt and misery, and his end was shame and death: love him there. Thy love is not required only in the hosanna's of Christ, when Christ is magnified, and his Gospel advanced and men preferred for loving it, no, nor only in the transfiguration of Christ, when Christ appears to thee in some particular beams and manifestation of his glory, but to love him in his *crucifigatur*, then when it is a scornful thing to love him. And love him in the *nunquid et tu*, when thou must pass that examination, "Wert not thou one of them?",[51] and in the *nonne ego te vidi*, if witnesses come in against thee for the love of Christ, love him when it is a suspicious thing, a dangerous thing to love him. And love him not only in spiritual transfigurations, when he visits thy soul with glorious consolations, but even in his inward eclipses, when he withholds his comforts and withdraws his cheerfulness, even when he makes as though he loved not thee, love him. Love him all the way, to his end, and to thy end too, to the laying down of thy life for him.

Mortificatio

Love him then in the laying down of the pleasures of this life for him, and love him in the laying down of the life itself, if his love need that testimony. Of the first case, of crucifying himself to the world, St. Augustine had occasion to say much to a young gentleman, young, and noble, and rich, so he was learned in other learnings, and upon that strength withdrew and kept off from Christ. It was Licentius, to whom St. Augustine writes his 39th Epistle. He had sent to St. Augustine a handsome elegy of his making, in which poem he had said as much of the vanity and deceivableness of this world as St. Augustine could have looked for, or perchance have said in a homily; and he ends his elegy thus, *"Hoc opus, ut jubeas,"* all this concerning this world I know already; do you but tell me, do you command me, what I shall do. *"Jubebit Augustinus conservo suo?"* says that sensible and blessed father: shall I, shall Augustine command his fellow servant? ... Must not Augustine rather lament that the Lord hath commanded thee, and is not obeyed? Wouldst thou hear me? Canst thou

---

50. James 5:11.
51. John 18:25, 26.

164

pretend that? . . . Thou that art inexorable against the persuasions of thine own soul, hard against the tenderness of thine own heart, deaf against the charms of thine own verses, canst thou pretend a willingness to be led by me? . . . How well disposed a soul, how high pitched a wit is taken out of my hands, that I may not sacrifice that soul, that I may not direct that wit upon our God, because, with all these good parts, thou turnest upon the pleasure of the world? . . . Do not speak out of wit, nor out of a love to elegant expressions, nor do not speak in jest of the dangerous vanities of this world; *mentiuntur,* they are false, they perform not their promises; *moriuntur,* they are transitory, they stay not with thee; and *in mortem trahunt,* they die, and they die of the infection, and they transfuse the venom into thee, and thou diest with them. . . . Nothing will deal truly with thee but the truth itself, and only Christ Jesus is this truth. He follows it thus much farther, . . . If thou foundest a chalice of gold in the earth, so good a heart as thine would say, surely this belongs to the Church, and surely thou wouldst give it to the Church. . . . God hath given thee a wit, an understanding, not of the gold of Ophir, but of the gold of the heavenly Jerusalem . . . In that chalice once consecrated to God, wilt thou drink a health to the devil, and drink a health to him in thine own blood, in making thy wit, thy learning, thy good-parts advance his kingdom? He ends all thus, . . . If thou undervalue thyself, if thou think not thyself worth hearing, if thou follow not thine own counsels, yet *misereris mei,* have mercy upon me, me, whose charge it is to bring others to heaven, me, who shall not be received there, if I bring nobody with me. Be content to go with me that way, which by the inspiration of the Holy Ghost I do show, and that way, which by the conduct of the Holy Ghost I would fain go. All bends to this: First, love Christ so far as to lay down the pleasures of this life for him, and so far as to lay down the life itself for him.

Martyrium

Christ did so for thee, and his blessed servants, the martyrs in the Primitive Church, did so for him, and thee, for his glory, for thy example. Can there be any ill, any loss, in giving thy life for him? Is it not part of the reward itself, the honor, to suffer for him? When Christ says, "Whosoever loses anything for my sake, and the Gospel's, he shall have a hundred-fold in houses, and lands, with persecutions,"[52] we need not limit that clause of the promise ("with persecutions") to be, that in the midst of persecutions God will give us temporal blessings, but that in the midst of

---

52. Mark 10:30.

temporal blessings, God will give us persecutions; that it shall be a part of his mercy, to be delivered from the danger of being puffed up by those temporal abundances, by having a mixture of adversity and persecutions; and then, what ill, what loss, is there in laying down this life for him?

Dominus

Love him then as he is presented to thee here. Love the "Lord," love "Christ," love "Jesus." If when thou lookest upon him as the "Lord," thou findest frowns and wrinkles in his face, apprehensions of him, as of a judge, and occasions of fear, do not run away from him, in that apprehension. Look upon him in that angle, in that line awhile, and that fear shall bring thee to love. And as he is "Lord," thou shalt see him in the beauty and loveliness of his creatures, in the order and succession of causes and effects, and in that harmony and music of the peace between him and thy soul. As he is "the Lord," thou wilt fear him, but no man fears God truly, but that that fear ends in love.

Christus

Love him as he is the "Lord" that would have nothing perish that he hath made. And love him as he is "Christ," that hath made himself man too, that thou mightest not perish. Love him as the "Lord" that could show mercy; and love him as "Christ," who is that way of mercy which the Lord hath chosen. Return again and again to that mysterious person, "Christ"; and let me tell you, that though the fathers never forbore to call the blessed Virgin Mary *Deiparam*, the Mother of God, yet in Damascene's time, they would not admit that name, *Christiparam*, that she was the Mother of Christ. Not that there is any reason to deny her that name now; but because then that great heretic Nestorius, to avoid that name in which the rest agreed, *Deiparam* (for he thought not Christ to be God), invented a new name, *Christiparam*. Though it be true in itself that that blessed Virgin is *Christpara*, yet because it was the invention of a heretic . . . Damascene and his age refused that addition to the blessed Virgin; so reverently were they affected, so jealously were they enamored of that name, "Christ," the name which implied his unction, his commission, the decree by which he was made a person able to redeem thy soul. And in that contemplation, say with Andrew, to his brother Peter, . . . I have found the *Messias*;[53] I could find no means of salvation in myself, nay, no such means to direct God upon, by my prayer, or by a wish, as he hath taken; but God himself hath

---

53. [John 1:41].

found a way, a *Messias;* his Son shall be made man; and *inveni Messiam,* I have found him, and found that he who by his incarnation was made able to save me (so he was "Christ"), by his actual passion hath saved me, and so I love him as "Jesus."

Jesus

Christ loved Stephen all the way, for all the way Stephen was disposed to Christ's glory, but in the agony of death (death suffered for him) Christ expressed his love most, in opening the windows, the curtains of heaven itself, to see Stephen die, and to show himself to Stephen.[54] I love my Savior as he is "the Lord," he that studies my salvation; and as "Christ," made a person able to work my salvation; but when I see him in the third motion, "Jesus," accomplishing my salvation by an actual death, I see those hands stretched out, that stretched out the heavens, and those feet racked, to which they that racked them are foot-stools; I hear him, from whom his nearest friends fled, pray for his enemies, and him whom his Father forsook, not forsake his brethren; I see him that clothes this body with his creatures, or else it would wither, and clothes this soul with his righteousness, or else it would perish, hang naked upon the cross; and him that hath, him that is, "the fountain of the water of life,"[55] cry out, "He thirsts," when that voice overtakes me in my cross-ways in the world, "Is it nothing to you, all you that pass by? Behold, and see, if there be any sorrow, like unto my sorrow, which is done unto me, wherewith the Lord hath afflicted me, in the day of his fierce anger;"[56] when I conceit, when I contemplate my Savior thus, I love the "Lord," and there is a reverent adoration in that love, I love "Christ," and there is a mysterious admiration in that love, but I love "Jesus," and there is a tender compassion in that love, and I am content to suffer with him, and to suffer for him, rather than see any diminution of his glory by my prevarication. And he that loves not thus, that loves not the Lord God, and God manifested in Christ, "Anathema, Maranatha," which is our next and last part.

Part 3. *Imprecatio*

Whether this "Anathema" be denounced by the Apostle, by way of imprecation, that he wished it so, or pronounced by way of excommunication, that others should esteem them so, and avoid them, as such persons, is some times debated among in our books. If the Apostles say it by way of

---

54. Acts 7:56.
55. [Revelation 21:6].
56. Lamentations 1:12.

imprecation, if it sound so, you are to remember first, that many things are spoken by the prophets in the Scriptures, which sound as imprecations, as execrations, which are indeed but prophecies. They seem to be spoken in the spirit of anger, when they are in truth but in the spirit of prophesy. So in very many places of the Psalms, David seems to wish heavy calamities upon his and God's enemies, when it is but a declaration of those judgments of God which he prophetically foresees to be imminent upon them. They seem imprecations, and are but prophecies. . . . If they be truly imprecations, you are to remember also that the prophets and apostles had in them a power extraordinary, and in execution of that power might do that which every private man may not do. So the prophets rebuked, so they punished kings. . . .[57] But upon imprecations of this kind, we as private men, or as public persons but limited by our commission, may not adventure . . . But take the prophets or the apostles in their highest authority, yet in an over-vehement zeal, they may have done some things some times not warrantable in themselves, many times many things not to be imitated by us.[58] . . . Since there is a possibility, a facility, a proclivity of erring herein, and so many conditions and circumstances required to make an imprecation just and lawful, the best way is to forebear them, or to be very sparing in them.

Excommunicatio

But we rather take this in the text to be an excommunication denounced by the Apostles, than an imprecation; so Christ himself, "If he will not hear the Church, let him be to thee as a heathen, or a publican,"[59] that is, have no conversation with him. So says the Apostle, speaking of an angel's, "Anathema." If any man, if we ourselves, if an angel from heaven, preach any other gospel, let him be accursed.[60] Now the excommunication is in the "Anathema," and the aggravating thereof in the other words, "Maranatha." The word "Anathema" had two significations; they are expressed thus, "*Quod Deo dicatum, Quod a Deo per vitium alienatum,*"[61] that which for some excellency in it was separated from the use of man to the service of God, or that which for some great fault in it was separated from God and man too. . . . From the first kind men abstained because they were consecrated to God, and from the other, because they were alienated from

57. 2 Kings 2:24; Acts 5:1; Acts 13:8.
58. Exodus 32:39; Romans 9:3; Luke 9:55.
59. Matthew 18:17.
60. Galatians 1:8.
61. Justin Martyr.

God;[62] and in that last sense, irreligious men such as love not the Lord Jesus Christ, are "Anathema," alienated from God. . . . By the light of nature, by the light of grace, we should separate ourselves from irreligious and from adolatrous persons; and that with that earnestness which the Apostle expresses in the last words, "Maran Atha."

Maran Atha

In the practice of the Primitive Church, by those canons which we call the Apostles' Canons, and those which we call the penitential canons, we see there were different penances inflicted upon different faults, and there were, very early, relaxations of penances, indulgences; and there were reservations of cases; in some any priest, in some a bishop only might dispense. It is so in our Church still. Impugners of the [Royal] Supremacy are excommunicated and not restored but by the archbishop. Impugners of the Common Prayer Book excommunicated too, but may be restored by the bishop of the place. . . . There was ever, there is yet a reserving of certain cases and a relaxation or aggravating of ecclesiastical censures, for their weight, and for their time. And because "Not to love the Lord Jesus Christ" was the greatest, the Apostle inflicts this heaviest excommunication, "Maran Atha."

The word seems to be a proverbial word among the Jews after their return, and vulgarly spoken by them, and so the Apostle takes it out of common use of speech. "Maran" is *Dominus,* "the Lord," and "Atha" is *Venit;* and so "Anathema, Maran Atha" will be, "Let him that loveth not the Lord Jesus Christ, be as an accursed person to you, even till the Lord come." . . . It is not only a censorious speech, it is a shame for them, and an inexcusable thing in them, if they do not love the Lord Jesus Christ, but it is a judiciary speech, thus much more, since they do not love the Lord, "The Lord judge them when he comes." I, says the Apostle, take away none of his mercy when he comes, but I will have nothing to do with them, till he comes; to me, he shall be "Anathema, Maran Atha," separated from me, till then; then, the Lord who shews mercy in minutes, do his will upon him. . . .

Conclusion

To end all, if a man love not the Lord, if he loves not God, which is, which was, and which is to come, what will please him, whom will he love? If he love the "Lord," and love not "Christ," and so love a God in general, but

---

62. Chrysostom.

lay no hold upon a particular way of salvation, *"Sine Christo, sine Deo,"* says the Apostle to the Ephesians, when we were without Christ, ye were without God.[63] A non-Christian is an atheist in that sense of the Apostle. If any man find a "Christ," a Savior of the world, but find not a "Jesus," an actual Savior, that this Jesus hath saved him, "Who is a liar," says another Apostle, "but he that denieth that Jesus is the Christ?" And (he says after), "Whosoever believeth that Jesus is the Christ, is born of God."[64] From the presumptuous atheist that believes no God manifested in Christ, from the melancholic atheist that believes no Jesus applied to him, from him of no religion, from him of no Christian religion, from him that errs fundamentally in the Christian religion, the Apostle enjoins a separation, not till the clouds of persecution come, and then join, not till beams of preferment come, and then join, not till laws may have been slumbered some years, and then join, not till the parties grow somewhat near an equality, and then join, but "Maran Atha, *donec Dominus venit,*" till the Lord come to his declaration in judgement, "If any man love not the Lord Jesus Christ, let him be accursed. Amen."

63. Ephesians 2:12.
64. Ephesians 2:22.

"In the Shadow of Thy Wings"[1]

Psalm 63:7. Because thou hast been my help, therefore in the shadow of thy wings will I rejoice.

The Psalms are the manna of the Church. As manna tasted to every man like that that he liked best, so do the Psalms minister instruction and satisfaction to every man in every emergency and occasion.[2] David was not only a clear prophet of Christ himself, but a prophet of every particular Christian; he foretells what I, what any, shall do and suffer and say. And as the whole book of Psalms is *oleum effusum*[3] (as the Spouse speaks of the name of Christ), an ointment poured out upon all sorts of sores, . . . a balm that searches all wounds; so are there some certain psalms that are imperial psalms, that command over all affections and spread themselves over all occasions, catholic, universal psalms that apply themselves to all necessities. This is one of those.

Divisio

Now as the spirit and soul of the whole book of Psalms is contracted into this psalm, so is the spirit and soul of this whole psalm contracted into this verse. The key of the psalm (as St. Jerome calls the titles of the psalms), tells us that David uttered this psalm "when he was in the wilderness of Judah." There we see the present occasion that moved him. And we see what was passed between God and him before, in the first clause of our text: "Because thou hast been my help." And then we see what was to come, by the rest: "Therefore in the shadow of thy wings will I rejoice." So that we have here the whole compass of time: past, present and future. And these three parts of time shall be at this time the three parts of this exercise: first, what David's distress put him upon for the present, and that lies in the context; secondly, how David built his assurance upon that

---

[1]. Donne wrote: "The second of my Prelent Sermons upon my five Psalms. Preached at S. Pauls, January 29, 1625 [1625/6]." *Sermons*, Potter and Simpson eds., 7:51–71.

2. Wisdom 16:20.

3. Song of Solomon 1:3.

which was past ("Because thou hast been my help"); and thirdly, what he established to himself for the future ("Therefore in the shadow of thy wings will I rejoice").

First, his distress in the wilderness, his present estate, carried him upon the memory of that which God had done for him before; and the remembrance of that carried him upon that of which he assured himself after. Fix upon God anywhere and you shall find him a circle. He is with you now, when you fix upon him; he was with you before, for he brought you to this fixation; and he will be with you hereafter, for, "He is yesterday, and today, and the same forever."[4]

For David's present condition, who was now in a banishment, in a persecution in the wilderness of Judah, we shall only insist . . . that in all those temporal calamities David was only sensible of his spiritual loss. It grieved him not that he was kept from Saul's court, but that he was kept from God's Church. For when he says, by way of lamentation, "That he was in a dry and thirsty land, where no water was,"[5] he expresses what penury, what barrenness, what drought and what thirst he meant: . . . that spiritual losses are incomparably heavier than temporal, and that therefore the restitution to our spiritual happiness, or the continuation of it, is rather to be made the subject of our prayers to God, in all pressures and distresses, than of temporal. . . .

Part 1. *Afflictio universalis:* the comparing of temporal and spiritual afflictions

In the way of this comparison, falls first the consideration of the universality of afflictions in general, and the inevitableness thereof. It is a blessed metaphor that the Holy Ghost has put into the mouth of the Apostle, . . . that our afflictions are but light, because there is an exceeding, and an eternal weight of glory attending them.[6] If it were not for that exceeding weight of glory, no other weight in this world could turn the scale, or weigh down those infinite weights of afflictions that oppress us here. . . .

It is not only Job that complains that he was a burden to himself,[7] but even Absalom's hair was a burden to him, till it was polled.[8] It is not only Jeremiah that complains . . . that God had made their fetters and their

---

4. Hebrews 13:8.
5. Psalm 63:1.
6. 2 Corinthians 4:17.
7. Job 7:20.
8. 2 Samuel 14:26.

chains heavy to them,[9] but the workmen in harvest complain that God had made a fair day heavy unto them ("We have borne the heat, and the burden of the day").[10] Sand is heavy, says Solomon.[11] And how many suffer so, under a sand-hill of crosses, daily, hourly afflictions that are heavy by their number if not by their single weight? And a stone is heavy, says he in the same place. And how many suffer so? How many, without any former preparatory cross, even in the midst of prosperity and security fall under some one stone, some grindstone, some millstone, some one unsupportable cross that ruins them? But then, says Solomon there, "A fool's anger is heavier than both." And how many children, and servants, and wives suffer under the anger, and moroseness, and peevishness, and jealousy of foolish masters, and parents, and husbands, though they must not say so? David and Solomon have cried out that all this world is vanity and levity; and God knows all is weight, and burden, and heaviness, and oppression; and if there were not a weight of future glory to counterpoise it, we should all sink into nothing.

I ask not Mary Magdalene whether lightness were not a burden, for sin is certainly, sensibly a burden. But I ask Susanna whether even chaste beauty were not a burden to her; and I ask Joseph whether personal comeliness were not a burden to him. I ask not Dives, who perished in the next world, the question; but I ask them who are made examples of Solomon's rule, of that "sore evil," as he calls it, "riches kept to the owners thereof for their hurt," whether riches be not a burden.[12]

All our life is a continual burden, yet we must not groan; a continual squeezing, yet we must not pant. And as in the tenderness of our childhood we suffer, and yet are whipped if we cry, so we are complained of if we complain, and made delinquents if we call the times ill. And that which adds weight to weight and multiplies the sadness of this consideration is this: that still the best men have had the most laid upon them. As soon as I hear God say that he hath found "an upright man, that fears God, and eschews evil," in the next lines I find a commission to Satan to bring in Sabeans and Chaldeans upon his cattle and servants, and fire and tempest upon his children, and loathsome diseases upon himself. As soon as I hear God say that he hath found "a man according to his own heart,"[13] I see his

---

9. Lamentations 3:7.
10. Matthew 20:12.
11. Proverbs 27:3.
12. Ecclesiastes 5:13.
13. [1 Samuel 13:14].

sons ravish his daughters, and then murder one another, and then rebel against the Father and put him into straits for his life. As soon as I hear God testify of Christ at his baptism, "This is my beloved Son in whom I am well pleased,"[14] I find that Son of his "led up by the Spirit to be tempted of the Devil."[15] And after I hear God ratify the same testimony again, at his Transfiguration,[16] . . . I find that beloved Son of his deserted, abandoned, and given over to scribes and Pharisees, and publicans, and Herodians, and priests, and soldiers, and people, and judges, and witnesses and executioners; and he that was called the beloved Son of God and made partaker of the glory of Heaven in this world, in his Transfiguration, is made now the sewer of all the corruption, of all the sins of this world, as no Son of God but a mere man; as no man, but a contemptible worm. As though the greatest weakness in this world were man, and the greatest fault in man were to be good, man is more miserable than other creatures, and good men more miserable than any other men. . . .

Afflictio spiritualis

They who write of natural story,[17] propose that plant for the greatest wonder in nature which, being no firmer than a bullrush or a reed, produces and bears for the fruit thereof no other but an entire and very hard stone. That temporal affliction should produce spiritual stoniness and obduration is unnatural yet ordinary. Therefore does God propose it as one of those greatest blessings which he multiplies upon his people, "I will take away your stony hearts, and give you hearts of flesh."[18] And, Lord, let me have a fleshy heart in any sense, rather than a stony heart. We find mention among the observers of rarities in nature,[19] of hairy hearts, hearts of men that have been overgrown with hair; but of petrified hearts, hearts of men grown into stone, we read not; for this petrefaction of the heart, this stupefaction of a man, is the last blow of God's hand upon the heart of man in this world. . . .

Let me wither and wear out my age in a discomfortable, in an unwholesome, in a penurious prison, and so pay my debts with my bones and recompense the wastefulness of my youth with the beggary of my age. Let me wither under sharp and foul and infamous diseases, and so recompense the wantonness of my youth with that loathesomeness in my age. Yet if

14. Matthew 3:17.
15. Matthew 4:1.
16. Matthew 17:5.
17. Pliny, Book 27.11.
18. Ezekiel 11:19 and 36:26.
19. Pliny and Plutarch.

God withdraw not his spiritual blessings, his grace, his patience; if I can call my suffering his doing, my passion his action, all this that is temporal is but a caterpillar got into one corner of my garden, but a mildew fallen upon one acre of my corn. The body of all, the substance of all, is safe as long as the soul is safe.

But when I shall trust to that which we call a good spirit, and God shall deject, and impoverish, and evacuate that spirit; when I shall rely upon a moral constancy and God shall shake, and enfeeble, and enervate, destroy and demolish that constancy; when I shall think to refresh myself in the serenity and sweet air of a good conscience and God shall call up the damps and vapors of hell itself and spread a cloud of diffidence and an impenetrable crust of desperation upon my conscience; when health shall fly from me, and I shall lay hold upon riches to succor me and comfort me in my sickness, and riches shall fly from me and I shall snatch after favor and good opinion to comfort me in my poverty; when even this good opinion shall leave me and calumnies and misinformation shall prevail against me; when I shall need peace because there is none but thou, O Lord, that should stand for me, and then shall find that all the wounds have come from thy hand, all the arrows that stick in me from thy quiver; when I shall see that because I have given myself to my corrupt nature, thou hast changed thine; and because I am all evil towards thee, therefore thou hast given over being good towards me; when it comes to this height, that the fever is not in the humors but in the spirits, that mine enemy is not an imaginary enemy (fortune) nor a transitory enemy (malice in great persons), but a real, and an irresistible, and an inexorable, and an everlasting enemy, the Lord of Hosts himself, the Almighty God himself—the Almighty God himself only knows the weight of this affliction. And except he put in that *pondus gloriæ*, exceeding weight of an eternal glory, with his own hand, into the other scale, we are weighed down, we are swallowed up, irreparably, irrevocably, irrecoverably, irremediably.

This is the fearful depth, this is spiritual misery, to be thus fallen from God. But was this David's case? Was he fallen thus far into a diffidence in God? No. But the danger, the precipice, the slippery sliding into that bottomless depth, is to be excluded from the means of coming to God, or staying with God. And this is what David laments here, that by being banished and driven into the wilderness of Judah, he had not access to the sanctuary of the Lord, to sacrifice his part in the praise and to receive his part in the prayers of the congregation. For Angels pass not to ends but by ways and means, nor men to the glory of the Triumphant Church but by participation of the Communion of the Militant.

To this note David sets his harp in many, many psalms. Sometimes

JOHN DONNE

that God had suffered his enemies to possess his Tabernacle ("He forsook the Tabernacle of Shiloh, He delivered his strength into captivity, and his glory into the enemy's hands").[20] But most commonly he complains that God disabled him from coming to the sanctuary. In which one thing he has summed up all his desires, all his prayers ("One thing have I desired of the Lord, that will I look after; That I may dwell in the house of the Lord, all the days of my life, to behold the beauty of the Lord, and to enquire in his temple").[21] His vehement desire of this he expresses again ("My soul thirsteth for God, for the living God; when shall I come and appear before God?").[22] He expresses a holy jealousy, a religious envy, even to the sparrows and swallows ("Yea, the sparrow hath found a house, and the swallow a nest for herself, and where she may lay her young, Even thine altars, O Lord of Hosts, my King and my God").[23] Thou art my King and my God, and yet excludest me from that which thou affordest to sparrows, "And are not we of more value than many sparrows?"[24]

And as though David felt some false ease, some half-temptation, some whispering that way, that God is in the wilderness of Judah, in every place as well as in his sanctuary, there is in the original in that place a pathetic, a vehement, a broken expression: "O thine Altars." It is true (says David) thou art here in the wilderness, and I may see thee here and serve thee here, but, "O thine Altars, O Lord of Hosts, my King and my God."[25] When David could not come in person to that place, yet he bent towards the temple. . . .

For, as in private prayer, when (according to Christ's command) we are shut up in our chamber, there is exercised the modesty and bashfulness of our faith, not pressing upon God in his house: so in the public prayers of the congregation there is exercised the fervor and holy courage of our faith, for . . . it is a mustering of our forces and a besieging of God.[26] Therefore does David so much magnify their blessedness that are in this house of God ("Blessed are they that dwell in thy house, for they will be still praising thee").[27] Those that look towards it may praise thee sometimes, but those men who dwell in the Church, and whose whole service lies in the Church, have certainly an advantage of all other men (who are

---

20. Psalm 78:60.
21. Psalm 27:4.
22. Psalm 42:2.
23. Psalm 84:3.
24. Luke 12:7.
25. Psalm 84:3.
26. Tertullian.
27. [Psalm 84:4].

necessarily withdrawn by worldly businesses) in making themselves acceptable to almighty God, if they do their duties and observe their Church services aright.

Excommunicatio

Man being therefore thus subject naturally to manifold calamities, and spiritual calamities being incomparably heavier than temporal, and the greatest danger of falling into such spiritual calamities being in our absence from God's Church, where only the outward means of happiness are ministered unto us, certainly there is much tenderness and deliberation to be used before the Church doors be shut against any man.

If I would not direct a prayer to God to excommunicate any man from the Triumphant Church (which were to damn him), I would not oil the key, I would not make the way too slippery for excommunications in the Militant Church; for that is to endanger him. I know how distasteful a sin to God contumacy and contempt and disobedience to order and authority is; and I know (and all men that choose not ignorance may know) that our excommunications (though calumniators impute them to small things, because, many times, the first complaint is of some small matter) never issue but upon contumacies, contempts, disobediences to the church. But they are real contumacies, not interpretative, apparent contumacies, not presumptive, that excommunicate a man in heaven. And much circumspection is required and (I am far from doubling it) exercised in those cases upon earth; for, though every excommunication upon earth be not sealed in heaven, though it damn not the man, yet it dams up that man's way by shutting him out of that Church through which he must go to the other.

Which being so great a danger, let every man take heed of excommunicating himself. The impersuasible recusant does so; the negligent libertine does so; the fantastic separatist does so; the half-present man, he whose body is here and mind away, does so; and he whose body is but half here, his limbs are here upon a cushion but his eyes, his ears are not here, does so. All these are self-excommunicators and keep themselves from hence. Only he enjoys that blessing, the want whereof David deplores, that is here entirely, and glad he is here, and glad to find this kind of service here that he does, and wishes no other.

And so we have done with our first part, David's aspect, his present condition, and his danger of falling into spiritual miseries because his persecution and banishment amounted to an excommunication, an excluding of him from the service of God in the Church. And we pass, in our order proposed at first, to the second, his retrospect, the consideration, what God had done for him before, "Because thou hast been my help."

JOHN DONNE

Part 2. *Assurance based on that which is Past*

Through this second part we shall pass by these three steps. First, that it behoves us in all our purposes and actions, to propose to ourselves a copy to write by, a pattern to work by, a rule or example to proceed by, because it has been thus heretofore, says David, "I will resolve upon this course for the future." And secondly, that the copy, the pattern, the precedent which we are to propose to ourselves is the observation of God's former ways and proceedings upon us; because God has already gone this way, this way I will await his going still. And then, thirdly and lastly, in this second part, the way that God had formerly gone with David, which was that he had been his help ("Because thou hast been my helpe").

First then, from the meanest artificer through the wisest philosopher to God himself, all that is well done or wisely undertaken, is undertaken and done according to preconceptions, fore-imaginations, designs and patterns proposed to ourselves beforehand. A carpenter builds not a house but that he first sets up a frame in his own mind, what kind of house he will build. The little great philosopher Epictetus would undertake no action but he would first propose to himself what Socrates, or Plato, what a wise man would do in that case, and according to that, he would proceed. Of God himself it is safely resolved in the School, that he never did anything in any part of time, of which he had not an eternal preconception, an eternal idea in himself before. Of which ideas, that is preconceptions, predeterminations in God, St. Augustine pronounces . . . there is so much truth and so much power in these ideas, as that without acknowledging them no man can acknowledge God, for he does not allow God counsel and wisdom and deliberation in his actions, but sets God on work before he have thought what he will do. And therefore he, and others of the Fathers read that place (which we read otherwise), "*Quod factum est, in ipso vita erat;*"[28] That is, in all their expositions, whatsoever is made, in time, was alive in God before it was made, that is, in that eternal Idea and pattern which was in him. So also do divers of those Fathers read those words to the Hebrews (which we read, "The things that are seen, are not made of things that do appear"), "*Ex invisibilibus visibilia facta sunt:* Things formerly invisible, were made visible;"[29] that is, we see them not till now, till they are made, but they had an invisible being in that Idea, in that pre-notion, in that purpose of God before, for ever before.

Of all things in Heaven and earth, but of himself, God had an Idea, a

---

28. John 1:3–4.
29. Hebrews 11:3.

pattern in himself, before he made it. And therefore let him be our pattern for that, to work after patterns; to propose to ourselves rules and examples for all our actions; and the more, the more immediately, the more directly our actions concern the service of God. If I ask God by what Idea he made me, God produces his . . . ["Let us make man in our image,"][30] that there was a concurrence of the whole Trinity to make me in Adam, according to that image which they were and according to that Idea which they had predetermined.

If I pretend to serve God, and he ask me for my idea, how I mean to serve him, shall I be able to produce none? If he ask me an idea of my religion and my opinions, shall I not be able to say, It is that which thy word and thy Catholic Church hath imprinted in me? If he asks me an idea of my prayers, shall I not be able to say, It is that which my particular necessities, that which the form prescribed by thy Son, that which the care and piety of the church in conceiving fit prayers hath imprinted in me? If he ask me an idea of my sermons, shall I not be able to say, It is that which the analogy of faith, the edification of the congregation, the zeal of thy work, the meditations of my heart have imprinted in me?

But if I come to pray or to preach without this kind of idea; if I come to extemporal prayer and extemporal preaching, I shall come to an extemporal faith and extemporal religion. And then I must look for an extemporal Heaven, a Heaven to be made for me; for to that Heaven which belongs to the Catholic Church I shall never come, except I go by the way of the Catholic Church, by former ideas, former examples, former patterns, to believe according to ancient beliefs, to pray according to ancient forms, to preach according to former meditations. God does nothing, man does nothing well, without these ideas, these retrospects, this recourse to preconceptions, pre-deliberations.

Via Domini

Something then I must propose to myself to be the rule and the reason of my present and future actions, which was our first branch in this second part; and then the second is, that I can propose nothing more availably than the contemplation of the history of God's former proceedings with me, which is David's way here. Because this was God's way before I will look for God in this way still. That language in which God spake to man, the Hebrew, has no present tense. They form not their verbs as our western languages do, in the present (*I hear*, or *I see*, or *I read*), but they begin at

---

30. [Genesis 1:26].

that which is past: *I have seen* and *heard* and *read.* God carries us in his language, in his speaking, upon that which is past, upon that which he has done already. I cannot have better security for present, nor future, than God's former mercies exhibited to me. . . .

There is no state, no church, no man, that has not this tie upon God, that has not God in these bands, that God by having done much for them already hath bound himself to do more. . . . Carry it up to the first sense and apprehension that ever thou hadst of God's working upon you, either in yourself when you came first to the use of reason, or in others in your behalf, in your baptism, yet when you think you are at the first, God had done something for your first before all that. . . . God had thee before he made thee. He loved thee first and then created thee, that thou loving him, he might continue his love to thee. The surest way and the nearest way to lay hold upon God is the consideration of that which he had done already. So David does. And that which he takes knowledge of in particular, in God's former proceedings towards him is, because God had been his help, which is our last branch in this part, "Because thou hast been my help."

Quia auxilium

From this one word, that God hath been my *help,* I make account that we have both these notions: first, that God hath not left me to myself, he hath come to my succor, he hath helped me; and then, that God hath not left out myself. He hath been my help, but he hath left something for me to do with him and by his help. My security for the future, in this consideration of that which is past, lies not only in this, that God hath delivered me, but in this also, that he hath delivered me by way of a help, and help always presumes an endeavor and co-operation in him that is helped.

God did not elect me as a helper, nor create me, nor redeem me, nor convert me, by way of helping me; for he alone did all, and he had no use at all of me. God infuses his first grace, the first way, merely as a giver, entirely, all himself; but his subsequent graces, as a helper; therefore we call them auxiliant graces, helping graces; and we always receive them when we endeavor to make use of his former grace. "Lord, I believe," says the man in the Gospel to Christ, "help mine unbelief."[31] If there had not been unbelief, weakness, imperfectness in that faith, there had needed no help; but if there had not been a belief, a faith, it had not been capable of help and assistance, but it must have been an entire act, without any concurrence on man's part.

---

31. Mark 9:24.

So that if I have truly the testimony of a rectified conscience, that God hath helped me, it is in both respects: first, that he hath never forsaken me, and then that he hath never suffered me to forsake myself. He hath blessed me with that grace, that I trust in no help but his, and with this grace too, that I cannot look for his help, except I help myself also. God did not help Heaven and earth to proceed out of nothing in the Creation, for they had no possibility of any disposition towards it, for they had no being. But God did help the earth to produce grass and herbs; for, for that, God had infused a seminal disposition into the earth which, for all that, it could not have perfected without his farther help. . . . If I will make God's former working upon me an argument of his future gracious purposes, as I must acknowledge that God hath done much for me, so I must find that I have done what I could, by the benefit of that grace with him; for God promises to be but a helper.

"Lord open thou my lips," says David: that is God's work entirely. And then, "My mouth shall shew forth thy praise":[32] there enters David into the work with God. And then, says God to him, . . . "Open thy mouth" (it is now made "thy mouth" and therefore do thou open it) "and I will fill it."[33] All incohations and consummations, beginnings and perfectings, are of God, of God alone; but in the way there is a concurrence on our part (by a successive continuation of God's grace), in which God proceeds as a helper; and I put him to more than that, if I do nothing. But if I pray for his help, and apprehend and husband his graces well when they come, then he is truly, properly my helper; and upon that security I can proceed to David's confidence for the future, "Because thou hast been my help, therefore in the shadow of thy wings will I rejoice;" Which is our third, and last general part.

Part 3. *Confidence for the Future*

In this last part, which is (after David's aspect and consideration of his present condition, which was, in the effect, an exclusion from God's Temple, and his retrospect, his consideration of God's former mercies to him, that he had been his help) his prospect, his confidence for the future, we shall stay a little upon these two steps: first, that that which he promises himself, is not an immunity from all powerful enemies, nor a sword of revenge upon those enemies. It is not that he shall have no adversary, nor that that adversary shall be able to do him no harm, but that he should have

---

32. Psalm 51:15.
33. Psalm 81:10.

a refreshing, a respiration . . . under the shadow of God's wings. And then, in the second place, that this way which God shall be pleased to take, this manner of refreshing, which God shall vouchsafe to afford (though it amount not to a full deliverance), must produce a joy, a rejoicing in us; we must not only not decline to a murmuring, that we have no more, no nor rest upon a patience for that which remains, but we must ascend to a holy joy, as if all were done and accomplished, "In the shadow of thy wings will I rejoice."

Umbra alarum

First then, lest any man in his dejection of spirit, or of fortune, should stray into a jealousy or suspicion of God's power to deliver him, as God hath spangled the firmament with stars, so hath he his Scriptures with names, and metaphors, and denotations of power. Sometimes he shines out in the name of a sword, and of a target, and of a wall, and of a tower, and of a rock, and of a hill; and sometimes in that glorious and manifold constellation of all together: . . . "The Lord of Hosts." God, as God, is never represented to us with defensive arms; he needs them not. . . . God is invulnerable in himself. . . . But though God need not, nor receive not defensive arms for himself, yet God is to us a helmet, a breastplate, a strong tower, a rock, everything that may give us assurance and defence. And as often as he will, he can refresh that proclamation, . . . "Our enemies shall not so much as touch us."[34]

But here, by occasion of his metaphor in this text, . . . "In the shadow of thy wings," we do not so much consider an absolute immunity, that we shall not be touched, as a refreshing and consolation when we are touched, though we be pinched and wounded. The names of God, which are most frequent in the Scriptures, are these three, *Elohim* and *Adonai* and *Jehovah;* And to assure us of his power to deliver us, two of these three are names of power. *Elohim* is *Deus fortis,* the mighty, the powerful God. . . . The second name of God is a name of power too, *Adonai.* For *Adonai* is *Dominus,* the Lord, such a Lord as is Lord and proprietary of all his creatures, and all creatures are his creatures. And then, *Dominum est potestas tum utendi, tum abutendi,* says the Law: to be absolute Lord of any thing gives that Lord a power to do what he will with that thing. God, as he is *Adonai,* the Lord, may give and take, quicken and kill, build and throw down, where and whom he will. But then his third name, and that name which he chooses to himself . . . is not a name of power, but only of

---

34. Psalm 105:15.

essence, of being, of subsistence, and yet in vertue of that name, God relieved his people. And if, in my afflictions, God vouchsafe to visit me in that name, to preserve me in my being, in my subsistence in him, that I be not shaked out of him, disinherited in him, excommunicated from him, divested of him, annihiliated towards him, let him at his good pleasure reserve his *Elohim* and his *Adonai*, the exercises and declarations of his mighty power, to those great public causes that more concern his glory, than any thing that can befall me. But if he impart his *Jehovah*, enlarge himself so far towards me as that I may live and move and have my being in him, though I be not instantly delivered, nor mine enemies absolutely destroyed, yet this is as much as I should promise myself, this is as much as the Holy Ghost intends in this metaphor, . . . "Under the shadow of thy wings": that is a refreshing, a respiration, a conservation, a consolation in all afflictions that are inflicted upon me.

Yet is not this metaphor of wings without a denotation of power. No act of God's, though it seem to imply but spiritual comfort, is without a denotation of power. . . . So that, if I have the shadow of his wings, I have the earnest of the power of them too. If I have refreshing and respiration from them, I am able to say (as those three confessors did to Nebuchad-nezzar), "My God is able to deliver me," I am sure he has power; "And my God will deliver me," when it conduces to his glory, I know he will; "But, if he do not, be it known unto thee, O King, we will not serve thy gods."[35] Be it known unto thee, O Satan, how long soever God defer my deliverance, I will not seek false comforts, the miserable comforts of this world. I will not, for I need not; for I can subsist under this shadow of these wings, though I have no more. . . .

Though God do not actually deliver us, nor actually destroy our enemies, yet if he refresh us in the shadow of his wings, if he maintain our subsistence (which is a religious constancy) in him, this should not only establish our patience (for that is but half the work), but it should also produce a joy, and rise to an exultation: "Therefore in the shadow of thy wings, I will rejoice."

Gaudium

I would always raise your hearts and dilate your hearts to a holy joy, to a joy in the Holy Ghost. There may be a just fear that men do not grieve enough for their sins. But there may be a just suspicion, too, that they may fall into inordinate griefs and diffidence of God's mercy. And God hath

---

35. Daniel 3:17.

reserved us to such times, as being the later times, give us even the dregs and lees of misery to drink. For, God hath not only let loose into the world a new spiritual disease; which is an equality and an indifferency, which religion our children, or our servants, or our companions profess . . . but God hath accompanied and complicated almost all our bodily diseases of these times, with an extraordinary sadness, a predominant melancholy, a faintness of heart, a cheerlessness, a joylessness of spirit. And therefore I return often to this endeavor of raising your hearts, dilating your hearts with a holy joy, joy in the Holy Ghost, for "under the shadow of his wings" you may, you should, "rejoice."

If you look upon this world in a map you find two hemispheres, two half worlds. If you crush heaven into a map you may find two hemispheres too, two half heavens; half will be joy and half will be glory, for in these two, the joy of heaven and the glory of heaven, is all heaven often represented unto us. And as of those two hemispheres of the world, the first has been known long before but the other (that of America, which is the richer in treasure), God reserved for later discoveries; so though he reserve that hemisphere of heaven which is the glory thereof, to the Resurrection, yet the other hemisphere, the joy of heaven, God opens to our discovery and delivers for our habitation even while we dwell in this world. As God has cast upon the unrepentant sinner two deaths, a temporal and a spiritual death, so he has breathed into us two lives. As the word for death is doubled, . . . "Thou shalt die the death,"[36] so is the word for life expressed in the plural, "God breathed into his nostrils the breath of lives," of divers lives.

Though our natural life were no life, but rather a continual dying, yet we have two lives besides that; an eternal life reserved for heaven, but yet a heavenly life too, a spiritual life, even in this world. And as God doth thus inflict two deaths and infuses two lives, so doth he also pass two judgments upon man, or rather repeats the same judgment twice. For that which Christ shall say to your soul at the last judgment, "Enter into thy Master's joy," he says to your conscience now, "Enter into thy Master's joy."[37] The everlastingness of the joy is the blessedness of the next life, but the entering, the inchoation is afforded here. For that which Christ shall say then to us, . . . "Come ye blessed,"[38] are words intended to persons that are coming, that are upon the way, though not at home. Here in this world he bids us, "Come"; there in the next he shall bid us, "Welcome."

---

36. Genesis 2:17.
37. Matthew 25:23.
38. Matthew 25:34.

The angels of heaven have joy in thy conversion,[39] and canst thou be without that joy in thyself? If thou desire revenge upon thine enemies, as they are God's enemies, that God would be pleased to remove and root out all such as oppose him, that affection appertains to glory. Let that alone till thou come to the hemisphere of glory. There join with those martyrs under the altar, . . . "How long O Lord, dost thou defer judgment?"[40] and thou shalt have thine answer there for that. Whilst thou art here, here join with David and the other saints of God in that holy increpation of a dangerous sadness, "Why art thou cast down O my soul? why art thou disquieted in me?"[41]

That soul that is dissected and anatomized to God, in a sincere confession, washed in the tears of true contrition, embalmed in the blood of reconciliation, the blood of Christ Jesus, can assign no reason, can give no just answer to that interrogatory, "Why art thou cast down O my soul? why art thou disquieted in me?" No man is so little as that he can be lost under these wings; no man so great as that they cannot reach to him. . . . To what temporal, to what spiritual greatness soever we grow, still pray we him to shadow us under his wings; for the poor need those wings against oppression, and the rich against envy.

The Holy Ghost, who is a dove, shadowed the whole world under his wings. He hovered over the waters,[42] he sat upon the waters, and he hatched all that was produced; and all that was produced so, was good. Be thou a mother where the Holy Ghost would be a father; conceive by him and be content that he produce joy in thy heart here. First think that as a man must have some land, or else he cannot be in a wardship, so a man must have some of the love of God, or else he could not fall under God's correction. God would not give him his physic, God would not study his cure, if he cared not for him. And then think also, that if God afford thee the shadow of his wings, that is, consolation, respiration, refreshing, though not a present and plenary deliverance in thine afflictions, not to thank God is a murmuring, and not to rejoice in God's ways is an unthankfulness.

Howling is the noise of hell, singing the voice of heaven; sadness the damp of hell, rejoicing the serenity of heaven. And he that has not this joy here lacks one of the best pieces of evidence for the joys of heaven, and has neglected or refused that earnest by which God uses to bind his bargain,

---

39. Luke 15:10.
40. Revelation 6:10.
41. Psalm 42:5.
42. [Genesis 1:2].

that true joy in this world shall flow into the joy of heaven, as a river flows into the sea. This joy shall not be put out in death and a new joy kindled in me in heaven; but as my soul, as soon as it is out of my body, is in heaven, and does not stay for the possession of heaven, nor for the fruition of the sight of God, till it be ascended through air and fire and moon and sun and planets and firmament, to that place which we conceive to be heaven, but without the thousandth part of a minute's stop, as soon as it issues, is in a glorious light, which is heaven (for all the way to heaven is heaven; and as those angels which came from heaven bring heaven with them and are in heaven here, so that soul that goes to heaven, meets heaven here; and as those angels do not divest heaven by coming, so those souls invest heaven, in their going). As my soul shall not go towards heaven, but go by heaven to heaven, to the heaven of heavens; and we go thither, not that being without joy we might have joy infused into us, but that as Christ says, "Our joy might be full,"[43] perfected, sealed with an everlastingness. For as he promises "that no man shall take our joy from us,"[44] so neither shall death itself take it away, nor so much as interrupt it, or discontinue it. But as in the face of death when he lays hold upon me, and in the face of the Devil when he attempts me, I shall see the face of God (for everything shall be a glass to reflect God upon me), so in the agonies of death, in the anguish of that dissolution, in the sorrows of that valediction, in the irreversibleness of that transmigration, I shall have a joy which shall no more evaporate than my soul shall evaporate; a joy that shall pass up and put on a more glorious garment above, and be joy super-invested in glory. *Amen.*

43. John 16:24.
44. John 16:22.

Prayer and the Divine Mercy[1]

Luke 23:34. Father, forgive them, for they know not what they do.

The word of God is either the co-eternal and co-essential Son, our Savior, which took flesh. . . ,[2] or it is the spirit of his mouth, by which we live, and not by bread only.[3] And so, in a large acceptation, every truth is the Word of God; for truth is uniform, and irrepugnant, and indivisible, as God. . . . More strictly the Word of God is that which God has uttered, either in writing, as twice in the Tables to Moses; or by ministry of angels, or prophets, in words; or by the unborn, in action, as in John the Baptist's exultation within his mother; or by new-born, from the mouths of babes and sucklings; or by things unreasonable, as in Balaam's ass; or insensible, as in the whole book of such creatures, "The heavens declare the glory of God, etc."[4] But nothing is more properly the Word of God to us than that which God himself speaks in those organs and instruments which himself has assumed for his chief work, our redemption. For in creation God spoke, but in redemption he did; and more, he suffered. And of that kind are these words. God in his chosen manhood says, "Father forgive them, for they know not what they do."

These words shall be fitliest considered, like a goodly palace, if we rest a little, as in an outward court, upon consideration of prayer in general; and then draw near the view of the palace, in a second court, considering this special prayer in general as the face of the whole palace. Thirdly, we will pass through the chief rooms of the palace itself; and then insist upon four steps: 1. Of whom he begs (Father). 2. What he asks (forgive them). 3. That he prays upon reason (for). 4. What the reason is

---

[1]. In *Fifty Sermons* this sermon is described as "Preached to the Nobility." We have no sure date for this sermon, but it was most likely delivered before 1622. See *Sermons*, Potter and Simpson eds., 5:18, and, for the sermon itself, pp. 231–44.

2. [John 1:14].

3. [Deuteronomy 8:3; Matthew 4:4].

4. [Psalm 19:1].

187

(they know not). And lastly, going into the backside of all, we will cast the objections: as why only Luke remembers this prayer: and why this prayer (as it seems by the punishment continuing upon the Jews to this day) was not obtained at God's hand.

Of Prayer

So therefore prayer is our first entry, for when it is said, "Ask and it shall be given," it is also said, "Knock and it shall be opened,"[5] showing that by prayer our entrance is. And not the entry only, but the whole house: "My house is the house of prayer."[6] Of all the conduits and conveyances of God's graces to us, none has been so little subject to cavillations as this of prayer. The sacraments have fallen into the hands of flatterers and robbers. Some have attributed too much to them, some detracted. Some have painted them, some have withdrawn their natural complexion. It has been disputed whether they be, how many they be, what they be, and what they do. The preaching of the Word has been made a servant of ambitions and a shop of many men's new-fangled wares. Almost every means between God and man suffers some adulteratings and disguises; but prayer least; and it has most ways and addresses. It may be mental, for we may think prayers. It may be vocal, for we may speak prayers. It may be actual, for we do prayers. For deeds have voice; the vices of Sodom did cry,[7] and the alms of Tobit.[8] And if it were proper for St. John in the first of the Revelations[9] to turn back and to see a voice, it is more likely God will look down to hear a work. So then to do the office of your vocation sincerely is to pray. How much the favorites of princes and great personages labor that they may be thought to have been in private conference with the prince. And though they be forced to wait upon his purposes, and talk of what he will, how fain they would be thought to have solicited their own, or their dependent's business. With the Prince of Princes, this every man may do truly; and the sooner, the more beggar he is: for no man is heard here but in forma pauperis [as a beggar].

Here we may talk long, welcomely, of our own affairs, and be sure to speed. You cannot whisper so low alone in your chamber but he hears you, nor sing so loud in the congregation but he distinguishes you. He grudges not to be chidden and disputed with, by Job. "The arrows of the Almighty

5. [Matthew 7:7].
6. [Luke 19:46].
7. [Genesis 18:20].
8. [Tobit 12:9].
9. [Revelations 1:12].

are in me, and the venom thereof hath drunk up my spirit. Is my strength the strength of stones, or is my flesh of brass, etc."[10] Not to be directed and counselled by Jonah, who was angry and said, "Did not I say, when I was in my country, thou wouldest deal thus?" And when the Lord said, "Doest thou well to be angry?" he replied, "I do well to be angry to the death."[11] Nor almost to be threatened and neglected by Moses: "Do this, or blot my name out of thy book."[12] It is an honor to be able to say to servants, "Do this": but to say to God, "Lord, do this," and prevail, is more; and yet more easy.

God is replenishingly everywhere; but most contractedly and work-ingly in the temple. Since then every rectified man is the temple of the Holy Ghost, when he prays; it is the Holy Ghost itself that prays; and what can be denied where the asker gives? He plays with us, as children, shows us pleasing things, that we may cry for them, and have them. "Before we call, he answers and when we speak, he hears:" so Isaiah 65:24. Physicians observe some symptoms so violent that they must neglect the disease for a time and labor to cure the accident; as burning fevers, in dysenteries. So in the sinful consumption of the soul, a stupidity and indisposition to prayer must first be cured. For "Ye lust, and have not, because ye ask not," James 4:2. The adulterous mother of the three great brothers, Gratian, Lombard, and Comestor, being warned by her confessor to be sorry for her act, said she could not, because her fault had so much profited the Church. "At least," said he, "be sorry that you cannot be sorry." So whosoever you be, that cannot readily pray, at least pray that you may pray. For, as in bodily, so in spiritual diseases, it is a desperate state to be speechless.

Of this Prayer. Father

It were unmannerliness to hold you longer in the entry. One turn in the inner court, of this special prayer in general, and so enter the palace. This is not a prayer for his own ease, as that in his agony seems. It has none of those infirmities which curious schismatics find in that. No suspicion of ignorance, as there ("if it be possible").[13] No tergiversation nor abandon-ing the noble work which he had begun, as there ("let this cup pass"). It is not an exemplar, or form, for us to imitate precisely (otherwise than in the doctrine), as that prayer (Matthew 6) which we call the Lord's Prayer, not because he said it, for he could never say "forgive us our trespasses," but

---

10. [Job 6:4, 12].
11. [Jonah 4:2, 9].
12. [Exodus 32:32].
13. [Matthew 26:39].

189

because he commanded us to say it. For though by Matthew, which says, "After this manner pray," we seem not bound to the words, yet Luke says, "When you pray, say, Our Father which art, etc."[14] But this is a prayer of God, to God; . . . as when foreign merchandise is misported, the prince may permit or inhibit his subjects to buy it, or not to buy it. Our blessed Savior arriving in this world freighted with salvation, a thing which this world never had power to have without him, except in that short time between man's creation and fall, he by this prayer begs that even to these despisers of it, it may be communicable, and that their ignorance of the value of it may not deprive them of it. Teaching that by example here, which he gave in precept before, (Matthew 5:44) "Pray for them which persecute you, that you may be the children of your Father which is in heaven." Therefore, doing so now, he might well say, "Father, forgive them," which is the first room in this glorious palace.

And in this contemplation, O my unworthy soul, you are presently in the presence. No passing of guards, nor ushers. No examination of your degree or habit. The prince is not asleep, nor private, nor weary of giving, nor refers to others. He puts you not to prevail by angels nor archangels. But lest anything might hinder you from coming into his presence, his presence comes into you. And lest majesty should dazzle you, you are to speak but to your Father. Of which word, *Abba*, the root is "to will"; from which root, the fruit also must be willingness and propenseness to grant. God is the Father of Christ, by that mystical and eternal unexpressible generation, which never began nor ended. Of which incomprehensible mystery, Moses and the ancient prophets spake so little, and so indirectly, that till the dawning of the day of Christ, after Esdras' time, those places seem not to be intended of the Trinity. Nay, a good while after Christ they were but tenderly applied to that sense. And at this day, the most of the writers in the reformed Churches, considering that we need not such far-fetched and such forced helps, and withal weighing how well the Jews of these times are provided with other expositions of those places, are very sparing in using them, but content themselves modestly herein with the testimonies of the New Testament.

Truly, this mystery is rather the object of faith than reason; and it is enough that we believe Christ to have ever been the Son of God, by such generation, and ourselves his sons by adoption. So that God is Father to all; but yet so, that though Christ say, (John 10) "My Father is greater than all," he adds, "I and my Father are all one," to show his eternal interest;

---

14. [Luke 11:2].

and (John 20) he seems to put a difference, "I go to my Father, and your Father, my God and your God." The Roman stories have that when Claudius saw it conduce to his ends to get the tribuneship, of which he was incapable because a patrician, he suffered himself to be adopted. But against this adoption two exceptions were found; one, that he was adopted by a man of lower rank, a plebeian; which was unnatural; and by a younger man than himself, which took away the presentation of a father. But our adoption is regular. For first, we are made the sons of the Most High, and thus also by the Ancient of Days. There was no one word, by which he could so nobly have maintained his dignity, kept his station, justified his cause, and withal expressed his humility and charity, as this, "Father." They crucified him for saying himself to be the Son of God. And in the midst of torments, he both professes the same still, and lets them see that they have no other way of forgiveness, but that he is the Son of that Father, "For no man cometh to the Father but by the Son."[15]

Forgive them

And at this voice (Father) O most blessed Savior, your Father, which is so fully yours that for your sake he is ours too; which is so wholly yours that he is yourself; which is all mercy, yet will not spare you; all justice, yet will not destroy us. And that glorious army of Angels, which hitherto by their own integrity maintained their first and pure condition, and by this work of yours, now near the *Consummatum est* [it is finished][16] attend a confirmation and infallibility of ever remaining so. And that faithful company of departed saints, to whom your merit must open a more inward and familiar room in your Father's Kingdom, stand all attentive to hear what you will ask of this Father. And what shall they hear? What do you ask? "Forgive them," forgive them? Must murderers be forgiven? Must the offended ask it? And must a Father grant it? And must he be solicited and remembered by the name of Father to do it? Was not your passion enough, but you must have compassion? And is your mercy so violent, that you will have a fellow feeling of their imminent afflictions, before they have any feeling? The Angels might expect a present employment for their destruction: the Saints might be out of fear, that they should be assumed or mingled in their fellowship. But you will have them pardoned. And yet dost not out of your own fulness pardon them, as you did the thief upon the cross, because he did already confess you; but you tell them, that they may be forgiven but at

---

15. [John 14:6].
16. [John 19:30].

your request, and if they acknowledge their advocate to be the Son of God. "Father, forgive them."

I that cannot revenge your quarrel cannot forgive them. I that could not be saved, but by their offence, cannot forgive them. And must a Father, Almighty, and well pleased in you, forgive them? You are more charitable towards them, than by your direction we may be to ourselves. We must pray for ourselves limitedly: forgive us, as we forgive. But you will have their forgiveness illimited and unconditioned. You seem not so much as to presume a repentance; which is so essential and necessary in all transgressions, as where by man's fault the actions of God are diverted from his appointed ends, God himself is content to repent the doing of them. As he repented first the making of man,[17] and then the making of a king.[18] But God will have them within the arms of his general pardon. And we are all delivered from our debts; for God has given his word, his co-essential word, for us all. And though (as in other prodigal debts, the interest exceed the principal) our actual sins exceed our original, yet God by giving his word for us has acquitted all.

For

But the affections of our Savior are not inordinate, nor irregular. He has a "for" for his prayer: "Forgive them, for, etc." And where he has not this "for," as in his prayer in his agony, he quickly interrupts the violence of his request, with a but, "Father, let this cup pass, but not my will." In that form of prayer which himself taught us, he has appointed a "for," on God's part, which is ever the same unchangeable: "For thine is the Kingdom." Therefore supplications belong to you: the power, "Thou openest thy hand and fillest every living thing": the glory, "for thy Name is glorified in thy grants."[19] But because on our part the occasions are variable, he has left our "for" to our religious discretion. For when it is said, (James 4) "You lust and have not, because you ask not," it follows presently, "You ask and miss, because you ask amiss." It is not a fit "for," for every private man to ask much means for he would do much good. I must not pray, Lord put into my hands the strength of Christian Kings, for out of my zeal I will employ your benefits to your advantage, your soldiers against your enemies, and be a bank against that deluge wherewith your enemy the Turk threatens to overflow your people. I must not pray, "Lord fill my heart with knowledge and understanding," for I would compose the schisms in

17. [Genesis 6:6].
18. [1 Samuel 15:11].
19. [Psalm 145:16].

your Church, and reduce your garment to the first continual and seamless integrity; and redress the deafnesses and oppressions of judges, and officers. But he gave us a convenient scantling for our "fors," who prayed, "Give me enough, for I may else despair, give me not too much, for so I may presume."[20]

Of Schoolmen, some affirm prayer to be an act of our will; for we would have that which we ask. Others, of our understanding; for by it we ascend to God, and better our knowledge, which is the proper aliment and food of our understanding; so that is a perplexed case. But all agree that it is an act of our reason, and therefore must be reasonable. For only reasonable things can pray; for the beasts and ravens are not said to pray for food, but "to cry."

Two things are required to make a prayer: 1. *Pius affectus* [good effect], which was not in the Devil's request, (Matthew 8:31) "Let us go into the swine"; nor (Job 1:11) "Stretch out thy hand, and touch all he hath"; and "Stretch out thy hand, and touch his bones";[21] and therefore these were not prayers. And it must be *rerum decentium* [of things which are good], for our government in that point, this may inform us. Things absolutely good, as remission of sins, we may absolutely beg: and to escape things absolutely ill, as sin. But mean and indifferent things, qualified by the circumstances, we must ask conditionally and referringly to the giver's will. For (2 Cor. 12:8) when Paul begged *stimulum carnis* [the thorn in the flesh] to be taken from him, it was not granted, but he had this answer, "My grace is sufficient for thee."

They know not: Ignorance

Let us now (not in curiosity but for instruction) consider the reason: "They know not what they do." First, if ignorance excuse and then, if they were ignorant.

Have you, O God, filled all your Scriptures, both of your recorders and notaries, which have penned the history of your love to your people; and of your secretaries the prophets, admitted to the foreknowledge of your purposes, and instructed in your cabinet; have you filled these with phrases and persuasions of wisdom and knowledge, and must these persecutors be pardoned for their ignorance? Have you bid Isaiah to say, (27:11) "It is a people of no understanding, therefore he that made them, shall not

20. [Proverbs 30:8, 9].
21. [Job 2:5].

have compassion of them." And Hosea (4:6) "My people are destroyed for lack of knowledge"; and now do you say, "Forgive them because they know not?" Shall ignorance, which is often the cause of sin, often a sin itself, often the punishment of sin, and ever an infirmity and disease contracted by the first great sin, advantage them? "Who can understand his faults?" said the man according to your heart, (Psalm 19:12) "Lord cleanse me from my secret faults." He durst not make his ignorance the reason of his prayer, but prayed against ignorance.

But your mercy is as the sea: both before it was the sea, for it overspreads the whole world: and since it was called into limits: for it is not the less infinite for that. And as by the sea the most remote and distant nations enjoy one another by traffic and commerce, East and West becoming neighbors: so by mercy the most different things are united and reconciled: sinners have heaven; traitors are in the prince's bosom: and ignorant persons are in the spring of wisdom, being forgiven, not only though they be ignorant, but because they are ignorant. But all ignorance is not excusable; nor any less excusable than not to know what ignorance is not to be excused. Therefore, there is an ignorance which they call *nescientiam,* a not knowing of things not appertaining to us. This we had had, though Adam had stood; and the angels have it, for they know not the latter day, and therefore for this we are not chargeable. They call the other privation, which if it proceed merely from our own sluggishness, in not searching the means made for our instruction, is ever inexcusable. If from God, who for his own just ends has cast clouds over those lights which should guide us, it is often excusable. For (1 Tim. 1:13) Paul says, "I was a blasphemer, and a persecutor, and an oppressor, but I was received to mercy, for I did it ignorantly, through unbelief." So though we are all bound to believe, and therefore faults done by unbelief cannot escape the name and nature of sin, yet since belief is the immediate gift of God, faults done by unbelief, without malicious concurrences and circumstances, obtain mercy and pardon from that abundant fountain of grace, Christ Jesus.

And therefore it was a just reason, "Forgive them, for they know not." If they knew not, which is evident both by this speech from truth itself, and by, (1 Cor. 2:8) "Had they known it, they would not have crucified the Lord of glory"; and (Acts 3:17) "I know that through ignorance ye did it." And though after so many powerful miracles, this ignorance were vincible, God having revealed enough to convert them, yet there seems to be enough on their parts to make it a perplexed case, and to excuse, though not a malicious persecuting, yet a not consenting to his doctrine. For they had a law, "Whosoever shall make himself the son of

God, let him die."[22] And they spoke out of their laws, when they said, "We have no other King but Caesar."[23] There were therefore some among them reasonable and zealously ignorant. And for those, the Son ever-welcome and well heard, begged of his Father, ever accessible and exorable, a pardon ever ready and natural.

[*Why St. Luke Alone*]

We have now passed through all those rooms which we unlocked and opened at first. And now may that point, why this prayer is remembered only by one evangelist, and why by Luke, be modestly inquired. For we are all admitted and welcomed into the acquaintance of the Scriptures, upon such conditions as travellers are into other countries: if we come as praisers and admirers of their commodities and government, not as spies into the mysteries of their state, nor searchers, not calumniators of their weaknesses. For though the Scriptures, like a strong rectified state, be not endangered by such a curious malice of any, yet he which brings that, deserves no admittance. When those great commissioners which are called the Septuagint, sent from Jerusalem to translate the Hebrew Scriptures into Greek, had perfected their work, it was and is an argument of divine assistance, that writing severally, they differed not. The same may prove even to weak and faithless men that the Holy Ghost superintended the four evangelists, because they differ not; as they which have written their harmonies make it evident.

But to us, faith teaches the other way. And we conclude not, because they agree, the Holy Ghost directed; for heathen writers and malefactors in examinations do so; but because the Holy Ghost directed, we know they agree and differ not. For as an honest man, ever of the same thoughts, differs not from himself, though he do not ever say the same things, if he say not contraries; so the four evangelists observe the uniformity and sameness of their guide, though all did not say all the same things, since none contradicts any. And as, when my soul, which enables all my limbs to their functions, disposes my legs to go, my whole body is truly said to go, because none stays behind; so when the Holy Spirit, which had made himself as a common soul to their four souls, directed one of them to say anything, all are well understood to have said it. And therefore when to that place in Matthew 27:9, where the evangelist cites the prophet Jere-

22. [John 19:7].
23. [John 19:15].

195

miah for words spoken by Zacharia, many medicines are applied by the Fathers, as that many copies have no name, that Jeremiah might be binominous and have both names, a thing frequent in the Bible, that it might be the error of a transcriber, that there was extant an apocryphal book of Jeremiah in which these words were, and sometimes things of such books were vouched, as Jannes and Jambres by Paul.[24] St. Augustine . . . teaches . . . that it is more wonderful that all the prophets spake one by Spirit, and so agreed, than if any one of them had spoken all those things; and therefore he adds, . . . "All say what any of them say." And in this sense most congruously is that of St. Jerome appliable, that the four Evangelists are *Quadriga Divina*, that as the four chariot wheels, though they look to the four corners of the world, yet they move to one end and one way, so the evangelists have both one scope and one way. . . .

Other singularities of Luke, of form or matter, I omit and end with one like this in our text. As in the apprehending of our blessed Savior, all the evangelists record that Peter cut off Malchus' ear, but only Luke remembers the healing of it again:[25] (I think) because that act of curing was most present and obvious to his consideration, who was a physician: so he was therefore most apt to remember this prayer of Christ, which is the physic and *balsamum* of our soul, and must be applied to us all (for we do all crucify him, and we know not what we do). And therefore St. Jerome gave a right character of him, in his Epistle to Paulinus, . . . "As he was a physician, so all his words are physic for a languishing soul."

The Effect of This Prayer

Now let us dispatch the last consideration of the effect of this prayer. Did Christ intend the forgiveness of the Jews, whose utter ruin God (that is, himself) had fore-decreed? And which he foresaw and bewailed even then hanging upon the cross? For those divines which reverently forbear to interpret the words, "Lord, Lord, why hast thou forsaken me?"[26] of a suffering hell in his soul, or of a departing of the Father from him; (for John 16 it is, "I am not alone, for the Father is with me") offer no exposition of those words more convenient than that the foresight of the Jews' imminent calamities expressed and drew those words from him: "In their affliction, were all kinds, and all degrees of misery." So that as one writer of the Roman story says elegantly, "He that considers the acts of

---

24. [2 Timothy 3:8].
25. [Matthew 26:51; Mark 14:47; Luke 22:50–51; John 18:10].
26. [Matthew 27:46].

Rome, considers not the acts of one people, but of mankind": I may truly say of the Jews' afflictions, he that knows them is ignorant of nothing that this world can threaten. For to that which the present authority of the Romans inflicted upon them, our Schools have added upon their posterity; that they are as slaves to Christians, and their goods subject to spoil, if the laws of the princes where they live did not out of indulgency defend them. Did he then ask, and was not heard? God forbid. A man is heard, when that is given which his will desired; and our will is ever understood to be a will rectified, and concurrent with God. This is *voluntas,* a discoursed and examined will. That which is upon the first sight of the object, is *velleitas,* a willingness, which we resist not only because we thought not of it. And such a willingness had Christ, when suddenly he wished that the cup might pass: but quickly conformed his will to his Father's. But in this prayer his will was present, therefore fulfilled.

Briefly then, in this prayer he commended not all the Jews, for he knew the chief to sin knowingly, and so out of the reach of reason ("for they know not"). Nor any, except they repented after: for it is not ignorance, but repentance, which derives to us the benefit of God's pardon. For he that sins of ignorance may be pardoned if he repent; but he that sins against his conscience, and is thereby impenitible, cannot be pardoned. And this is all which I will say of these words, "Father forgive them, for they know not what they do."

O eternal God, look down from thy Throne to thy footstool: from thy blessed company of Angels and saints, to us, by our own faults made more wretched and contemptible than the worms which shall eat us, or the dust which we were, and shall be. O Lord, under the weight of thy justice we cannot stand. Nor had any other title to thy mercy, but the name of Father, and that we have forfeited. That name of sons of God, thou gavest to us, all at once in Adam; and he gave it away from us all by his sin. And thou hast given it again to every one of us, in our regeneration by baptism, and we have lost it again by our transgressions. And yet thou wert not weary of being merciful, but didest choose one of us, to be a fit and worthy ransom for us all; and by the death of thy Christ, our Jesus, gavest us again the title and privilege of thy Sons; but with conditions, which though easy, we have broke, and with a yoke, which though light, and sweet, we have cast off. How shall we then dare to call thee Father? Or to beg that thou wilt make one trial more of us? These hearts are accustomed to rebellions, and hopeless. But, O God, create in us new hearts, hearts capable of the love and fear due to a Father. And then we shall dare to say, "Father," and to say, "Father forgive us." Forgive us, O Father, and all which are engaged, and accountable to thee for us: forgive our parents, and those which undertook for us in baptism. Forgive the civil magistrate, and the minister. Forgive them their negligences, and us our stubbornnesses. And give us the grace that we may ever sincerely say, both this prayer of example and counsel, "Forgive our enemies," and that other precept, "Our Father which art in Heaven, etc."

The Virtue of Praise[1]

Psalm 90:14. O satisfy us early with thy mercy, that we may rejoice and be glad all our days.

. . . If we require exactly an unanimous consent, that all agree in the author of this psalm, we can get no farther, then that the Holy Ghost is the author. All agree the words to be canonical scripture, and so from the Holy Ghost; and we seek no farther. The words are his, and they offer us these considerations: first, that the whole psalm being in the title thereof called a prayer, "A Prayer of Moses the man of God," it puts us justly and pertinently upon the consideration of many dignities and prerogatives of that part of our worship of God, prayer. For there we shall see that though the whole psalm be not a prayer, yet because there is a prayer in the psalm, that denominates the whole psalm, the whole psalm is a prayer. When the psalm grows formally to be a prayer our text enters, "O satisfy us early with thy mercy, that we may rejoice and be glad all our days." And in that there will be two parts more, the prayer itself, "O satisfy us early with thy mercy," and the affect thereof, "That we may rejoice and be glad all our days." So that our parts are three, first prayer, then this prayer, and lastly the benefits of all prayer.

Part 1. *Prayer*

For the first, which is prayer in general, I will thrust no farther then the text leads me in, that is, that prayer is so essential a part of God's worship, as that all is called prayer . . . Remember you of thus much of the method or elements of prayer, that whereas the whole book of psalms is called . . . the book of praise, yet this psalm and all that follow to the hundredth psalm, and divers others besides these (which make us a fair limb of this body, and a considerable part of the book) are called prayers. The book is praise, the parts are prayer. The name changes not the nature; prayer and

---

[1]. Preached at St. Paul's probably at some time between November, 1621, and the end of 1622. See *Sermons*, Potter and Simpson eds., 5:23–24, and for the sermon, pp. 268–95.

199

praise is the same thing. The name scarce changes the name; prayer and praise is almost the same word. As the duties agree in the heart and mouth of a man, so the names agree in our ears, and not only in the language of translation, but in the language of the Holy Ghost himself, for that which with us differs but so, prayer and praise, in the original differs no more than so, "*tehillim,*" and "*tephilloth.*"

And this concurrence of these two parts of our devotion, prayer and praise, that they accompany one another, nay this co-incidence that they meet like two waters and make the stream of devotion consist together, but constitute one another, is happily expressed in this part of the prayer, which is our text. For that which in the original language is expressed in the voice of prayer, "O satisfy us, etc." in the first translation, that of the Septuagint, is expressed in the voice of praise, "*saturasti,* Thou hast satisfied us." The original makes it a prayer, the translation a praise. . . . That prayer which our Savior gave us (for as he meant to give us all for asking, so he meant to give us words by which we should ask), as that prayer consists of seven petitions, and seven is infinite, so by being at first begun with glory and acknowledgement of his reigning in heaven, and then shut up in the same manner, with acclamations of power and glory, it is made a circle of praise, and a circle is infinite too. The prayer and the praise is equally infinite. Infinitely poor and needy man, that ever needest infinite things to pray for; infinitely rich and abundant man, that ever hast infinite blessings to praise God for.

God's house in this world is called the house of prayer, but in heaven it is the house of praise: no surprisal with any new necessities there, but one even, incessant, and everlasting tenor of thanksgiving. And it is a blessed incohation of that state here, here to be continually exercised in the commemoration of God's former goodness towards us. "My voice shalt thou hear in the morning, O Lord," says David. What voice? The voice of his prayer; it is true; "In the morning will I direct my prayer unto thee," says David there.[2] And not only then, but at noon and at night he vows that sacrifice, "Evening and morning, and at noon will I pray, and cry unto thee."[3] But David's devotion began not when his prayers began. One part of his devotion was before morning: "At midnight will I rise, and give thanks unto thee, O Lord," he says.[4] Doubtless when he lay down and closed his eyes, he had made up his account with God, and had received his *quietus est* then. And then the first thing that he does when he wakes again,

---

2. Psalm 5:3.
3. Psalm 55:17.
4. Psalm 119:62.

is not to importune God for more, but to bless God for his former blessings. And as this part of his devotion, praise, began all, so it passes through all: "I will bless the Lord at all times, and his praise shall be continually in my mouth."[5] He extends it through all times, and all places, and would fain do so through all persons, too, as we see by that adprecation which is so frequent with him: "O that men would therefore praise the Lord, and declare the wondrous works that he doth for the children of men!"[6]

If we compare these two incomparable duties, prayer and praise, it will stand thus: Our prayers besiege God (as Tertullian speaks, especially of public prayer in the congregation . . .) but our praises prescribe in God, we urge him, and press him, with his ancient mercies, his mercies of old. By prayer we incline him, we bend him, but by praise we bind him; our thanks for former benefits, is a producing of a specialty, by which he hath contracted with us for more. In prayer we sue to him, but in praise we sue him himself. Prayer is our petition, but praise is as our evidence. In that we beg, in this we plead. God hath no law upon himself, but yet God himself proceeds by precedent, and whensoever we present to him with thanksgiving what he hath done, he does the same, and more again. Neither certainly can the church institute any prayers more effectual for the preservation of religion, or of the state, then the collects for our deliverances, in the like cases before. And when he hears them, though they have the nature of praise only, yet he translates them into prayers. And when we ourselves know not how much we stand in need of new deliverances, he delivers us from dangers which we never suspected, from armies and navies which we never knew were prepared, and from plots and machinations which we never knew were brought into consultation, and diverts their forces and dissipates their counsels with an untimely abortion. And farther I extend not this first part of prayer in general, in which, to that which you may have heard often and usefully of the duty and dignity of prayer, I have only added this of the method and elements thereof, that prayer consists as much of praise for the past, as of supplication for the future.

Part 2. *This particular prayer*

We pass now to the second part, to this particular prayer, and those limbs that make up this body, those pieces that constitute this part. There are many, as many as words in it: "Satisfy," and "satisfy us," and do that

---

5. Psalm 34:1.
6. [Psalm 107:8.].

"early," and do that which is "thine," and let that be "mercy." So that first it is a prayer for fulness and satisfaction, "*satura,* satisfy," and then it is a prayer not only of appropriation to ourselves, "satisfy me," but of a charitable dilatation and extension to others, "satisfy us," all us, all thy servants, all thy church. And then, thirdly, it is a prayer of dispatch and expedition, "*satura nos mane,* satisfy us early," and after that, it is a prayer of evidence and manifestation. And then, lastly, it is a prayer of limitation even upon God himself, that God will take no other way herein, but the way of "mercy," "satisfy us early with thy mercy."

And because these are the land-marks that must guide you in this voyage, and the places to which you must resort to assist your memory, be pleased to take another survey and impression of them. I may have an apprehension of a conditional promise of God and I may have some fair credulity and testimony of conscience, of an endeavor to perform those conditions, and so some incohations of those promises, but yet this is not a fulness, a satisfaction, and this is a prayer for that, "*satura,* satisfy." I may have a full measure in myself, find no want of temporal conveniencies, or spiritual consolation even in inconveniencies, and so hold up a holy alacrity and cheerfulness for all concerning myself, and yet see God abandon greater persons and desert whole churches and states, upon whom his glory and gospel depends much more than upon me, but this is a prayer of charitable extension, "*satura nos,*" not "me," but "us," all us that profess thee aright. This also I may be sure that God will do at last, he will rescue his own honor in rescuing or establishing his servants, he will bring Israel out of Egypt and out of Babylon, but yet his Israel may lie long under the scourge and scorn of his and their enemies, 300 years before they get out of Egypt, 70 years before they get out of Babylon, and so fall into tentations of conceiving a jealousy and suspicion of God's good purpose towards them. And this is a prayer of dispatch and expedition, "*satura mane,* satisfy us early," "O God make speed to save us, O Lord make haste to help us." But he may derive help upon us by means that are not his, not avowed by him. He may quicken our counsels by bringing in an Achitophel, he may strengthen our armies by calling in the Turk, he may establish our peace and friendships by remitting or departing with some parts of our religion; at such a dear price we may be helped, but these are not his helps, and this is a prayer of manifestation, that all the way to our end he will be pleased to let us see that the means are from him. "*satura nos tua,* satisfy us" with that which is "thine," and comes from "thee," and so directs us to "thee." All this may be done too, and yet not that done which we pray for here. God may send that which is his, and yet without present comfort therein. God may multiply corrections and judgements and tribulations upon us, and intend to help us that way by, whipping and beating us into the way, and this is his way. But this is a prayer of limitation even upon God himself, that our way may be his, and that his way may be the way of "mercy." "Satisfy us early with thy mercy."

Satura

First then, the first word "*satura*," implies a fulness, and it implies a satisfaction, a quietness, a contentedness, an acquiescence in that fulness. "Satisfy" is, let us be full, and let us feel it and rest in that fulness. These two make up all heaven, all the joy and all the glory of heaven, fulness and satisfaction in it. And therefore St. Jerome refers this prayer of our text to the resurrection and to that fulness and that satisfaction which we shall have then, and not till then. For though we shall have a fulness in heaven, as soon as we come thither, yet that is not fully a satisfaction because we shall desire and expect a fuller satisfaction in the reunion of body and soul. And when heaven itself cannot give us this full satisfaction till then, in what can we look for it in this world, where there is no true fulness nor any satisfaction in that kind of fulness which we seem to have? Pleasure and sensuality and the giving to ourselves all that we desire cannot give this. You hear God reproaches Israel so, "You have multiplied your fornications, and yet are not satisfied."[7] Labor for profit, or for preferment, cannot do it. You see God reproaches Israel for that too, "Ye have sown much and bring in little, ye eat but have not enough, ye drink but are not filled, ye clothe you but are not warm, and he that earneth wages putteth it into a broken bag,"[8] that is, it runs out as fast as it comes in. He finds nothing at the year's end, his Midsummer will scarce fetch up Michaelmas, and if he have brought about his year and made up his circle, yet he hath raised up nothing, nothing appears in his circle.

If these things could fill yet they could not satisfy us, because they cannot stay with us, or not we with them: "He hath devoured substance, and he shall vomit it."[9] He devoured it by bribery, and he shall vomit it by a fine. He devoured it by extortion, and he shall vomit it by confiscation. He devoured it in other courts, and shall vomit it in a Star-chamber. If it stay some time, it shall be with an anguish and vexation: "When he shall be filled with abundance, it shall be a pain to him," as it is in the same place. Still his riches shall have the nature of a vomit, hard to get down and hard to keep in the stomach when it is there; hardly got, hardly kept when they

---

7. Ezekiel 16[:29].
8. Haggai 1[:6].
9. Job 20[:15].

are got. If all these could be overcome, yet it is clogged with a heavy curse: "Wo be unto you that are full, for ye shall be hungry."[10] Where, if the curse were only from them who are poor by their own sloth or wastefulness, who for the most part delight to curse and malign the rich, the curse might be contemned by us, and would be thrown back by God into their own bosomes; but "*Os Domini locutum*, The mouth of the Lord hath spoken it," Christ himself hath denounced this curse upon worldly men, that they shall be hungry, not only suffer impairment and diminution, but be reduced to hunger.

There is a spiritual fulness in this life, of which St. Jerome speaks, . . . "A happy excess and a wholesome surfet . . . in which the more we eat the more temperate we are, and the more we drink, the more sober." In which (as St. Bernard also expresses it, in his mellifluence) . . . "By a mutual and reciprocal, by an undeterminable and unexpressible generation of one another . . . the desire of spiritual graces begets satiety," if I would be, I am full of them. And then this satiety begets a farther desire, still we have a new appetite to those spiritual graces. This is a holy ambition, a sacred covetousness, and a wholesome dropsy. Napthali's blessing, "O Napthali satisfied with favor and full with the blessing of the Lord";[11] St. Stephen's blessing, "Full of faith and of the Holy Ghost";[12] the blessed Virgin's blessing, "Full of grace";[13] Dorcas' blessing, "Full of good works and of almsdeeds";[14] the blessing of him, who is blessed above all, and who blesseth all, Christ Jesus, "Full of wisdom,"[15] "Full of the Holy Ghost,"[16] "Full of grace and truth."[17] But so far are all temporal things from giving this fulness or satisfaction, as that even in spiritual things, there may be, there is often an error or mistaking.

Even in spiritual things there may be a fulness and no satisfaction. And there may be satisfaction and no fulness. I may have as much knowledge as is presently necessary for my salvation, and yet have a restless and unsatisfied desire to search into unprofitable curiosities, unrevealed mysteries, and inextricable perplexities. And, on the other side, a man may be satisfied and think he knows all when, God knows, he knows nothing at all. For I know nothing if I know not Christ crucified, and I know not that

---

10. Luke 6[:25].
11. Deuteronomy 33:23.
12. Acts 6:5.
13. [Luke 1:28].
14. Acts 9:36.
15. Luke 2:40.
16. Luke 4:1.
17. John 1:14.

SERMONS

if I know not how to apply him to myself. Nor do I know that if I embrace him not in those means which he hath afforded me in his church, in his Word and Sacraments. If I neglect this means, this place, these exercises, howsoever I may satisfy myself with an over-valuing mine own knowledge at home, I am so far from fulness as that vanity itself is not more empty.

In the wilderness every man had one and the same measure of manna, the same gomer went through all, for manna was a meat that would melt in their mouths, and of easy digestion. But then for their quails, birds of a higher flight, meat of a stronger digestion, it is not said, that every man had an equal number. Some might have more, some less, and yet all their fulness. Catechistical divinity, and instructions in fundamental things, is our manna. Every man is bound to take his gomer, his explicit knowledge of articles necessary to salvation. The simplest man, as well as the greatest doctor, is bound to know that there is one God in three persons, that the second of those, the Son of God, took our nature and died for mankind. And that there is a Holy Ghost, which in the Communion of Saints, the church established by Christ, applies to every particular soul the benefit of Christ's universal redemption. But then for our quails, birds of a higher pitch, meat of a stronger digestion, which is the knowledge how to rectify every straying conscience, how to extricate every entangled and scrupulous and perplexed soul, in all emergent doubts, how to defend our church and our religion from all the mines and all the batteries of our adversaries, and to deliver her from all imputations of heresy and schism which they impute to us, this knowledge is not equally necessary in all. In many cases a master of servants and a father of children is bound to know more than those children and servants, and the pastor of the parish more than parishioners. They may have their fulness, though he have more, but he hath not his except he be able to give them satisfaction.

This fulness then is not an equality in the measure; our fulness in heaven shall not be so . . . In a word, the fulness that is inquired after, and required by this prayer, carry it upon temporal, carry it upon spiritual things, is such a proportion of either, as is fit for that calling in which God hath put us. And then the satisfaction in this fulness is not to hunt and pant after more worldly possessions by undue means, or by macerating labor, as though we could not be good, or could do no good in the world except all the goods of the world passed our hands, nor to hunt and pant after the knowledge of such things as God by his scriptures hath not revealed to his church, nor to wrangle contentiously and uncharitably about such points as do rather shake others' consciences then establish our own, as though we could not possibly come to heaven except we knew what God meant to do with us before he meant to make us. St. Paul expresses fully what this fulness is, and satisfies us in this satisfaction, ... "That ye may be filled according to the will of God."[18] What is the will of God? How shall I know the will of God upon me? God hath manifested his will in my calling, and a proportion, competent to this calling, is my fulness and should be my satisfaction, that so God may have "*odorem quietis,*" (as it is said in Noah's sacrifice, after he came out of the ark, "that God had smelt a savor of rest")[19] a sacrifice, in which he might rest himself, for God hath a sabbath in the sabbaths of his servants, a fulness in their fulness, a satisfaction when they are satisfied, and is well pleased when they are so.

Nos

So then this prayer is for fulness and fulness is a competency in our calling, and a prayer for satisfaction, and satisfaction is a contentment in the competency. And then this prayer is not only a prayer of appropriation to ourselves, but of a charitable extention to others too, "*satura nos,* satisfy us," all us, all thy church. Charity begins in ourselves, but it does not end there but dilates itself to others. The saints in heaven are full, as full as they can hold, and yet they pray. Though they want nothing, they pray that God would pour down upon us graces necessary for our peregrination here, as he hath done upon them in their station there. We are full, full of the gospel, present peace and plenty in the preaching thereof, and fair appearances of a perpetuall succession. We are full, and yet we pray. We pray that God would continue the gospel where it is, restore the gospel where it was, and transfer the gospel where it hath not yet been preached.

Charity desires not her own, says the Apostle,[20] but much less doth charity desire no more then her own, so as not to desire the good of others too. True love and charity is to do the most that we can, all that we can for the good of others. So God himself proceeds, when he says, "What could I do that I have not done?"[21] And so he seems to have begun at first, when God bestowed upon man his first and greatest benefit, his making, it is expressed so, "*faciamus hominem,* Let us," all us, "make man."[22] God seems to summon himself, to assemble himself, to muster himself, all himself, all the persons of the Trinity, to do what he could in the favor of man. So also when he is drawn to a necessity of executing judgement, and

---

18. Colossians 4:12.
19. Genesis 8:21.
20. [1 Corinthians 13:5].
21. [Isaiah 5:4].
22. [Genesis 1:26].

for his own honor, and consolidation of his servants, puts himself upon a revenge, he proceeds so too. When man had rebelled and began to fortify in Babel, then God says, "*venite,* Let us," all us come together, and "*descendamus, et confundamus,* Let us," all us, "go down and confound their language," and their machinations and fortifications.[23]

God does not give patterns; God does not accept from us acts of half-devotion, and half-charities; God does all that he can for us. And therefore when we see others in distress, whether national or personal calamities, whether princes be dispossessed of their natural patrimony and inheritance, or private persons afflicted with sickness or penury or banishment, let us go God's way, all the way. First, "*faciamus hominem ad imaginem nostram,*" let us make that man according unto our image, let us consider ourselves in him and make our case his, and remember how lately he was as well as we and how soon we may be as ill as he, and then "*descendamus et confundamus,*" let us, us with all the power we have, remove or slacken those calamities that lie upon them.

This only is charity, to do all, all that we can. And something there is which every man may do. There are armies, in the levying whereof every man is an absolute prince and needs no commission. There are forces in which every man is his own muster-master, the force which we spoke of before, out of Tertullian, the force of prayer. In public actions we obey God when we obey them to whom God hath committed the public. In those things which are in our own power, the subsidies and contributions of prayer, God looks that we should second his "*faciamus*" with our "*dicamus,*" that since he must do all, we would pray him that he would do it, and his "*descendamus*" with our "*ascendamus,*" that if we would have him come down and fight our battles, or remove our calamities, we should first go up to him, in humble and fervent prayer, that he would continue the gospel where it is, and restore it where it was, and transfer it where it was never yet heard. Charity is to do all to all, and the poorest of us all can do this to any.

Mane

I may then, I must pray for this fulness (and fulness is sufficiency) and for this satisfaction (and satisfaction is contentment) and that God would extend this, and other his blessings, upon others too. And if God do leave us in Egypt, in a Babylon, without relief, for some time I may proceed to

---

23. Genesis 11:7.

this holy importunity, which David intimates here, "*satura nos mane*," O Lord, make haste to help us, "satisfy us early with thy mercy," and God will do so. "Weeping may endure for a night," says David.[24] David does not say, it must endure for a night, that God will by no means shorten the time. Perchance God will wipe all tears from thine eyes, at midnight, if thou pray. Try him that way then. If he do not, "If weeping do endure for a night," all night, "yet joy commeth in the morning," saith David. And then he doth not say, joy may come in the morning, but it commeth certainly, infallibly it comes, and comes in the morning. God is an early riser, "In the morning-watch, God looked upon the host of the Egyptians."[25] He looked upon their counsels to see what they would do, and upon their forces to see what they could do. He is not early up, and never nearer. "His going forth is prepared as the morning," (there is his general providence in which he visits every creature) "and he shall come to us in the former, and later rain upon the earth."[26] He makes haste to us in the former and seconds his former mercies to us, in more mercies. And as he makes haste to refresh his servants, so goes he the same pace, to the ruin of his enemies. "*In matutino interficiam*, I will early destroy all the wicked of the land."[27] It is not a weakening of them, it is a destruction. It is not a squadron or regiment, it is all. It is not only upon the land, but the wicked of the land, he will destroy upon the sea too. This is his promise, this is his practice, this is his pace . . .

Now if we look for this early mercy from God, we must rise betimes too and meet God early. God hath promised to give "*matutinam stellam*," the morning-star.[28] But they must be up betimes in the morning that will take the morning-star. "I Jesus am the bright and morning star."[29] God will give us Jesus, him and all his, all his tears, all his blood, all his merits. But to whom and upon what conditions? That is expressed there, "*Vincenti dabo*, to him that overcommeth I give the morning-star." Our life is a warfare, our whole life. It is not only with lusts in our youth and ambitions in our middle years, and in devotions in our age, but with agonies in our body and tentations in our spirit upon our death-bed that we are to fight. And he cannot be said to overcome, that fights not out the whole battle. If he enters not the field in the morning, that is apply not himself to God's service in his youth, if he continue not to the evening, if he faint in the way

24. Psalm 30:5.
25. Exodus 14:24.
26. Hosea 6:3.
27. Psalm 101:8.
28. Revelation 2:28.
29. Revelation 22:16.

and grow remiss in God's service, for collateral respects, God will overcome his cause and his glory shall stand fast, but that man can scarce be said to have overcome.

It is the counsel of the wise man, "Prevent the sun to give thanks to God, and at the day-spring pray unto him."[30] You see still, how these two duties are marshalled and disposed, first praise and then prayer, but both early. And it is placed in the Lamentations, as though it were a lamentable negligence to have omitted it, "It is good for a man, that he bear his yoke in his youth."[31] Rise as early as you can, you cannot be up before God, no, nor before God raise you. Howsoever you prevent this sun, the sun of the firmament, yet the Son of heaven hath prevented you, for without his grace you could not stir. Have any of you slept out their morning, resisted his private motions to private prayer at home, neglected his callings so? Though a man do sleep out his forenoon, the sun goes on his course, and comes to his meridional splendor, though that man have not looked towards it. That Son which hath risen to you at home, in those private motions, hath gone on his course and hath shined out here in this house of God, upon Wednesday, and upon Friday, and upon every day of holy convocation. All this, at home and here, yee have slept out and neglected.

Now, upon the sabbath, and in these holy exercises, this Son shines out as at noon. The grace of God is in the exaltation, exhibited in the powerfulest and effectualest way of his ordinance, and if you will but wake now, rise now, meet God now, now at noon, God will call even this early. Have any of you slept out the whole day and are come in that drowsiness to your evening, to the closing of your eyes, to the end of your days? Yet rise now, and God shall call even this an early rising. If you can make shift to deceive your own souls and say, "We never heard God call us," if you neglected your former callings so as that you have forgot that you have been called, yet is there one amongst you that denies God calls him now? If he neglect this calling now, tomorrow he may forget that he was called today, or remember it with such a terror as shall blow a damp, and a consternation upon his soul, and a lethargy worse then his former sleep. But if he will wake now, and rise now, though this be late in his evening, in his age, yet God shall call this early. Be but able to say with Isaiah this night, "My soul hath desired thee in the night,"[32] and thou mayest be bold to say with David tomorrow morning, "*satura nos mane,* satisfy us early with thy mercy," and he shall do it.

---

30. Wisdom 16:28. ["prevent," that is came before, awoke before sunrise].
31. Lamentations 3:27.
32. Isaiah 26:9.

JOHN DONNE

But yet no prayer of ours, howsoever made in the best disposition, in the best testimony of a rectified conscience, must limit God in his time, or appoint him in what morning, or at what hour in the morning, God shall come to our deliverance. The Son of man was not less the Son of God, nor the less a beloved Son, though God hid from him the knowledge of the day of the general judgement. Thou art not less the servant of God, nor less rewarded by him, though he keep from thee the knowledge of thy deliverance from any particular calamity. All God's deliverances are in the morning because there is a perpetual night, and an invincible darkness upon us, till he deliver us. God is the God of that climate where the night is six months long, as well as of this where it is but half so many hours. The highest hill hinders not the roundness of the earth, the earth is round for all that hill. The lowest vaults and mines hinder not the solidness of the earth, the earth is solid for all that. Much less hath a year, or ten years, or all our three-score years and ten, any proportion at all to eternity. And therefore God comes early in a sort to me, though I lost abundance of my reward by so long lingering, if he come not till he open me the gate of heaven, by the key of death. There are Indies at my right hand, in the East; but there are Indies at my left hand too, in the West. There are testimonies of God's love to us in our East, in our beginnings; but if God continue tribulation upon us to our West, to our ends, and give us the light of his presence then, if he appear to us at our transmigration, certainly he was favorable to us all our peregrination, and though he show himself late, he was our friend early. The prayer is that he would come early, but it is, if it be rightly formed, upon both these conditions: first that I rise early to meet him, and then that I magnify his hour as early, whensoever he shall be pleased to come.

Tua

All this I shall do the better, if I limit my prayer, and my practise, with the next circumstances in David's prayer, "*tua*, satisfy us early with" that which is thine, "thy mercy." For there are mercies (in a fair extent and accommodation of the word, that is refreshings, eases, deliverances) that are not his mercies, nor his satisfactions. How many men are satisfied with riches (I correct myself, few are satisfied; but how many have enough to satisfy many?) and yet have never a penny of his money? Nothing is his that comes not from him, that comes not by good means. How many are there that are easy to admit scruples, and jealousies, and suspicions in matter of religion . . . and yet have never a dram of satisfaction from his word, whose word is preached upon the house top, and avowed, and not in corners? How many men are anguished with torturing diseases, racked

SERMONS

with the conscience of ill-spent estates, oppressed with inordinate melan-
cholies and irreligious dejections of spirit, and then repair and satisfy
themselves with wine, with women, with fools, with commedies, with
mirth and music, and with all Job's miserable comforters, and all this while
have no beams of his satisfaction . . . ? In losses of worldly goods, in
sicknesses of children, or servants, or cattle, to receive light or ease from
witches, this is not his mercy. It is not his mercy except we go by good
ways to good ends, except our safety be established by alliance with his
friends, except our peace may be had with the perfect continuance of our
religion, there is no safety, there is no peace. But let me feel the effect of
this prayer, as it is a prayer of manifestation, let me discern that that is
done upon me is done by the hand of God and I care not what it be. I had
rather have God's vinegar then man's oil, God's wormwood then man's
manna, God's justice then any man's mercy, for therefore did Gregory of
Nyssa call St. Basil in a holy sense "*ambidextrum*," because he took every
thing that came by the right handle, and with the right hand, because he
saw it to come from God. Even afflictions are welcome, when we see them
to be his, though the way that he would choose, and the way that this
prayer entreats, be only mercy, "Satisfy us early with thy mercy." . . .

Misericordia
God's corrections are his acts as the physician is his creature, God created
him for necessity. When God made man his first intention was not that
man should fall and thus need a Messias, nor that man should fall sick and
so need a physician, nor that man should fall into rebellion by sin and so
need his rod, his staff, his scourge of afflictions, to whip him into the way
again. But yet says the Wiseman, "Honor the physician for the use you
may have of him; slight him not, because thou hast no need of him yet."[33]
So though God's corrections were not from a primary, but a secondary
intention, yet, when you see those corrections fall upon another, give a
good interpretation of them, and believe God's purpose to be not to
destroy but to recover that man. Do not thou make God's rhubarb thy
ratsbane, and poison thine own soul with an uncharitable misinterpretation
of that correction, which God hath sent to cure him. And then, in thine
own afflictions, fly evermore to this prayer, "Satisfy us with thy mercy."
First, "satisfy us," make it appear to us that thine intention is mercy,
though thou enwrap it in temporal afflictions. In this dark cloud let us
discern thy Son and though in an act of displeasure, see that thou art

___
33. Ecclesiasticus 38:1.

211

pleased with us. "Satisfy us" that there is mercy in thy judgements, and then "satisfy us" that thy mercy is mercy. For such is the stupidity of sinful man, that as in temporal blessings, we discern them best by wanting them, so do we the mercies of God too. . . .

Part 3. *What this Prayer produces: Joy*

There remains yet a third part, what this prayer produces, and it is joy, and continual joy, "that we may rejoice and be glad all our days." The words are the parts, and we invert not, we trouble not the order. The Holy Ghost hath laid them fitliest for our use, in the text itself, and so we take them. First then, the gain is joy. Joy is God's own seal, and his keeper is the Holy Ghost. We have many sudden ejaculations in the form of prayer, sometimes inconsiderately made, and they vanish so. But if I can reflect upon my prayer, ruminate, and return again with joy to the same prayer, I have God's seal upon it. And therefore it is not so very an idle thing, as some have misimagined it, to repeat often the same prayer in the same words. Our Savior did so. He prayed a third time, and in the same words. This reflecting upon a former prayer is that that sets to this seal, this joy, and if I have joy in my prayer, it is granted so far as concerns my good and God's glory. . . .

This joy we shall see when we see him who is so in it, as that he is this joy itself. But here in this world, as far as I can enter into my master's sight, I can enter into my master's joy. I can see God in his creatures, in his church, in his Word and Sacraments, and Ordinances. Since I am not without this sight, I am not without this joy. Here a man may "*transilire mortalitatem,*" says that divine moral man [Seneca]. I cannot put off mortality, but I can look upon immortality. I cannot depart from this earth, but I can look into heaven. So I cannot possess that final and accomplished joy here, but as my body can lay down a burden or a heavy garment, and joy in that ease, so my soul can put off my body so far as that the concupisencies thereof, and the manifold and miserable encumbrances of this world, cannot extinguish this holy joy. And this inchoative joy David derives into two branches, "To rejoice," and "to be glad."

Exultatio

The Holy Ghost is an eloquent author, a vehement and an abundant author, but yet not luxuriant. He is far from a penurious, but as far from a superfluous style too. And therefore we do not take these two words in the text, "To rejoice," and "to be glad," to signify merely one and the same thing, but two beams, two branches, two effects, two expressings of this joy. We take them therefore as they offer themselves in their roots, and first natural propriety of the words. The first, which we translate "To rejoice," is "*ranan*." And "*ranan*" denotes the external declaration of internal joy. For the word signifies "*cantare*," to sing, and that with an extended and loud voice, for it is the word which is oftenest used for the music of the church and the singing of psalms; which was a declaration of their zealous alacrity in the primitive church, as that, when to avoid discovery in the times of persecution, they were forced to make their meetings in the night, they were also forced to put out their candles because by that light in the windows they were discovered. After that this meeting in the dark occasioned a scandal and ill report upon those Christians, that their meetings were not upon so holy purposes as they pretended, they discontinued their vigils and night meetings, yet their singing of psalms, when they did meet, they never discontinued, though that many times exposed them to danger and to death itself, as some of the authors of the secular story of the Romans have observed and testified unto us.

And some ancient decrees and constitutions we have in which such are forbidden to be made priests as were not perfect in the psalms. And though St. Jerome tell us this, with some admiration, and note of singularity, that Paula could say the whole book of psalms without book, in Hebrew, yet he presents it as a thing well known to be their ordinary practise.... In the village where I dwell, says he, where Christ was born, in Bethlehem, if you cannot sing the psalms you must be silent. Here you shall hear nothing but psalms, for (as he pursues it) ... the husbandman that follows the plough, he that sows, that reaps, that carries home, all begin and proceed in all their labors with singing of psalms. Therefore he calls them there, *cantiones amatorias,* those that make or entertain love, that seek in the holy and honorable way of marriage to make themselves acceptable and agreeable to one another by no other good parts nor conversation but by singing of psalms....

And this universal use of the psalms, that they served all for all, gives occasion to one author, in the title of the book of psalms, to depart from the ordinary reading, which is *sephir tehillim,* the book of praise, and to read it *sephir telim,* which is *acervorum,* the book of helps, where all assistances to our salvation are heaped and treasured up. And our countryman Bede found another title, in some copies of this book ... the book of meditations upon Christ, because this book is (as Gregory of Nyssa calls it) *Clavis David,* that key of David which lets us in to all the mysteries of our religion; which gave the ground to that which St. Basil says, that if all the other books of Scripture could be lost, he would ask no more than the book of psalms, to catechize children, to edify congregations, to convert gentiles, and to convince heretics.

But we are launched into too large a sea, that consideration of this book of psalms. I mean but this, in this, that if we take that way with God, the way of prayer, prayer so elemented and constituted, as we have said, that consists rather of praise and thanksgiving than supplication for future benefits, God shall infuse into us, a zeal of expressing our consolation in him by outward actions, to the establishing of others. We shall not disavow nor grow slack in our religion, nor in any parts thereof. God shall neither take from us the candle and the candlestick, the truth of the gospel, which is the light, and the cheerful and authorized, and countenanced, and rewarded preaching of the gospel, which is the candlestick that exalts the light. Nor take from us our zeal to this outward service of God that we come to an indifferancy, whether the service of God be private or public, sordid or glorious, allowed and suffered by way of connivency or commanded and enjoined by way of authority. God shall give us this *"ranan,"* this rejoicing, this external joy. We shall have the public preaching of the gospel continued in us, and we shall show that we rejoice in it, by frequenting it, and by instituting our lives according unto it.

Delectabimur

But yet this *"ranan,"* this *"rejoicing,"* this outward expressing of our inward zeal, may admit interruptions, receive interceptions, intermissions, and discontinuances; for, without doubt in many places there live many persons well affected to the truth of religion that dare not avow it, express it, declare it, especially where that fearful vulture, the Inquisition, hovers over them. And therefore the Holy Ghost hath added here another degree of joy, which no law, no severe execution of law, can take from us, in another word of less extent, *"shamach,"* which is an inward joy, only in the heart, which we translate here to be "glad." ...

Though we lose our *"ranan,"* our public rejoicing, we shall never lose our *"shamach,"* our inward gladness, that God is our God, and we his servants for all this. God will never leave his servants without this internal joy, which shall preserve them from suspicions of God's power, that he cannot maintain or not restore his cause, and from jealousies, that he hath abandoned or deserted them in particular. God shall never give them over to an indifferency, nor to a stupidity, nor to an absence of tenderness and holy affections, that it shall become all one to them how God's cause prospers or suffers. But if I continue in that way, prayer, and prayer so qualified; if I lose my *"ranan,"* my outward declarations of rejoicing; if I be tied to a death-bed in a consumption, and cannot rejoice in coming to these public congregations to participate of their prayers, and to impart to them my meditations; if I be ruined in my fortune and cannot rejoice in an

214

open distribution to the relief of the poor, and a preaching to others, in that way, by example of doing good works; if at my last minute I be not able to edify my friends nor catechize my children with anything that I can do or say; if I be not able so much as with hand or eye to make a sign, though I have lost my "*ranan*," all the eloquence of outward declaration, yet God will never take from me my "*shamach*," my internal gladness and consolation, in his undeceivable and undeceiving Spirit, that he is mine and I am his. And this joy, this gladness, in my way and in my end, shall establish me; for that is that which is intended in the next, and last word, "*omnibus diebus*," we shall "rejoice and be glad all our days."

Omnibus diebus

Nothing but this testimony, "That the Spirit bears witness with my spirit," that upon my prayer so conditioned, of praise and prayer, I shall still prevail with God, could imprint in me the "joy, all my days."[34] The seals of his favor in outward blessings, fail me in the days of shipwreck, in the days of fire, in the days of displacing my potent friends, or raising mine adversaries. In such days I cannot rejoice and be glad. The seals of his favor in outward blessings and holy cheerfulness, fail me in a present remorse after a sin newly committed. But yet in the strength of a Christian hope, as I can pronounce out of the grounds of nature, in an eclipse of the sun, that the sun shall return to his splendor again, I can pronounce out of the grounds of God's Word (and God's Word is much better assurance than the grounds of nature, for God can and does shake the grounds of nature by miracles, but no jot of his Word shall ever perish) that I shall return again on my hearty penitence, if I delay it not, and rejoice and be glad all my days, that is, what kind of day soever overtake me.

In the days of our youth, when the joys of this world take up all the room, there shall be room for this holy joy, that my recreations were harmless and my conversation innocent. And certainly to be able to say that in my recreations, in my conversation, I neither ministered occasion of tentation to another nor exposed myself to tentations from another, is a fair beam of this rejoicing in the days of my youth. In the days of our age, when we become incapable, insensible of the joys of this world, yet this holy joy shall season us, not with a sinful delight in the memory of our former sins, but with a re-juveniscence, a new and a fresh youth, in being come so near to another, to an immortal life. In the days of our mirth, and of laughter, this holy joy shall enter. And as the sun may say to the stars at

34. [Romans 8:16].

noon, how frivolous and impertinent a thing is your light now, so this joy shall say "unto laughter, thou art mad, and unto mirth, what dost thou?"[35] And in the mid-night of sadness, and dejection of spirit, this joy shall shine out and chide away that sadness with David's holy charm, "My soul, why art thou cast down, why art thou disquieted within me?" ...

And to end with the end of all, "*In die mortis*," in the day of my death, and that which is beyond the end of all and without end in itself, the day of judgement, if I have the testimony of a rectified conscience, that I have accustomed myself to the access to God by prayer, and such prayer as though it have had a body of supplication and desire of future things, yet the soul and spirit of that prayer, that is my principal intention in that prayer, hath been praise and thanksgiving. If I be involved in St. Chrysostom's patent, ... that those who pray so, that is pray by way of praise (which is the most proper office of angels), as they shall be better than angels in the next world (for they shall be glorifying spirits, as the angels are, but they shall also be glorified bodies, which the angels shall never be), so in this world they shall be as angels, because they are employed in the office of angels, to pray by way of praise. If as St. Basil reads those words of that psalm, not "*spiritus meus*," but "*respiratio mea laudet Dominum*," not only my spirit, but my very breath, not my heart only, but my tongue and my hands be accustomed to glorify God, "*in die mortis*," in the day of my death, when a mist of sorrow and sighs shall fill my chamber, and a cloud exhaled and condensed from tears shall be the curtains of my bed, when those that love me shall be sorry to see me die, and the devil himself that hates me, sorry to see me die so in the favor of God. And "*in die judicii*," in the day of judgement when as all time shall cease, so all measures shall cease. The joy and the sorrow that shall be then, shall be eternal, no end, and infinite, no measure, no limitation, when every circumstance of sin shall aggravate the condemnation of the unrepentent sinner and the very substance of my sin shall be washed away in the blood of the Savior, when I shall see them who sinned for my sake perish eternally because they proceeded in that sin, and I myself who occasioned their sin received into glory because God upon my prayer and repentence had satisfied me early with his mercy, early that is, before my transmigration, "*in omnibus diebus*," in all these days, the days of youth, and the wantonnesses of that, the days of age, and the tastelessness of that, the days of mirth, and the sportfulness of that, and of inordinate melancholy, and the disconsolateness of that, the days of such miseries as astonish us with their suddenness,

---

35. Eccles. 2:2.

and such as aggravate their own weight with a heavy expectation. In the day of death, which pieces up that circle, and in that day which enters another circle that hath no pieces, but is one equal everlastingness, the day of judgement, either I shall rejoice, be able to declare my faith and zeal to the assistance of others, or at least be glad in mine owne heart, in a firm hope of mine own salvation.

And therefore beloved, as they whom lighter affections carry to showes and masks and commedies; as you yourselves, whom better dispositions bring to these exercises, conceive some contentment and some kind of joy, in that you are well and commodiously placed, they to see the show, you to hear the sermon, when time comes, though your greater joy be reserved to the coming of that time; so though the fulness of joy be reserved to the last times in heaven, yet rejoice and be glad that you are well and commodiously placed in the mean time, and that you sit but in expectation of the fulness of those future joys. Return to God with a joyful thankfulness that he hath placed you in a church which withholds nothing from you that is necessary to salvation, whereas in another church they lack a great part of the Word and half the Sacrament. And which obtrudes nothing to you that is not necessary to salvation, whereas in another church the additional things exceed the fundamental, the occasional, the original, the collateral, the direct. And the traditions of men, the commandments of God. Maintain and hold up this holy alacrity, this religious cheerfulness. For inordinate sadness is a great degree and evidence of unthankfulness, and the departing from joy in this world is a departing from one piece of our evidence, for the joys of the world to come.

The Grace of Repentance[1]

Psalm 32:5. "I acknowledged my sin unto thee, and mine iniquity have I not hid. I said, I will confess by transgressions unto the Lord, and thou forgavest the iniquity of my sin."

This is the Sacrament of Confession. So we may call it in a safe meaning. That is, the mystery of confession: for true confession is a mysterious art. As there is a "mystery of iniquity,"[2] so there is a "mystery of the Kingdom of Heaven."[3] And the mystery of the Kingdom of Heaven is this, that no man comes thither, but in a sort as he is a notorious sinner. One mystery of iniquity is that in this world, though I multiply sins, yet the judge cannot punish me if I can hide them from other men, though he know them. But if I confess them he can, he will, he must. The mystery of the Kingdom of Heaven is that only the declaring, the publishing, the notifying, and confessing of my sins possesses me of the Kingdom of Heaven. There is a case in which the notoriety of my sin, by way of glory in that sin, casts a scandal upon others and leads them into tentation; for so my sin becomes theirs because they sin my sin by example. And their sin becomes mine because I gave the example, and we aggravate one another's sin, and both sin both. But there is a publication of sin that both alleviates, nay annihilates my sin, and makes him that hates sin, Almighty God, love me the better for knowing me to be such a sinner, than if I had not told him of it. Therefore do we speak of the mystery of confession; for it is not delivered in one rule, nor practised in one act.

Divisio

In this confession of David's ("I acknowledged my sin unto thee, &c.) we shall see more then so; for, though our two parts be but the two acts,

---

[1]. One of eight sermons given on Psalm 32, most likely before the middle of 1623, and at St. Paul's. See *Sermons*, Potter, Simpson eds., 9:38–44; and, for the sermon, pp. 296–315.

2. 2 Thessalonians 2:7.

3. Matthew 13:11.

David's act and God's act, confession and absolution, yet is there more than one single action to be considered in each of them. For first, in the first, there is a reflected act, that David doth upon himself before he come to his confession to God; something David had done before he came to say, "I will confess," as he did "confess," before God "forgave the iniquity of his sin." Now that which he did in himself, and which preceded his confession to God, was the "*notum feci,* I acknowledged my sin"; which was not his bringing it to the knowledge of God by way of confession. For (as you see by the method of the Holy Ghost in the frame of the text) it preceded his purpose of confessing, but it was the taking knowledge of his sin in himself. It was his first quickening and inanimation, that grace gave his soul, as the soul gives the child in the mother's womb. And then in David's act upon himself, follows the "*non operui,* I have not hid mine iniquity," none of mine iniquities from mine own sight. I have displayed to myself, anatomized mine own conscience, left no corner unsearched, I am come to a perfect understanding of mine own case, "*non operui.*" This is David's act upon himself, the recalling and recollecting of his sins, in his own memory. And then finding the number, the weight, and so the oppression of those sins there, he considers where he may discharge himself of them. And "*dixi,*" says David, which is a word that implies both deliberation and resolution, and execution, too, I thought what was best to do and I resolved upon this and did it. "*Dixi Confitebor,*" that I would make a true, a full, a hearty confession to God of all those sins; for such we see the elements and the extent of his confession to be. He will confess "peccata," transgressions, sins; neither by an overtenderness, and diffidence, and scrupulosity to call things sins that are not sin nor by indulgent flattering and sparing of himself to forbear those things which are truly so. He will confess "*peccata,* sins," and "*peccata sua,* his sins." First "*sua,*" that is "*a se perpetrata,*" he will acknowledge them to have proceeded, and to have been committed by himself, he will not impute them to any other cause, least of all to God. And then *sua, non aliena,* he will confess sins that are his own sins and not meddle with the sins of other men, that appertain not to him.

This is the subject of his confession, "sins," and "his sins," and then "*peccata sua Domino,* His sins unto the Lord," both in that consideration, that all sins are committed against the Lord, and in that also, that confession of all sins is to be made unto the Lord. And lastly, all this (as St. Jerome reads this text, and so also did our former translation) "*adversum se,* against himself," that is, without any hope of relief or reparation in himself. He begins to think of his own sinful state and he proceeds to a particular inquisition upon his conscience; there is his preparation. Then he considers and thereupon resolves, and thereupon proceeds to confess things that are truly sins. And then all them as his own, without imputing them to others, if they be his own, without meddling with others, and these to the Lord against whom all sin is committed, and to whom all confession is to be directed. And all this still against himself, without any hope from himself. All this is in David's action, preparatorily in himself and then declaratorily towards God, and do but make up our first part.

In the other, which is God's act towards David, the absolution, the remission, the forgiveness, we shall consider first the fulness. For it is both of the sin and the punishment of the sin, for the word imports both . . . And then we shall consider the seasonableness, the speed, the acceleration of God's mercy in the absolution, for in David it is but *actus inchoatus*, and *actus consummatus* in God. David did but say, I will confess and God forgave the iniquity and the punishment of his sin. Now as this distribution is paraphrase enough upon the text, so a little larger paraphrase upon every piece of paraphrase will be as much as will fall into this exercise. For, as you see, the branches are many and full of fruit, and I can but shake them and leave every one to gather his own portion, to apply those notes which may most advance his edification.

Part 1. *Notum feci*

First then in this mystery of confession, we consider David's reflected act, his preparatory act, preceding his confession to God and transacted in himself, of which the first motion is the *notum feci*, I acknowledged in myself, I came to a feeling in myself what my sinful condition was. This is our quickening in our regeneration and second birth. And till this come a sinner lies as the chaos in the beginning of the creation, before the "Spirit of God had moved upon the face of the waters, dark," and "void," and "without form." He lies, as we may conceive out of the authors of natural story, the slime and mud of the river Nilus to lie, before the sun-beams strike upon it; which after, by the heat of those beams, produces several shapes and forms of creatures. So till this first beam of grace, which we consider here, strike upon the soul of a sinner, he lies in the mud and slime, in the dregs and lees and tartar of his sin. He cannot as much as wish that that sun would shine upon him. He does not so much as know that there is such a sun that has that influence and impression. But if this first beam of grace enlighten him to himself, reflect upon himself, *notum facit*, (as the text says), if it acquaint him with himself, then, as the creatures in the creation, then, as the new creatures at Nilus, his sins begin to take their forms, and their specifications, and they appear to him in their particular true shapes, and that which he hath in a general name called pleasure or wantonness now calls itself in his conscience a direct adultery, a direct incest. And that which he hath called frugality and providence for family and posterity, tells him plainly, my name is oppression and I am the spirit of covetousness. . . .

God by his ordinance, executed by us, brings him to this *notum feci*, into company with himself, unto an acquaintance and conversation with himself, and he sees his sins look with other faces, and he hears his sins speak with other voices, and he finds them to call one another by other names. And when he is thus come to that consideration, Lord! how I have mistaken myself. Am I that thought myself and passed with others for a sociable, a pleasurable man, and good company; am I a leprous adulterer; is that my name? Am I that thought myself a frugal man and a good husband, I whom fathers would recommend to their children and say, mark how he spares, how he grows up, how he gathers; am I an oppressing extortioner; is that my name?

Blessed be thy name, O Lord, that hast brought me to this *notum feci*, to know mine own name, mine own miserable condition. He will also say, may that blessing of thine enlarge itself farther, that as I am come to this *notum feci*, to know that I mistook myself all this while, so I may proceed to the *non operui*, to a perfit sifting of my conscience, in all corners: which is David's second motion in his act of preparation, and our next consideration, "I acknowledged my sin," and I hid none, disguised none, *non operui*.

Non operui

Sometimes the magistrate is informed of an abuse and yet proceeds to no farther search nor inquisition. This word implies a sifting of the conscience. He doth not only take knowledge of his sins than when they discover themselves; of his riot and voluptuousness than when he burns in a fever occasioned by his surfets; nor of his licentiousness than when he is under the anguish and smart of corrosives; nor of his wastefulness and pride than when he is laid in prison for debt: He doth not seek his sins in his belly nor in his bones nor in his purse, but in his conscience, and he unfolds that, rips up that, and enters into the privatest and most remote corners thereof. And there is much more in this negative circumstance, *non operui*, I hid nothing, than in the former acknowledgement, *notum feci*, I took knowledge of my sins. . . .

But any thing serves for a cover of sin, even from a net, that every man sees through, to such a cloud of darkness as none but the prince of darkness, that cast that cloud upon us, can see us in it, nor we see ourselves. That we should hide lesser sins with greater is not strange; that in

JOHN DONNE

an adultery we should forget the circumstances in it and the practices to
come to it. But we hide greater sins with lesser, with a manifold and
multiplied throng and cloud of lesser sins. . . . Easiness of conversation
with a woman seems no great harm. Adorning themselves to please those
with whom they converse, is not much more. To hear them whom they are
thus willing to please, praise them and magnify their perfections, is little
more then that. To allow them to sue and solicit for possession of that
which they have so much praised, is not much more neither. Nor will it
seem much at last, to give them possession of that they sue for; nay it will
seem a kind of injustice to deny it them. We hide lesser sins with greater,
greater with lesser. Nay we hide the devil with God, we hide all the week's
sins with a sabbath's solemnity: and . . . this is a possessing of God, a
making the devil to enter into God, when we hide our sins with an
outward sanctity and call God to witness and testify to the congregation
that we are saints, when we are devils; for this is a subborning of God, and
a drawing of God himself into a perjury. . . .

Dixi meditando

This word, "*Dixi, Amar,* I said," is a word that implies first meditation,
deliberation, considering, and then upon such meditation, a resolution too,
and execution after all. When it is said of God, "*dixit*," and "*dixit*," God
said this and said that in the first creation, "*cave ne cogites strepitum*,"[4] do
not think that God uttered a sound; his speaking was inward, his speaking
was thinking. So David uses this word in the person of another, "*dixit
insipiens,* the fool hath said," that is, "*in corde,* said in his heart," that is,
thought "that there is no God."[5] There speaking is thinking; and speaking
is resolving too. So David's son Solomon uses the word, "Behold I purpose
to build a house unto the Lord,"[6] where the word is "I say," I will do it,
speaking is determining; and speaking is executing too, "*Dixi custodiam,* I
said I will take heed to my ways,"[7] that is, I will proceed and go forward in
the paths of God. And such a premeditation, such a preconsideration, do
all our approaches and accesses to God, and all our acts in his service
require.

God is the rock of our salvation. God is no occasional God, no
accidental God; neither will God be served by occasion, nor by accident,
but by a constant devotion. Our communication with God must not be in

---

4. Basil.
5. Psalm 14:1.
6. 1 Kings 5:5.
7. Psalm 39:1.

interjections that come in by chance, nor our devotions made up of parentheses that might be left out. They err equally that make a god of necessity and that make a god of contingency; they that with the Manichees make an ill god, a god that forces men to do all the ill that they do, and they that with the Epicures make an idle god, an indifferent god, that cares not what is done. God is not destiny; then there could be no reward or punishment; but God is not fortune neither, for then there were no providence. If God have given reason only to man, it were strange that man should exercise that reason in all his moral and civil actions and only do the acts of God's worship casually. . . . Not to consider the nature of confession and absolution, not to consider the nature of the sins we should confess and be absolved of, is a stupidity against David's practice here. "*Dixit*," he said, he meditated, he considered God's service is no extemporal thing. But then "*dixit*," he resolved too, for so the word signifies, consideration, but resolution upon it; and then, that he resolved, he executed.

Dixi statuendo

This is not only David's "*dixi in corde*," where speaking is thinking, nor only Solomon's "*dixi aedificabo*," I resolved how I might build, but it is also the Prodigal's "*Dixi revertar*, I said I will go to my Father,"[8] a resolving and executing of that resolution for that, that execution crowns all. How many think to come hither when they wake and are not ready when the hour comes? And even this morning's omission is an abridgement, or an essay of their whole lives. They thinke to repent every day and are not ready when the bell tolls. . . .

Confitebor

It is but a homely metaphor, but it is a wholesome and a useful one, "*confessio vomitus*,"[9] confession works as a vomit. It shakes the frame and it breaks the bed of sin, and it is an ease to the spiritual stomach, to the conscience, to be thereby disburdened. It is an ease to the sinner, to the patient; but that that makes it absolutely necessary is that it is a glory to God; for in all my spiritual actions, apprecations or deprecations, whether I pray for benefits or against calamities, still my Alpha and Omega, my first and last motive, must be the glory of God. Therefore Joshua says to Achan, "My Son, give I pray thee, glory unto the Lord God of Israel, and make confession unto him."[10] Now, the glory of God arises not out of the

---

8. Luke 15:18.
9. Origen.
10. Joshua 7:19.

confessing, but because every true confessing is accompanied with a detestation of the sin, as it hath separated me from God, and a sense of my reunion and redintegration with God, in the abjuration of my former sins (for to tell my sin by way of a good tale, or by boasting in it, though it be a revealing, a manifesting, it is not a confession). In every true confessing God hath glory, because he hath a strayed soul reunited to his kingdom. And to advance this glory, David confesses *peccata*, sins, which is our next consideration, "I said, I will confess my sins unto the Lord."

Peccata vera

First, he resents his state, all is not well. Then he examines himself, thus and thus it stands with me. Then he considers, then he resolves, then he executes, he confesses (so far are we gone), and now he confesses sins. For the Pharisee's (though he pretended a confession) was rather an exprobation, how much God had been beholden to him, for his sabbaths, for his alms, for his tithes, for his fasting. David confesses sins; first, such things as were truly sins. For as the element of air that lies between the water and the fire is sometimes condensed into water, sometimes rarified into fire: so lies the conscience of man between two operations of the devil. Sometimes he rarifies it, evaporates it, that is apprehends nothing, feels nothing to be sin; sometimes he condenses it, that everything falls and sticks upon it, in the nature, and takes the weight of sin, and he misinterprets the indifferent actions of others, and of his own, and destroys all Christian liberty, all conversation, all recreation, and out of a false fear of being undutiful to God is unjust to all the world and to his own soul, and consequently to God himself, who of all notions would not be received in the notion of a cruel or tyrannical God.

In an obdurate conscience that feels no sin, the devil glories most, but in the over-tender conscience he practices most. This is his triumphant, but this is his militant church. That is his sabbath, but this is his six days labor. In the obdurate he hath induced a security, in the scrupulous and over-tender he is working for desperation. There are few things in the Scriptures which the Holy Ghost hath expressed in so many names as sin: "sin, wickedness, iniquity, transgressions, offences," many, many more. And all this, that thereby we might reflect upon ourselves often, and see if our particular actions fell not under some of those names. But then, lest this should over-intimidate us, there are as many names given by the Holy Ghost to the Law of God: "Law, Statutes, Ordinances, Covenants, Testimony, Precept," and all the rest, of which there is some one at least repeated in every verse of the hundred and nineteenth psalm; that thereby we might still have a rule to measure and try our actions by, whether they be sins or no. For, as the Apostle says, "He had not known sin if he had not known the Law." So there had been no sin if there had been no Law. And therefore that soul that feels itself oppressed under the burden of a vow, must have recourse to the Law of God, and see whether that vow fall under the rule of that Law. For as an over-tender conscience may call things sins that are not, and so be afraid of things that never were, so may it also of things that were but are not now; of such sins as were truly sins and fearful sins but are now dead, dead by a true repentance and buried in the sea of the blood of Christ Jesus, and sealed up in that monument, under the seal of reconciliation, the blessed sacrament, and yet rise sometimes in this tender conscience, in a suspicion and jealousie, that God hath not truly, not fully forgiven them.

And as a ghost, which we think we see, affrights us more than an army that we do see: so these apparitions of sins, of things that are not against any Law of God, and so are not sins, or sins that are dead in a true repentance, and so have no being at all, by the devil's practice work dangerously upon a distempered conscience. For as God hath given the soul an imagination, and a fancy, as well as an understanding, so the devil imprints in the conscience a false imagination, as well as a fearful sense of true sin. David confesses sins, sins that are truly sins.

Omnia

But the more ordinary danger is in our not calling those things which are truly sins by that name. For, as sometimes when the baptism of a child is deferred for state, the child dies unbaptized: so the sinner defers the baptism of his sin, in his tears and in the blood of the Savior offered in the blessed sacrament, till he die nameless, nameless in the Book of Life. It is a character that one of the ancientest of poets gives of a well-bred and well-governed gentleman, that he would not tell such lies as were like truths, not probable lies; nor such truths as were like lies, not wonderful, not incredible truths. It is the constancy of a rectified Christian not to call his indifferent actions sins, for that is to slander God, as a cruel God; nor to call sins indifferent actions, for that is to undervalue God, as a negligent God. God doth not keep the conscience of man upon the wrack, in a continual torture and stretching; but God doth not stupify the conscience with an opiate in an insensibleness of any sin. The Law of God is the balance and the *criterium*. By that try thine actions, and then confess. David did so. "*Peccata,*" he confessed sins; nothing that was not so as such; neither omitted he anything that was so. And then they were, "*peccata sua,*" his sins, "I said, I will confess my sins unto the Lord."

Sua

First, "*sua*, his sins," that is "*a se perpetrata*," sins which he confesses to have been of his voluntary committing. He might, and did not, avoid them. When Adam said, by way of alienation and transferring his fault, "The woman whom thou gavest me"; and the woman said, "The serpent deceived me";[11] God took this by way of information to find out the principal, but not by way of extenuation or alleviation of their faults. Every Adam eats with as much sweat of his brow and every Eve brings forth her children with as much pain in her travail, as if there had been no serpent in the case. If a man sin against God, who shall plead for him? If a man lay his sins upon the serpent, upon the devil, it is no plea, but if he lay them upon God, it is blasphemy. . . . David confesses "his sins," that is, he confesses them to be his. And then he confesses "his," he meddles not with those that are other men's.

Non aliena

The magistrate and the minister are bound to consider the sins of others. For their sins become *quodammodo nostra*, in some sort ours . . . All men are bound to confess and lament the sins of the people. It was then when Daniel was in that exercise of his devotion, "confessing his sin, and the sin of his people,"[12] that he received that comfort from the Angel Gabriel; and yet, even then, the first thing that fell under his confession was his own sin, "my sin," and then "the sin of my people." . . . National calamities are induced by general sins, and where they fall, we cannot so charge the laity as to free the clergy, nor so charge the people as to free the magistrate. But as great sums are raised by little personal contributions; so a little true sorrow from every soul would make a great sacrifice to God, and a few tears from every eye a deeper and a safer sea about this island, then that that doth wall it. Let us therefore never say, that is *aliena ambitio*, the immoderate ambition of a pretending monarch that endangers us; that it is *aliena perfidia*, the falsehood of perfidious neighbors that hath disappointed us; that it is *aliena fortuna*, the growth of others who have shot up under our shelter that may overtop us: they are *peccata nostra*, our own pride, our own wantonness, our own drunkenness, that makes God shut and close his hand towards us, withdraw his former blessings from us and then strike us. . . . We dispute what is our own, as though we would but know what to give. Alas, our sins are our own, let us give them. Our sins

---

11. Genesis 3:12.
12. Daniel 9:20.

are our own; that we confess. And we confess them, according to David's method, *Domino*, to the Lord. "I will confess my sins to the Lord."

Domino peccavi

After he had deliberated and resolved upon his course, what he would do, he never stayed upon the person, to whom. His way being confession, he stayed not long in seeking his ghostly Father, his confessor, *confitebor Domino*. And first, *peccata Domino*, that his sins were sins against the Lord. For, as every sin is a violation of a law, so every violation of a law reflects upon the law-maker. It is the same offence to coin a penny, and a piece. The same to counterfeit the seal of a subpoena, or of a pardon. The second table was writ by the hand of God, as well as the first; and the majesty of God, as he is the Law-giver, is wounded in an adultery, and a theft, as well as in an idolatry, or a blasphemy. It is not enough to consider the deformity and the foulness of an action so as that an honest man would not have done it; but so as it violates a law of God, and his majesty in that law. The shame of men is one bridle that is cast upon us. It is a moral obduration, and in the suburbs, next door to a spiritual obduration, to be voice-proof, not to be afraid, nor ashamed, what the world says. He that relies upon his *plaudo domi*, though the world hiss, I give myself a *plaudite* at home, I have him at my table, and her in my bed, whom I would have, and I care not for rumor. He that rests in such a *plaudite* prepares for a tragedy, a tragedy in the ampitheater, the double theater, this world and the next too. Even the shame of the world should be one bridle, but the strongest is the other, *peccata Domino*, to consider that every sin is a violation of the majesty of God.

Domino confitebor

And then, "*confitebor Domino*," says David, "I will confess my sins to the Lord." Sins are not confessed if they be not confessed to him. And if they be confessed to him, in case of necessity it will suffice, though they be confessed to no other. Indeed, a confession is directed upon God though it be to his minister. If God had appointed his angels, or his saints to absolve me, as he hath his ministers, I would confess to them. . . . The law of the leper is "That he shall be brought unto the priest."[13] Men come not willingly to this manifestation of themselves. Nor are they to be brought in chains, as they do in the Roman Church, by a necessity of an exact enumeration of all their sins. But to be led with that sweetness, with which our

---

13. Leviticus 14:2.

church proceeds, in appointing sick persons, if they feel their consciences troubled with any weighty matter, to make a special confession and to receive absolution at the hands of the priest; and then to be remembered that every coming to the communion is as serious a thing as our transmigration out of this world, and we should do as much here for the settling of our conscience as upon our death-bed; and to be remembered also that none of all the Reformed Churches have forbidden confession, though some practice it less than others. If I submit a cause to the arbitrement of any man to end it, *secundum voluntatem*, says the law, how he will, yet still ... his will must be regulated by the rules of common honesty, and general equity. So when we lead men to this holy ease of discharging their heavy spirits, by such private confessions, yet this is still limited by the law of God, so far as God hath instituted this power by his Gospel in his church, and far from inducing amongst us that torture of the conscience, that usurpation of God's power, that spying into the counsels of princes, and supplanting of their purposes, with which the Church of Rome hath been deeply charged.

Adversum me

And this useful and un-misinterpretable confession, which we speak of, is the more recommended to us, in that with which David shuts up his act (as out of St. Jerome and out of our former translation we intimated unto you), that he doth all this *"adversum se*, I will confess my sins unto the Lord, against myself"; the more I find confession, or any religious practice to be against myself, and repugnant to mine own nature, the farther I will go in it. For still the *adversum me* is *cum Deo*. The more I say against myself, the more I vilify myself, the more I glorify my God. As St. Chrysostom says, every man is *spontaneus Satan*, a Satan to himself. As Satan is a Tempter, every man can tempt himself. So I will be *spontaneus Satan*. As Satan is an accuser, an adversary, I will accuse myself. I consider often that passionate humiliation of St. Peter, *"Exi a me Domine*," He fell at Jesus' knees, saying, "Depart from me, for I am a sinful man, O Lord."[14] And I am often ready to say so and more: Depart from me, O Lord, for I am sinful enough to infect thee. As I may persecute thee in thy children, so I may infect thee in thine ordinances. Depart, in withdrawing thy word from me, for I am corrupt enough to make even thy saving gospel the savor of death unto death. Depart in withholding thy sacrament, for I am leprous enough to taint thy flesh and to make the balm of thy blood poison to my soul. Depart

---

14. Luke 5:8.

in withdrawing the protection of thine angels from me, for I am vicious enough to imprint corruption and rebellion into their nature. And if I be too foul for God himself to come near me, for his ordinances to work upon me, I am no companion for myself, I must not be alone with myself; for I am as apt to take, as to give infection. I am a reciprocal plague; passively and actively contagious. I breath corruption and breath it upon myself; and I am the Babylon that I must go out of, or I perish. . . .

And so you have the whole mystery of David's confession, in both his acts; preparatory, in resenting his sinful condition in general, and surveying his conscience in particular; and then his deliberation, his resolution, his execution, his confession; confession of true sins, and of them only, and of all them, of his sins, and all this to the Lord, and all that against himself. That which was proposed for the second part, must fall into the compass of a conclusion, and a short one, that is God's act, "Thou forgavest the iniquity of my sin."

Part 2

This is a wide door, and would let out armies of instructions to you; but we will shut up this door, with these two leaves thereof: the fulness of God's mercy, "He forgives the sin and the punishment"; and the seasonableness, the acceleration of his mercy in this expression of our text, that David's is but "*actus inchoatus*," he says "he will confess," and God's is "*actus consummatus*, Thou forgavest," thou hadst already forgiven the iniquity and punishment of my sin. These will be the two leaves of this door. And let the hand that shuts them be this "and," this particle of connection which we have in the text, "I said, and thou didst." For though this remission of sin be not presented here as an effect upon that cause of David's confession . . . yet it is at least as a consequent from an occasion, so assured, so infallible, as let any man confess as David did, and he shall be sure to be forgiven as David was. For though this forgiveness be a flower of mercy, yet the root grows in the justice of God. If we acknowledge our sin, he is faithful and just to forgive us our sin.[15] It grows out of his faithfulness, as he hath vouchsafed to bind himself by a promise, and out of his justice, as he hath received a full satisfaction for all our sins. So that this hand, this "and," in our text, is as a ligament, as a sinew, to connect and knit together that glorious body of God's preventing grace and his subsequent grace. If our confession come between and tie the knot, God that moved us to that act will perfect all.

---

15. 1 John 1:9.

JOHN DONNE

Plenitudo

Here enters the fulness of his mercy, at one leaf of this door; well expressed at our door in that *"Ecce sto, et pulso,"* Behold, I stand at the door and knock;[16] for first he comes; here is no mention of our calling of him before; he comes of himself; and then he suffers not us to be ignorant of his coming. He comes so as that he manifests himself, "Ecce," Behold. And then he expects not that we should wake with that light and look out of ourselves, but he knocks, solicits us, at least with some noise at our doors, some calamities upon our neighbors. And again he appears not like a lightning that passes away as soon as it is seen, that no man can read by it nor work by it, nor light a candle, nor kindle a coal by it, but he stands at the door and expects us all day; not only with a patience but with a hunger to effect his purpose upon us. He would come in and sup with us, accept our diet, our poor endeavors; and then would have us sup with him, (as it is there added) would feast us with his abundant graces, which he brings even home to our doors. But those he does not give us at the door; not till we have let him in, by the good use of his former grace. And as he offers his fulness of his mercy by these means before, so by way of pardon and remission, if we have been defective in opening the door upon his standing and knocking, this fulness is fully expressed in this word of this text, as our two translations (neither departing from the natural signification of the word) have rendered it.

Poena

This word is the same here, in David's sweetness, as in Cain's bitterness, *"gnavon."* And we cannot tell whether Cain speak there of a punishment too great to be borne, or of a sin too great to be pardoned;[17] nor which David means here. It fills up the measure of God's mercy if we take him to mean both. God, upon confession, forgives the punishment of the sin; so that the just terror of hell and the imaginary terror of purgatory, for the next world, is taken away. And for this world, what calamities and tribulations soever fall upon us, after these confessions, and remissions, they have not the nature of punishments, but they are fatherly corrections and medicinal assistances against relapses, and have their main relation and prospect upon the future.

---

16. Revelation 3:20.
17. Genesis 4:13.

Iniquitas

For not only the sin itself but the iniquity of the sin is said to be forgiven. God keeps nothing in his mind against the last day. But whatsoever is worst in the sin, the venom, the malignity of the sin, the violation of his law, the affrontings of his majesty residing in that law, though it have been a winking at his light, a resisting of his light, the ill nature, the malignity, the iniquity of the sin is forgiven. Only this remains, that God extinguishes not the right of a third person, or pardons a murder so as that he bars another from his appeal. Not that his pardon is not full, upon a full confession, but that the confession is no more full if it be not accompanied with satisfaction, that is restitution of all unjustly gotten, than if the confession lacked contrition and true sorrow. Otherwise the iniquity of the sin, and the punishment of the sin, are both fully pardoned. And so we have shut one leaf of this door, the fulness. The other is the speed and acceleration of his mercy, and that leaf we will clap to in a word.

Promptitudo

This is expressed in this, David is but at his *"dixit,"* and God at his *"remisit."* David was but saying, nay but thinking, and God was doing, nay perfecting his work. To the lepers that cried out for mercy, Christ said, Go, show yourselves to the priest.[18] So he put them into the way; and they went, says the text; and as they went they were healed upon the way. No man comes into the way but by illumination and direction of God. Christ put them into the way. The way is the Church. No man is cured out of the way; no man that separates himself from the Church; nor in the way neither, except he go. If he live negligently and trust only upon the outward profession; nor though he go, except he go according to Christ's bidding; except he conform himself to that worship of God, and to those means of sanctification, which God hath instituted in his church, without singularities of his own or traditions of other men's inventing and imposing. This, this submitting and conforming ourselves to God, so as God hath commanded us, the purposing of this and the endeavoring of this, is our *"dixit"* in the text, our saying that we will do it, and upon this *"dixit,"* this purposing, this endeavoring, instantly, immediately, infallibly, follows the *"remisit,"* God will, God does, God hath forgiven the iniquity and the punishment of the sin.

18. Luke 17:14.

Therefore to end all, "Pour out thy heart like water before the face of the Lord.[19] No liquor comes so clearly, so absolutely from the vessel, not oil, not milk, not wine, not honey, as that it leaves no taste behind; so may sweet sins. And therefore pour out, says the prophet, not the liquor, but the heart itself, and take a new heart of God's making. For thy former heart was never so of God's making as that Adam had not a hand in it. And his image was in it, in original sin as well as God's in creation. As liquors poured out leave a taste and a smell behind them, unperfected confessions (and who perfects his confession?) leave ill gotten goods sticking upon thine heir, and they leave a taste and a delight to think and speak of former sins, sticking upon thy self. But pour out thy heart like water; all ill impressions in the very root.

And for the accomplishment of this great mystery of godliness by confession, fix thy meditations upon those words, and in the strength of them come now (or when thou shalt be better strengthened by the meditation of them) to the table of the Lord. The Lord looketh upon men[20] and if any say, I have sinned and perverted that which was right and it profited me not, he will deliver his soul from going down into the pit, and his life shall see light. And it is added, Lo all these things worketh God twice and thrice. Here is a fulness of consolation, first plenary, and here is a present forgiveness. If man, if any man say, I have sinned, God doth, God forgives; and here is more than that, an iteration, if thou fall upon infirmity again God will on penitence more carefully performed forgive again. This he will do twice and thrice, says the Hebrew. Our translation might boldly say, as it doth, this God will do often. But yet if God find "*dolum in spiritu,*" an over-confidence in this, God cannot be mocked; and therefore take heed of trusting upon it too often, but especially of trusting upon it too late. And whatsoever the Holy Ghost may mean by the twice or thrice, be sure to do it once, do it now, and receive thy Savior there, and so as he offers himself unto thee in these ordinances this day, once, and twice, and thrice, that is in prayer, in preaching, in the sacrament. For this is thy trinity upon earth, that must bring thee to the Trinity in heaven: To which Trinity, &c.

---

19. Lamentations 2:19.
20. Job 33:27.

"Deaths Duell, or, A Consolation to the Soule, against the dying Life and living Death of the Body"[1]

Psalm 68:20. And unto God the Lord belong the issues of death.

Buildings stand by the benefit of their foundations that sustain and support them, and of their buttresses that comprehend and embrace them, and of their contignations that knit and unite them. The foundations suffer them not to sink, the buttresses suffer them not to swerve, and the contignation and knitting suffers them not to cleave. The body of our building is in the former part of this verse. It is this: "He that is our God is the God of salvation"; *ad salutes*, of salvations in the plural, so it is in the original; the God that gives us spiritual and temporal salvation too.

But of this building, the foundation, the buttresses, the contignations are in this part of the verse, which constitutes our text, and in the three divers acceptations of the words amongst our expositors. "Unto God the Lord belong the issues of death." For first the foundation of this building (that our God is the God of all salvations) is laid in this; that unto this "God the Lord belong the issues of death," that is, it is in his power to give us an issue and deliverance, even then when we are brought to the jaws and teeth of death, and to the lips of that whirlpool, the grave. And so in this

---

[1]. Delivered at the beginning of Lent, 1630, at Whitehall, in the presence of King Charles I. The title is seemingly Donne's own. *Sermons*, Potter and Simpson eds., 10:229–48.

acceptation, this *exitus mortis,* this issue of death is *liberatio a morte,* a deliverance from death, and this is the most obvious and most ordinary acceptation of these words, and that upon which our translation lays hold, "the issues from death."

And then secondly the buttresses that comprehend and settle this building, that he that is our God, is the God of all salvation, are thus raised. "Unto God the Lord belong the issues of death," that is, the disposition and manner of our death: what kind of issue and transmigration we shall have out of this world, whether prepared or sudden, whether violent or natural, whether in our perfect senses or shaken and disordered by sickness. There is no condemnation to be argued out of that, no judgment to be made upon that, for howsoever, they die, "precious in his sight is the death of his saints,"[2] and with him are "the issues of death," the ways of our departing out of this life are in his hands. And so in this sense of the words, this *exitus mortis,* the issue of death is *liberatio in morte,* a deliverance in death. Not that God will deliver us from dying, but that he will have a care of us in the hour of death, of what kind soever our passage be. . . .

And then lastly the contignation and knitting of this building, that he that is our God is the God of all salvations, consists in this, "Unto this God the Lord belong the issues of death," that is, that this God the Lord having united and knit both natures in one, and being God, having also come into this world, in our flesh, he could have no other means to save us, he could have no other issue out of this world, nor return to his former glory, but by death. And so in this sense, this *exitus mortis,* this issue of death is *liberatio per mortem,* a deliverance by death, by the death of this God, our Lord Christ Jesus. And this is St. Augustine's acceptation of the words, and those many and great persons that have adhered to him.

In all these three lines then, we shall look upon these words. First, as the God of power, the Almighty Father rescues his servants from the jaws of death. And then as the God of mercy, the glorious Son rescued us, by taking upon himself this issue of death. And then between these two, as the God of comfort, the Holy Ghost rescues us from all discomfort by his blessed impressions beforehand, that what manner of death soever be ordained for us, yet this *exitus mortis* shall be *introitus in vitam,* our issue in death shall be an entrance into everlasting life. And these three considerations, our deliverance *a morte, in morte, per morte,* from death, in death, and by death, will abundantly do all the offices of the foundations, of the butresses, of the contignation of this our building: that "He that is our God

---

2. [Psalm 116:15].

is the God of all salvation" because "unto this God the Lord belong the issues of death."

Part 1. *A morte*

First, then, we consider this *exitus mortis* to be *liberatio a morte*, that with God the Lord are the issues of death, and therefore in all our deaths, and deadly calamities of this life, we may justly hope of a good issue from him. And all our periods and transitions in this life are so many passages from death to death. Our very birth and entrance into this life is an issue from death, for in our mother's womb we are dead so, as that we do not know we live, not so much as we do in our sleep. Neither is there any grave so close, or so putrid a prison, as the womb would be unto us if we stayed in it beyond our time, or died there before our time. In the grave the worms do not kill us, we breed and feed, and then kill those worms which we ourselves produced. In the womb the dead child kills the mother that conceived it. . . . And if we be not dead so in the womb, so as that being dead we kill her that gave us our first life, our life of vegetation, yet we are dead so, as David's idols are dead.[3] In the womb we have "eyes and see not, ears and hear not." There in the womb we are fitted for works of darkness, all the while deprived of light. And there in the womb we are taught cruelty, by being fed with blood, and may be damned, though we be never born.

Of our very making in the womb, David says, "I am wonderfully and fearfully made,"[4] and "Such knowledge is too excellent for me,"[5] . . . for even that "is the Lord's doing, and it is wonderful in our eyes."[6] It is "he that hath made us, and not we ourselves,"[7] no, nor our parents neither. "Thy hands have made me and fashioned me round about," says Job, and (as the original word is) "thou hast taken pains about me," and yet, says he, "thou dost destroy me." Though I be the masterpiece of the greatest Master (man is so), yet if you do no more for me, if you leave me where you made me, destruction will follow. The womb which should be the house of life becomes death itself if God leave us there. That which God threatens so often, the shutting of the womb, is not so heavy, nor so discomfortable a curse in the first, as in the latter shutting, nor in the shutting of barrenness, as in the shutting of weakness, when children are come to the birth and there is not strength to bring forth.[8]

---

3. Psalm 115:[5,]6.
4. Psalm 139:14.
5. Psalm 139:6.
6. Psalm 118:23.
7. Psalm 100:3.
8. Isaiah 37:3.

It is the exaltation of misery to fall from a near hope of happiness. And in that vehement imprecation, the prophet expresses the highest of God's anger, "Give them O Lord, what wilt thou give them? give them a miscarrying womb."[9] Therefore as soon as we are men (that is, inanimated, quickened in the womb), though we cannot ourselves, our parents have reason to say in our behalf, "Wretched man that he is, who shall deliver him from this body of death?"[10] for even the womb is a body of death if there be no deliverer. It must be he that said to Jeremiah, "Before I formed thee I knew thee, and before thou camest out of the womb I sanctified thee."[11]

We are not sure that there was no kind of ship nor boat to fish in, nor to pass by, till God prescribed Noah that absolute form of the Ark. That word which the Holy Ghost, by Moses, uses for the Ark is common to all kinds of boats, *thebah,* and is the same word that Moses uses for the boat that he was exposed in, that his mother laid him in an ark of bulrushes.[12] But we are sure that Eve had no midwife when she was delivered of Cain, therefore she might well say, "I have gotten a man from the Lord," wholly, entirely from the Lord.[13] It is the Lord that enabled me to conceive, the Lord that infused a quickening soul into that conception, the Lord that brought into the world that which himself had quickened. Without all this might Eve say, My body had been but the house of death, and . . . to "God the Lord belong the issues of death."

But then this *exitus a morte,* is but *introitus in mortem,* this issue, this deliverance from that death, the death of the womb, is an entrance, a delivering over to another death, the manifold deaths of this world. We have a winding sheet in our mother's womb, which grows with us from our conception, and we come into the world, wound up in that winding sheet, for we come to seek a grave. And as prisoners discharged of actions may lie for fees, so when the womb has discharged us, yet we are bound to it by cords of flesh, by such a string, as that we cannot go thence, nor stay there. We celebrate our own funerals with cries, even at our birth; as though our three score and ten years life were spent in our mother's labor, and our circle made up in the first point thereof; we beg one baptism, with another, a sacrament of tears. And we come into a world that lasts many ages, but we last not.

---

9. Hosea 9:14.
10. Romans 7:24.
11. Jeremiah 1:5.
12. Exodus 2:3.
13. Genesis 4:1.

SERMONS

In domo Patris [in my Father's house], says our blessed Savior, speaking of heaven, ... "there are many mansions,"[14] divers and durable, so that if a man cannot possess a martyr's house (he has shed no blood for Christ), yet he may have a confessor's, he has been ready to glorify God in the shedding of his blood. And if a woman cannot possess a virgin's house (she has embraced the holy state of marriage), yet she may have a matron's house, she has brought forth and brought up children in the fear of God. ... "In my Father's house," in heaven, "there are many mansions," but here upon earth, "the son of man hath not where to lay his head," says he himself.[15] ... How then has God given this earth to the sons of men?[16] He has given them earth for their materials, to be made of earth, and he has given them earth for their grave and sepulture, to return and resolve to earth, but not for their possession. "Here we have no continuing city,"[17] nay no cottage that continues, nay no persons, no bodies that continue. . . .

Even the Israel of God has no mansions, but journeys, pilgrimages in this life. By that measure did Jacob measure his life to Pharaoh: "the days of the years of my pilgrimage."[18] And though the Apostle would not say *morimur*, that, while we are in the body we are dead,[19] yet he says *peregrinamur*, while we are in the body, we are but in a pilgrimage, and we are absent from the Lord. He might have said dead, for this whole world is but an universal churchyard, but our common grave, and the life and motion that the greatest persons have in it is but as the shaking of buried bodies in the grave by an earthquake. That which we call life is but . . . a week of deaths, seven days, seven periods of our life spent in dying, a dying seven times over; and there is an end. Our birth dies in infancy, and our infancy dies in youth, and youth and the rest die in age, and age also dies, and determines all.

Nor do all these, youth out of infancy, age out of youth, arise so, as a Phoenix out of the ashes of another Phoenix formerly dead, but as a wasp or a serpent out of a carrion, or as a snake out of dung. Our youth is worse than our infancy, and our age worse than our youth. Our youth is hungry and thirsty after those sins which our infancy knew not. And our age is sorry and angry that it cannot pursue those sins which our youth did. And besides all the way, so many deaths, that is, so many deadly calamities accompany every condition and every period of this life as that death itself would be an ease to them that suffer them. Upon this sense does Job wish that God had

---

14. John 14:2.
15. Matthew 8:20.
16. [Psalm 115:16].
17. Hebrews 13:14.
18. Genesis 47:9.
19. 2 Corinthians 5:6.

not given him an issue from the first death, from the womb. "Wherefore hast thou brought me forth out of the womb? O that I had given up the ghost, and no eye seen me! I should have been as though I had not been."

And not only the impatient Israelites in their murmuring ("would to God we had died by the hand of the Lord in the land of Egypt"),[20] but Elijah himself, when he fled from Jezebel and went for his life, as that text says, under the juniper tree, requested that he might die, and said, "It is enough now, O Lord, take away my life."[21] So Jonah justifies his impatience, nay his anger towards God himself. "Now O Lord take, I beseech thee, my life from me, for it is better to die than to live."[22] And when God asked him, "doest thou well to be angry for this?" he replies, "I do well to be angry, even unto death." How much worse a death than death is this life, which so good men would so often change for death!

But if my case be as St. Paul's case, *quotidie morior*, that "I die daily,"[23] that something heavier than death falls upon me every day; if my case be David's case, . . . "all the day long we are killed,"[24] that not only every day, but every hour of the day something heavier than death falls upon me; though that be true of me, . . . "I was shapen in iniquity, and in sin did my mother conceive me"[25] (there I died one death), though that be true of me, I was born not only of the child of sin, but the child of wrath, of the wrath of God for sin,[26] which is a heavier death; yet . . . with "God the Lord are the issues of death," and after a Job, and a Joseph, and a Jeremiah, and a Daniel, I cannot doubt of a deliverance. And if no other deliverance conduce more to his glory and my good, yet he has the keys of death, and he can let me out at that door, that is, deliver me from the manifold deaths of this world, the every day's death and every hour's death, by that one death, the final dissolution of body and soul, the end of all.

But then is that the end of all? Is that dissolution of body and soul the last death that the body shall suffer? (For of spiritual death we speak not now.) It is not. Though this be *exitus a morte*, it is *introitus in mortem:* though it be an issue from the manifold deaths of this world, yet it is an entrance into the death of corruption and putrefaction and vermiculation and incineration, and dispersion in and from the grave, in which every dead man dies over again.

20. Exodus 16:3.
21. 1 Kings 19:4.
22. Jonah 4:3.
23. 1 Corinthians 15:31.
24. Psalm 44:22.
25. Psalm 51:5.
26. Ephesians 2:3.

It was a prerogative peculiar to Christ not to die this death, not to see corruption. What gave him this privilege? Not Joseph's great proportion of gums and spices, that might have preserved his body from corruption and incineration longer than he needed it, longer than three days, but it would not have done it forever. What preserved him then? Did his exemption and freedom from original sin preserve him from this corruption and incineration? 'Tis true that original sin has induced this corruption and incineration upon us. If we had not sinned in Adam, "mortality had not put on immortality" (as the Apostle speaks)[27] nor "corruption had not put on incorruption," but we had had our transmigration from this to the other world, without any mortality and corruption at all.

But yet since Christ took sin upon him, so far as made him mortal, he had it so far too as might have made him see this corruption and incineration, though he had no original sin in himself. What preserved him then? Did the hypostatical union of both natures, God and man, preserve him from this corruption and incineration? 'Tis true that this was a most powerful embalming, to be embalmed with the divine nature itself, to be embalmed with eternity, was able to preserve him from corruption and incineration forever. And he was embalmed so, embalmed with the divine nature itself even in his body as well as in his soul; for the Godhead, the divine nature, did not depart, but remained still united to his dead body in the grave.

But yet for all this powerful embalming, this hypostatical union of both natures, we see Christ did die; and for all this union which made him God and man, he became no man (for the union of the body and soul makes the man, and he whose soul and body are separated by death as long as that state lasts is properly no man). And therefore as in him the dissolution of body and soul was no dissolution of the hypostatical union, so is there nothing that constrains us to say, that though the flesh of Christ had seen corruption and incineration in the grave, this had been any dissolution of the hypostatical union, for the divine nature, the Godhead might have remained with all the elements and principles of Christ's body, as well as it did with the two constitutive parts of his person, his body and his soul.

This incorruption then was not in Joseph's gums and spices, nor was it in Christ's innocency and exemption from original sin, nor was it (that is, it is not necessary to say it was) in the hypostatical union. But this incorruptibleness of his flesh is most conveniently placed in that, . . . "thou wilt not suffer thy holy one to see corruption."[28] We look no

---

27. 1 Corinthians 15:33 [53–54].
28. Psalm 16:10.

JOHN DONNE

further for causes or reasons in the mysteries of religion, but to the will
and pleasure of God: Christ himself limited his inquisition in that, . . .
"even so Father, for so it seemeth good in thy sight."[29] Christ's body did
not see corruption, therefore, because God had decreed it should not.

The humble soul (and only the humble soul is the religious soul) rests
himself upon God's purposes and his decrees . . . which he has declared
and manifested, not such as are conceived and imagined in ourselves,
though upon some probability, some verisimilitude. So in our present case
Peter proceeded in his sermon at Jerusalem, and so Paul in his at Antioch.[30]
They preached Christ to have been risen without seeing corruption not
only because God had decreed it, but because he had manifested that
decree in his prophet. Therefore does St. Paul cite by special number the
second Psalm for that decree. And therefore both St. Peter and St. Paul cite
for it that place in the 16th Psalm,[31] for when God declares his decree and
purpose in the express words of his prophet, or when he declares it in the
real execution of the decree, then he makes it ours, then he manifests it to
us. And therefore as the mysteries of our religion are not the objects of our
reason, but by faith we rest on God's decree and purpose (It is so, O God,
because it is thy will it should be so), so God's decrees are ever to be
considered in the manifestation thereof.

All manifestation is either in the word of God, or in the execution of
the decree. And when these two concur and meet, it is the strongest
demonstration that can be. When therefore I find those marks of adoption
and spiritual filiation, which are delivered in the Word of God to be upon
me, when I find that real execution of his good purpose upon me, as that
actually I do live under the obedience, and under the conditions which are
evidences of adoption and spiritual filiation; then, and so long as I see these
marks and live so, I may safely comfort myself in a holy certitude and a
modest infallibility of my adoption. Christ determines himself in that, the
purpose of God was manifest to him. St. Peter and St. Paul determine
themselves in those two ways of knowing the purpose of God, the Word
of God before, the execution of the decree in the fullness of time. It was
prophesied before, say they, and it is performed now. Christ is risen
without seeing corruption.

Now this which is so singularly peculiar to him, that his flesh should
not see corruption, at his second coming, his coming to judgment, shall
extend to all that are then alive, their flesh shall not see corruption, because

29. Matthew 11:26.
30. Acts 2:31, 13:35.
31. Psalm 16:10.

as the Apostle says, and says as a secret, a mystery, "Behold I show you a mystery, we shall not all sleep" (that is, not continue in the state of the dead in the grave), "but we shall all be changed in an instant."[32] We shall have a dissolution, and in the same instant a redintegration, a recompacting of body and soul, and that shall be truly a death and truly a resurrection, but no sleeping, no corruption. But for us that die now and sleep in the state of the dead, we must all pass this posthumous death, this death after death, nay this death after burial, the dissolution after dissolution, this death of corruption and putrefaction, of vermiculation and incineration, of dissolution and dispersion in and from the grave, when these bodies that have been the children of royal parents, and the parents of royal children, must say with Job, "Corruption thou art my father," and to the worm, "Thou art my mother and my sister."[33]

Miserable riddle, when the same worm must be my mother and my sister and myself. Miserable incest, when I must be married to my mother and my sister, and be both father and mother to my own mother and sister, beget and bear that worm which is all that miserable penury. When my mouth shall be filled with dust, and the worm shall feed, and feed sweetly upon me,[34] when the ambitious man shall have no satisfaction if the poorest alive tread upon him, nor the poorest receive any contentment in being made equal to princes, for they shall be equal but in dust.[35] One dies at his full strength, being wholly at ease and in quiet, and another dies in the bitterness of his soul, and never eats with pleasure, but they lie down alike in the dust and the worm covers them. In Job, and in Isaiah, it covers them and is spread under them, the worm is spread under you and the worm covers you.[36] There's the mats and the carpets that lie under, and there's the state and the canopy that hangs over the greatest of the sons of men. Even those bodies that were the temples of the Holy Ghost come to this delapidation, to ruin, to rubbish, to dust; even the Israel of the Lord, and Jacob himself has no other specification, no other denomination, but that *vermis Jacob*, thou "worm of Jacob."

Truly the consideration of this posthumous death, this death after burial, that after God (with whom are the issues of death) has delivered me from the death of the womb by bringing me into the world, and from the manifold deaths of the world by laying me in the grave, I must die again in

---

32. 1 Corinthians 15:51.
33. [Job] 17:14.
34. [Job] 24:20.
35. Job 21:23.
36. [Isaiah] 14:11.

an incineration of this flesh and in a dispersion of that dust. That that monarch who spread over many nations alive, must in his dust lie in a corner of that sheet of lead, and there but so long as that lead will last; and that private and retired man that thought himself his own forever, and never came forth, must in his dust of the grave be published and (such are the revolutions of the graves) be mingled with the dust of every highway, and of every dunghill, and swallowed in every puddle and pond: this is the most inglorious and contemptible vilification, the most deadly and peremptory nullification of man, that we can consider.

God seems to have carried the declaration of his power to a great height, when he sets the Prophet Ezekiel in the valley of dry bones and says, "Son of man can these bones live?"[37] as though it had been impossible, and yet they did. "The Lord laid sinews upon them, and flesh, and breathed into them, and they did live." But in that case there were bones to be seen, something visible, of which it might be said, Can this thing live? But in this death of incineration and dispersion of dust, we see nothing that we can call that man's. If we say, Can this dust live? perchance it cannot. It may be the mere dust of the earth, which never did live, nor never shall. It may be the dust of that man's worms, which did live, but shall no more. It may be the dust of another man, that concerns not him of whom it is asked. This death of incineration and dispersion is, to natural reason, the most irrecoverable death of all, and yet . . . "unto God the Lord belong the issues of death," and by recompacting this dust into the same body, and reanimating the same body with the same soul, he shall in a blessed and glorious resurrection give me such an issue from this death as shall never pass into any other death, but establish me into a life that shall last as long as the Lord of life himself.

And so have you that that belongs to the first acceptation of these words ("unto God the Lord belong the issues of death"), that though from the womb to the grave and in the grave itself we pass from death to death, yet, as Daniel speaks, "The Lord our God is able to deliver us, and he will deliver us."

Part 2. *Liberatio in morte*

And so we pass unto our second accommodation of these words ("unto God the Lord belong the issues of death"), that it belongs to God, and not to man, to pass a judgment upon us at our death, or to conclude a dereliction on God's part upon the manner thereof.

---

37. [Ezekiel 37:1].

Those indications which the physicians receive, and those presagitions which they give for death or recovery in the patient, they receive and they give out of the grounds and the rules of their art. But we have no such rule or art to give a presagition of spiritual death and damnation upon any such indication as we see in any dying man. We see often enough to be sorry, but not to despair. For the mercies of God work momentarily in minutes, and many times insensibly to bystanders or any other then the party departing, and we may be deceived both ways. We use to comfort ourself in the death of a friend, if it be testified that he went away like a lamb, that is, without any reluctation. But, God knows that he may be accompanied with a dangerous damp and stupefaction, and insensibility of his present state. Our blessed Savior suffered colluctations with death, and a sadness even in his soul to death, and an agony even to a bloody sweat in his body, and expostulations with God, and exclamations upon the cross.

He was a devout man, who said upon his death bed, or death turf (for he was a hermit) . . . "Hast thou served a good Master threescore and ten years, and now art thou loath to go into his presence?" Yet Hilarion was loath. He was a devout man,[38] that said that day he died, . . . "Consider this to be the first day's service that ever thou didst thy Master, to glorify him in a Christianly and a constant death, and if thy first day be thy last day too, how soon dost thou come to receive thy wages?" Yet Barlaam would have been content to have stayed longer for it.

Make no ill conclusions upon any man's loathness to die. And then, upon violent deaths inflicted, as upon malefactors, Christ himself has forbidden us by his own death to make any ill conclusion; for his own death had those impressions in it. He was reputed, he was executed as a malefactor, and no doubt many of them who concurred to his death did believe him to be so. Of sudden death there are scarce examples to be found in the Scriptures upon good men, for death in battle cannot be called sudden death. But God governs not by examples, but by rules, and therefore make no ill conclusion upon sudden death nor upon distempers neither, though perchance accompanied with some words of diffidence and distrust in the mercies of God.

The tree lies as it falls,[39] 'tis true, but yet it is not the last stroke that fells the tree, nor the last word nor gasp that qualifies the soul. Still pray we for a peaceable life against violent death, and for time of repentance against sudden death, and for sober and modest assurance against distempered and

---

38. Barlaam.
39. [Eccles. 11:3].

diffident death, but never make ill conclusions upon persons overtaken with such deaths; . . . "to God the Lord belong the issues of death." And he received Samson, who went out of this world in such a manner (consider it actively, consider it passively in his own death, and in those whom he slew with himself) as was subject to interpretation hard enough. Yet the Holy Ghost has moved St. Paul to celebrate Samson in his great catalogue, and so does all the Church.[40]

Our critical day is not the very day of our death but the whole course of our life. I thank him that prays for me when my bell tolls, but I thank him much more that catechises me, or preaches to me, or instructs me how to live. . . . There's my security, the mouth of the Lord has said it, do this and you shall live. But though I do it, yet I shall die too, die a bodily, a natural death. But God never mentions, never seems to consider that death, the bodily, the natural death. God does not say, live well and you shall die well, that is, an easy, a quiet death; but live well here, and you shall live well forever. As the first part of a sentence pieces well with the last, and never respects, never harkens after the parenthesis that comes between, so does a good life here flow into an eternal life, without any consideration what manner of death we die. But whether the gate of my prison be opened with an oiled key (by a gentle and preparing sickness), or the gate be hewn down by a violent death, or the gate be burned down by a raging and frantic fever, a gate into heaven I shall have, for from the Lord is the cause of my life, and with God the Lord are the issues of death. And further we carry not this second acceptation of the words, as this issue of death is a *liberatio in morte* God's care that the soul be safe, what agonies soever the body suffers in the hour of death.

Part 3. *Liberatio per mortem*

But pass to our third part and last part: as this issue of death is *liberatio per mortem*, a deliverance by the death of another, by the death of Christ. . . . "You have heard of the patience of Job" says St. James (5:11). All this while you have done that, for in every man, calamitous, miserable man, a Job speaks. Now see "the end of the Lord," says that Apostle, which is not that end that the Lord proposed to himself (salvation to us), nor the end which he proposes to us (conformity to him), but see "the end of the Lord," says he, the end that the Lord himself came to; death and a painful and a shameful death.

---

40. Hebrews 11[:32].

But why did he die? and why die so? . . . As St. Augustine interpreting this text answers that question: because to this "God our Lord belonged the issues of death."[41] . . . What can be more obvious, more manifest than this sense of these words. In the former part of this verse, it is said, "He that is our God, is the God of salvation," . . . so he reads it, the God that must save us. Who can that be, says he, but Jesus? for therefore that name was given him, because he was to save us.[42] And to this Jesus, says he, this Savior, belong the issues of death. . . . Being come into this life in our mortal nature, he could not go out of it any other way then by death. . . . Therefore it is said, "To God the Lord belong the issues of death"; . . . to show that his way to save us was to die. And from this text does St. Isidor prove that Christ was truly man (which as many sects of heretics denied as that he was truly God), because to him, though he were *Dominus Dominus* (as the text doubles it) God the Lord, yet to him, to God the Lord belonged the issues of death. . . . More cannot be said[43] than Christ himself says of himself, "These things Christ ought to suffer"; he had no other way but by death.

So then this part of our sermon must needs be a passion sermon. Since all his life was a continual passion, all our Lent may well be a continual Good Friday. Christ's painful life took off none of the pains of his death. He felt not the less then for having felt so much before. Nor will anything that shall be said before lessen, but rather enlarge the devotion to that which shall be said of his passion at the time of due soleminization thereof. Christ bled not a drop the less at the last for having bled at his circumcision before, nor will you shed a tear the less then, if you shed some now.

And therefore be now content to consider with me how to this God the Lord belonged the issues of death. That God, this Lord, the Lord of life could die, is a strange contemplation. That the Red Sea could be dry,[44] that the sun could stand still,[45] that an oven could be seven times heat and not[46] burn, that lions could be hungry and not bite,[47] is strange, miraculously strange, but super-miraculous that God could die. But that God would die is an exaltation of that. But even of that also it is a super-exaltation, that God should die, must die, and (said St. Augustine), "God the

---

41. De Civitate Dei lib. 17, c. 18.
42. Matthew 1:21.
43. Luke 24:26.
44. Exodus 14:21.
45. Joshua 10:12.
46. [Daniel 3:19].
47. [Daniel 6:22].

Lord had no issue but by death," and . . . (says Christ himself), "all this Christ ought to suffer," was bound to suffer. . . . Says David, God is the God of revenges, he would not pass over the sin of man unrevenged, unpunished.[48] But then . . . (says that place) the God of revenges works freely, he punishes, he spares whom he will. And would he not spare himself? He would not. . . . Love is strong as death,[49] stronger; it drew in death that naturally is not welcome. . . . "If it be possible," says Christ, "let this cup pass,"[50] when his love expressed in a former decree with his Father had made it impossible.

Many waters quench not love.[51] Christ tried many. He was baptized out of his love, and his love determined not there. He mingled blood with water in his agony and that determined not his love. He wept pure blood, all his blood at all his eyes, at all his pores, in his flagellation and thorns (to the Lord our God belonged the issues of blood) and these expressed, but these did not quench his love. He would not spare, nay he could not spare himself. There was nothing more free, more voluntary, more spontaneous than the death of Christ. 'Tis true, . . . he died voluntarily, but yet when we consider the contract that had passed between his Father and him, there was . . . a kind of necessity upon him. All this Christ ought to suffer. And when shall we date this obligation, . . . this necessity? When shall we say that began? Certainly this decree by which Christ was to suffer all this was an eternal decree, and was there anything before that, that was eternal? Infinite love, eternal love; be pleased to follow this home, and to consider it seriously, that what liberty soever we can conceive in Christ, to die or not to die, this necessity of dying, this decree is as eternal as that liberty; and yet how small a matter made he of this necessity and this dying?

His Father calls it but a bruise, and but a bruising of his heel ("the serpent shall bruise his heel")[52] and yet that was that the serpent should practice and compass his death. Himself calls it but a baptism, as though he were to be the better for it. "I have a baptism to be baptized with,"[53] and he was in pain till it was accomplished, and yet this baptism was his death. The Holy Ghost calls it joy ("for the joy which was set before him he endured the cross")[54] which was not a joy of his reward after his passion, but a joy that filled him even in the midst of those torments, and arose from

---

48. Psalm 94:1.
49. Song of Solomon 8:6.
50. [Matthew 26:39].
51. Song of Solomon 8:7.
52. Genesis 3:15.
53. Luke 12:50.
54. Hebrews 12:2.

him. When Christ calls his passion *calicem*, a cup, and no worse ("can ye drink of my cup"),[55] he speaks not odiously, not with detestation of it. Indeed it was a cup, . . . a health to all the world. And, . . . says David, "what shall I render to the Lord?" Answer you with David, . . . "I will take a cup of salvation."[56] Take it, that cup of salvation, his passion, if not into your present imitation, yet into your present contemplation.

And behold how that Lord that was God yet could die, would die, must die, for your salvation. That Moses and Elijah talked with Christ in the transfiguration both St. Matthew and St. Mark tell us,[57] but what they talked of only St. Luke. . . . Says he, "They talked of his decease, of his death which was to be accomplished at Jerusalem."[58] The word is of his *exodus*, the very word of our text, *exitus*, his issue by death. Moses, who in his exodus had prefigured this issue of our Lord, and in passing Israel out of Egypt through the Red Sea had foretold in that actual prophecy Christ's passing of mankind through the sea of his blood. And Elijah, whose exodus and issue out of this world was a figure of Christ's ascension, had no doubt a great satisfaction in talking with our blessed Lord . . . of the full consummation of all this in his death, which was to be accomplished at Jerusalem.

Our meditation of his death should be more visceral and affect us more because it is of a thing already done. The ancient Romans had a certain tenderness and detestation of the name of death, they could not name death, no, not in their wills. There they could not say . . . "if or when I die," but "when the course of nature is accomplished upon me." To us that speak daily of the death of Christ ("he was crucified, dead and buried"), can the memory or the mention of our own death be irksome or bitter? There are in these latter times amongst us those that name death freely enough, and the death of God, but in blasphemous oaths and execrations. Miserable men, who shall therefore be said never to have named Jesus, because they have named him too often, and therefore hear Jesus say, . . . "I never knew you,"[59] because they made themselves too familiar with him.

Moses and Elijah talked with Christ of his death only in a holy and joyful sense of the benefit which they and all the world were to receive by that. Discourses of religion should not be out of curiosity, but to edifica-

55. Matthew 20:22.
56. Psalm 116:12.
57. Matthew 17:3, Mark 9:4.
58. Luke 9:31.
59. [Matthew 7:23].

tion. And then they talked with Christ of his death at that time, when he was in the greatest height of glory that ever he admitted in this world, that is, his transfiguration. And we are afraid to speak to the great men of this world of their death, but nourish in them a vain imagination of immortality and immutability. But . . . (as St. Peter said there) it is good to dwell here, in this consideration of his death, and therefore transfer we our tabernacle (our devotions) through some of those steps which God the Lord made to his issue of death that day.

Take in the whole day from the hour that Christ received the Passover upon Thursday, unto the hour in which he died the next day. Make this present day that day in your devotion, and consider what he did, and remember what you have done. Before he instituted and celebrated the Sacrament (which was after the eating of the Passover), he proceeded to that act of humility, to wash his disciples' feet, even Peter's, who for a while resisted him. In your preparation to the holy and blessed Sacrament, have you with a sincere humility sought a reconciliation with all the world, even with those that have been averse from it, and refused that reconciliation from you? If so, and not else, you have spent that first part of his last day in a conformity with him.

After the Sacrament he spent the time till night in prayer, in preaching, in psalms. Have you considered that a worthy receiving of the Sacrament consists in a continuation of holiness after, as well as in a preparation before? If so, you have therein also conformed yourself to him. So Christ spent his time till night: "At night he went into the garden to pray,"[60] and . . . he spent much time in prayer. How much? Because it is literally expressed that he prayed there three several times, and that returning to his Disciples after his first prayer, and finding them asleep said, "Could ye not watch with me one hour?"[61] it is collected that he spent three hours in prayer. I dare scarce ask you where you went or how you disposed of yourself when it grew dark and after last night. If that time were spent in a holy recommendation of yourself to God and a submission of your will to his, it was spent in a conformity to him. In that time and in those prayers was his agony and bloody sweat. I will hope that you did pray, but not every ordinary and customary prayer; but prayer actually accompanied with shedding of tears, and dispositively in a readiness to shed blood for his glory in necessary case, puts you into a conformity with him.

About midnight he was taken and bound with a kiss. Are you not too

60. Luke 22:44.
61. Matthew 26:40.

conformable to him in that? Is not that too literally, too exactly your case? at midnight to have been taken and bound with a kiss? From thence he was carried back to Jerusalem, first to Annas, then to Caiaphas, and (as late as it was) then he was examined and buffeted and delivered over to the custody of those officers, from whom he received all those irrisions and violences, the covering of his face, the spitting upon his face, the blasphemies of words, and the smartness of blows which that Gospel mentions. In which compass fell ... that crowing of the cock which called up Peter to his repentance. How you passed all that time last night, you know. If you did anything then that needed Peter's tears, and have not shed them, let me be your cock, do it now. Now your Master (in the unworthiest of his servants) looks back upon you, do it now.

Betimes, in the morning, so soon as it was day, the Jews held a counsel in the High Priest's hall, and agreed upon their evidence against him, and then carried him to Pilate, who was to be his judge. Did you accuse yourself when you waked this morning, and were you content even with false accusations (that is) rather to suspect actions to have been sin, which were not, than to smother and justify such as were truly sins? Then you spent that hour in conformity to him. Pilate found no evidence against him, and therefore to ease himself and to pass a compliment upon Herod, Tetrarch of Galilee, who was at that time at Jerusalem (because Christ being a Galilean was of Herod's jurisdiction) Pilate sent him to Herod, and rather as a madman than a malefactor. Herod remanded him (with scorns) to Pilate to proceed against him; and this was about eight of the clock.

Have you been content to come to this inquisition, this examination, this agitation, this pursuit of your conscience, to sift it, to follow it from the sins of your youth to your present sins, from the sins of your bed to the sins of your board, and from the substance to the circumstance of your sins? That's time spent like your Savior's. Pilate would have saved Christ by using the privilege of the day in his behalf, because that day one prisoner was to be delivered, but they chose Barabbas. He would have saved him from death by satisfying their fury with inflicting other torments upon him, scourging and crowning with thorns, and loading him with many scornful and ignominious contumelies. But this redeemed him not, they pressed a crucifying.

Have you gone about to redeem your sin by fasting, by alms, by disciplines and mortifications, in way of satisfaction to the justice of God? That will not serve, that's not the right way; we press an utter crucifying of that sin that governs you: and that conforms you to Christ. Towards noon Pilate gave judgment, and they made such haste to execution, as that by noon he was upon the cross. There now hangs that sacred body upon the cross, rebaptized in his own tears and sweat, and embalmed in his own blood alive. There are those bowels of compassion, which are so conspicuous, so manifested, as that you may see them through his wounds. There those glorious eyes grew faint in their light: so as the sun, ashamed to survive them, departed with his light too. And then that Son of God, who was never from us, and yet had now come a new way unto us in assuming our nature, delivers that soul (which was never out of his Father's hands) by a new way, a voluntary emission of it into his Father's hands.

For though to this God our Lord, belonged these issues of death, so that considered in his own contract, he must necessarily die, yet at no breach or battery which they had made upon his sacred body issued his soul, but . . . "he gave up the Ghost," and as God breathed a soul into the first Adam, so this second Adam breathed his soul into God, into the hands of God. There we leave you in that blessed dependency, to hang upon him that hangs upon the cross, there bathe in his tears, there suck at his wounds, and lie down in peace in his grave, till he vouchsafe you a resurrection, and an ascension into the Kingdom, which he has purchased for you with the inestimable price of his incorruptible blood. *Amen.*

Devotions

I

The first Alteration, the first Grudging, of the Sickness

Meditation

Variable, and therefore miserable condition of man! this minute I was well, and am ill, this minute. I am surprised with a sudden change, and alteration to worse, and can impute it to no cause, nor call it by any name. We study health, and we deliberate upon our meats, and drink, and air and exercises, and we hew and we polish every stone that goes to that building; and so our health is a long and a regular work: but in a minute a cannon batters all, overthrows all, demolishes all. A sickness unprevented for all our diligence, unsuspected for all our curiosity, nay, undeserved, if we consider only disorder, summons us, seizes us, possesses us, destroys us in an instant. O miserable condition of man! which was not imprinted by God, who, as he is immortal himself, had put a coal, a beam of immortality into us, which we might have blown into a flame, but blew it out by our first sin. We beggared ourselves by hearkening after false riches, and infatuated ourselves by hearkening after false knowledge. So that now, we do not only die, but die upon the rack, die by the torment of sickness; nor that only, but are pre-afflicted, super-afflicted with these jealousies and suspicions and apprehensions of sickness, before we can call it a sickness. We are not sure we are ill; one hand asks the other by the pulse, and our eye asks our own urine how we do. O multiplied misery! We die, and cannot enjoy death, because we die in this torment of sickness. We are tormented with sickness, and cannot stay till the torment come, but pre-apprehensions and presages prophesy those torments which induce that death before either come; and our dissolution is conceived in these first changes, quickened in the sickness itself, and born in death, which bears date from these first changes. Is this the honour which man hath by being a little world, that he hath these earthquakes in himself, sudden shakings; these lightnings, sudden flashes; these thunders, sudden noises; these eclipses,

253

sudden offuscations and darkening of his senses; these blazing stars, sudden fiery exhalations; these rivers of blood, sudden red waters? Is he a world to himself only therefore, that he hath enough in himself, not only to destroy and execute himself, but to presage that execution upon himself; to assist the sickness, to antedate the sickness, to make the sickness the more irremediable by sad apprehensions, and, as if he would make a fire the more vehement by sprinkling water upon the coals, so to wrap a hot fever in cold melancholy, lest the fever alone should not destroy fast enough without this contribution, nor perfect the work (which is destruction) except we joined an artificial sickness of our own melancholy, to our natural, our unnatural fever. O perplexed discomposition, O riddling distemper, O miserable condition of man!

Expostulation

If I were but mere dust and ashes I might speak unto the Lord, for the Lord's hand made me of this dust, and the Lord's hand shall re-collect these ashes; the Lord's hand was the wheel upon which this vessel of clay was framed, and the Lord's hand is the urn in which these ashes shall be preserved. I am the dust and the ashes of the temple of the Holy Ghost, and what marble is so precious? But I am more than dust and ashes: I am my best part, I am my soul. And being so, the breath of God, I may breathe back these pious expostulations to my God: My God, my God, why is not my soul as sensible as my Body? Why hath not my soul these apprehensions, these presages, these changes, these antidates, these jealousies, these suspicions of a sin, as well as my body of a sickness? Why is there not always a pulse in my soul to beat at the approach of a temptation to sin? Why are there not always waters in mine eyes, to testify my spiritual sickness? I stand in the way of temptations, naturally, necessarily; all men do so; for there is a snake in every path, temptations in every vocation; but I go, I run, I fly into the ways of temptation which I might shun; nay, I break into houses where the plague is; I press into places of temptation, and tempt the devil himself, and solicit and importune them who had rather be left unsolicited by me. I fall sick of sin, and am bedded and bedrid, buried and putrified in the practice of sin, and all this while have no presage, no pulse, no sense of my sickness. O height, O depth of misery, where the first symptom of the sickness is hell, and where I never see the fever of lust, of envy, of ambition, by any other light than the darkness and horror of hell itself, and where the first messenger that speaks to me doth not say, "Thou mayest die," no, nor "Thou must die," but "Thou art dead"; and where the first notice that my soul hath of her sickness is irrecoverableness, irremediableness: But, O my God, Job did not charge thee foolishly in his temporal afflictions, nor may I in my spiritual. Thou hast imprinted a pulse in our soul, but we do not examine it; a voice in our conscience, but we do not hearken unto it. We talk it out, we jest it out, we drink it out, we sleep it out; and when we wake, we do not say with Jacob, "Surely the Lord is in this place, and I knew it not": but though we might know it, we do not, we will not. But will God pretend to make a watch, and leave out the spring? to make so many various wheels in the faculties of the soul, and in the organs of the body, and leave out grace, that should move them? or will God make a spring, and not wind it up? Infuse his first grace, and not second it with more, without which we can no more use his first grace when we have it, than we could dispose ourselves by nature to have it? But alas, that is not our case; we are all prodigal sons, and not disinherited; we have received our portion, and mispent it, not been denied it. We are God's tenants here, and yet here, he, our landlord, pays us rents; not yearly, nor quarterly, but hourly, and quarterly; every minute he renews his mercy, but we will not understand, lest that we should be converted, and he should heal us.[1]

Prayer

O Eternal and most gracious God, who, considered in thyself, art a circle, first and last, and altogether; but, considered in thy working upon us, art a direct line, and leadest us from our beginning, through all our ways, to our end, enable me by thy grace to look forward to mine end, and to look backward too, to the considerations of thy mercies afforded me from the beginning; that so by that practice of considering thy mercy, in my beginning in this world, when thou plantedst me in the Christian church, and thy mercy in the beginning in the other world, when thou writest me in the book of life, in my election, I may come to a holy consideration of thy mercy in the beginning of all my actions here: that in all the beginnings, in all the accesses and approaches, of spiritual sicknesses of sin, I may hear and hearken to that voice, "O thou man of God, there is death in the pot,"[2] and so refrain from that which I was so hungerly, so greedily flying to. "A faithful ambassador is health,"[3] says thy wise servant Solomon. Thy voice received in the beginning of a sickness, of a sin, is true health. If I can see that light betimes, and hear that voice early, "Then shall my light break

---

1. Matt. 13:16.
2. 2 Kings, 4:40.
3. Prov. 13:17.

forth as the morning, and my health shall spring forth speedily."[4] Deliver me therefore, O my God, from these vain imaginations; that it is an over-curious thing, a dangerous thing, to come to that tenderness, that rawness, that scrupulousness, to fear every concupiscence, every offer of sin, that this suspicious and jealous diligence will turn to an inordinate dejection of spirit, and a diffidence in thy care and providence; but keep me still established, both in a constant assurance, that thou wilt speak to me at the beginning of every such sickness, at the approach of every such sin; and that, if I take knowledge of that voice then, and fly to thee, thou wilt preserve me from falling, or raise me again, when by natural infirmity I am fallen. Do this, O Lord, for his sake, who knows our natural infirmities, for he had them, and knows the weight of our sins, for he paid a dear price for them, thy Son, our Saviour, Christ Jesus. Amen.

---

4. Isaiah, 58:8.

IV

The Physician Is Sent for

Meditation

It is too little to call man a little world; except God, man is a diminutive to nothing. Man consists of more pieces, more parts, than the world; than the world doth, nay, than the world is. And if those pieces were extended, and stretched out in man as they are in the world, man would be the giant, and the world the dwarf; the world but the map, and the man the world. If all the veins in our bodies were extended to rivers, and all the sinews to veins of mines, and all the muscles that lie upon one another, to hills, and all the bones to quarries of stones, and all the other pieces to the proportion of those which correspond to them in the world, the air would be too little for this orb of man to move in, the firmament would be but enough for this star; for, as the whole world hath nothing, to which something in man doth not answer, so hath man many pieces of which the whole world hath no representation. Enlarge this meditation upon this great world, man, so far as to consider the immensity of the creatures this world produces; our creatures are our thoughts, creatures that are born giants; that reach from east to west, from earth to heaven; that do not only bestride all the sea and land, but span the sun and firmament at once; my thoughts reach all, comprehend all. Inexplicable mystery; I their creator am in a close prison, in a sick bed, any where, and any one of by creatures, my thoughts, is with the sun, and beyond the sun, overtakes the sun, and overgoes the sun in one pace, one step, everywhere. And then, as the other world produces serpents and vipers, malignant and venomous creatures, and worms and caterpillars, that endeavour to devour that world which produces them, and monsters compiled and complicated of divers parents and kinds; so this world, ourselves, produces all these in us, in producing diseases, and sicknesses of all those sorts: venomous and infections diseases, feeding and consuming diseases, and manifold and entangled diseases made up of many several ones. And can the other world name so many venomous, so many consuming, so many monstrous creatures, as we can diseases of all these kinds? O miserable abundance, O beggarly riches! how much do we lack of having remedies for every disease, when as yet we have not names for them? But we have a Hercules against these giants, these monsters; that is, the physician; he musters up all the forces of the other world to succour this, all nature to relieve man. We have the physician, but we are not the physician. Here we shrink in our proportion, sink in our dignity, in respect of very mean creatures, who are physicians to themselves. The hart that is pursued and wounded, they say, knows an herb, which being eaten throws off the arrow: a strange kind of vomit. The dog that pursues it, though he be subject to sickness, even proverbially, knows his grass that recovers him. And it may be true, that the drugger is as near to man as to other creatures; it may be that obvious and present simples, easy to be had, would cure him; but the apothecary is not so near him, nor the physician so near him, as they two are to other creatures. Man hath not that innate instinct, to apply those natural medicines to his present danger, as those inferior creatures have; he is not his own apothecary, his own physician, as they are. Call back therefore thy meditation again, and bring it down: what's become of man's great extent and proportion, when himself shrinks himself and consumes himself to a handful of dust; what's become of his soaring thoughts, his compassing thoughts, when himself brings himself to the ignorance, to the thoughtlessness, of the grave? His diseases are his own, but the physician is not; he hath them at home, but he must send for the physician.

Expostulation

I have not the righteousness of Job, but I have the desire of Job: "I would speak to the Almighty, and I would reason with God."[1] My God, my God, how soon wouldst thou have me go to the physician, and how far wouldst thou have me go with the physician? I know thou hast made the matter, and the man, and the art; and I go not from thee when I go to the physician. Thou didst not make clothes before there was a shame of the nakedness of the body, but thou didst make physic before there was any grudging of any sickness; for thou didst imprint a medicinal virtue in many simples, even from the beginning. Didst thou mean that we should be sick when thou didst so? when thou madest them? No more than thou didst mean, that we

---

1. Job 13:3.

DEVOTIONS

should sin, when thou madest us: thou foresawest both, but causedst neither. Thou, Lord, promisest here trees, "whose fruit shall be for meat, and their leaves for medicine."[2] It is the voice of thy Son, "Wilt thou be made whole?"[3] that draws from the patient a confession that he was ill, and could not make himself well. And it is thine own voice, "Is there no physician?"[4] that inclines us, disposes us, to accept thine ordinance. And it is the voice of the wise man, both for the matter, physic itself, "The Lord hath created medicines out of the earth, and he that is wise shall not abhor them,"[5] and for the art, and the person, the physician cutteth off a long disease. In all these voices thou sendest us to those helps which thou hast afforded us in that. But wilt not thou avow that voice too, "He that hath sinned against his Maker, let him fall into the hands of the physician,"[6] and wilt not thou afford me an understanding of those words? Thou, who sendest us for a blessing to the physician, dost not make it a curse to us to go when thou sendest. Is not the curse rather in this, that only he falls into the hands of the physician, that casts himself wholly, entirely upon the physician, confides in him, relies upon him, attends all from him, and neglects that spiritual physic which thou also hast instituted in thy church. So to fall into the hands of the physician is a sin, and a punishment of former sins; so, as Asa fell, who in his disease "sought not to the Lord, but to the physician."[7] Reveal therefore to me thy method, O Lord, and see whether I have followed it; that thou mayest have glory, if I have, and I pardon, if I have not, and help that I may. Thy method is, "In time of thy sickness, be not negligent": wherein wilt thou have my diligence expressed? "Pray unto the Lord, and he will make thee whole."[8] O Lord, I do; I pray, and pray thy servant David's prayer, "Have mercy upon me, O Lord, for I am weak; heal me, O Lord, for my bones are vexed":[9] I know that even my weakness is a reason, a motive, to induce thy mercy, and my sickness an occasion of thy sending health. When art thou so ready, when is it so seasonable to thee, to commiserate, as in misery? But is prayer for health in season, as soon as I am sick? Thy method goes further: "Leave off from sin, and order thy hands aright, and cleanse thy heart from all wickedness."[10] Have

---

2. Ezek. 47:12.
3. John 5:6.
4. Jer. 8:22.
5. Ecclus. 38:4.
6. Ecclus. 38:15.
7. 1 Chron. 16:12.
8. Ecclus. 38:9.
9. Psalm 6:2.
10. Ecclus. 38:10.

I, O Lord, done so? O Lord, I have; by thy grace, I am come to a holy detestation of my former sin. Is there any more? In thy method there is more: "Give a sweet savour, and a memorial of fine flour, and make a fat offering, as not being."[11] And, Lord, by thy grace, I have done that, sacrificed a little of that little which thou lentest me, to them for whom thou lentest it: and now in thy method, and by thy steps, I am come to that, "Then give place to the physician, for the Lord hath created him; let him not go from thee, for thou hast need of him."[12] I send for the physician, but I will hear him enter with those words of Peter, "Jesus Christ maketh thee whole";[13] I long for his presence, but I look "that the power of the Lord should be present to heal me."[14]

Prayer

O most mighty and most merciful God, who art so the God of health and strength, as that without thee all health is but the fuel, and all strength but the bellows of sin; behold me under the vehemence of two diseases, and under the necessity of two physicians, authorized by thee, the bodily, and the spiritual physician. I come to both as to thine ordinance, and bless and glorify thy name that, in both cases, thou hast afforded help to man by the ministry of man. Even in the new Jerusalem, in heaven itself, it hath pleased thee to discover a tree, which is "a tree of life there, but the leaves thereof are for the healing of the nations."[15] Life itself is with thee there, for thou art life; and all kinds of health, wrought upon us here by thine instruments, descend from thence. "Thou wouldst have healed Babylon, but she is not healed."[16] Take from me, O Lord, her perverseness, her wilfulness, her refractoriness, and hear thy Spirit saying in my soul: Heal me, O Lord, for I would be healed. "Ephraim saw his sickness, and Judah his wound; then went Ephraim to the Assyrian, and sent to King Jareb, yet could not he heal you, nor cure you of your wound."[17] Keep me back, O Lord, from them who misprofess arts of healing the soul, or of the body, by means not imprinted by thee in the church for the soul, or not in nature for the body. There is no spiritual health to be had by superstition, nor bodily by witchcraft; thou, Lord, and only thou, art Lord of both. Thou in

---

11. Ecclus. 38:11.
12. Ecclus. 38:12.
13. Acts, 9:34.
14. Luke, 5:17.
15. Rev. 22:2.
16. Jer. 51:9.
17. Hosea, 5:13.

DEVOTIONS

thyself art Lord of both, and thou in thy Son art the physician, the applier of both. "With his stripes we are healed,"[18] says the prophet there; there, before he was scourged, we were healed with his stripes; how much more shall I be healed now, now when that which he hath already suffered actually is actually and effectually applied to me? Is there any thing incurable, upon which that balm drops? Any vein so empty as that that blood cannot fill it? Thou promisest to heal the earth;[19] but it is when the inhabitants of the earth "pray that thou wouldst heal it." Thou promisest to heal their waters, but "their miry places and standing waters," thou sayest there, "thou wilt not heal."[20] My returning to any sin, if I should return to the ability of sinning over all my sins again, thou wouldst not pardon. Heal this earth, O my God, by repentant tears, and heal these waters, these tears, from all bitterness, from all diffidence, from all dejection, by establishing my irremovable assurance in thee. "Thy Son went about healing all manner of sickness."[21] (No disease incurable, none difficult; he healed them in passing.) "Virtue went out of him, and he healed all,"[22] all the multitude (no person incurable), he healed them "every whit"[23] (as himself speaks), he left no relics of the disease; and will this universal physician pass by this hospital, and not visit me? not heal me? not heal me wholly? Lord, I look not that thou shouldst say by thy messenger to me, as to Hezekiah, "Behold, I will heal thee, and on the third day thou shalt go up to the house of the Lord."[24] I look not that thou shouldst say to me, as to Moses in Miriam's behalf, when Moses would have had her healed presently, "If her father had but spit in her face, should she not have been ashamed seven days? Let her be shut up seven days, and then return,"[25] but if thou be pleased to multiply seven days (and seven is infinite), if this day must remove me till days shall be no more, seal to me my spiritual health, in affording me the seals of they church; and for my temporal health, prosper thine ordinance, in their hands who shall assist in the sickness, in that manner, and in that measure, as may most glorify thee, and most edify those who observe the issues of thy servants, to their own spiritual benefit.

---

18. Isaiah, 53:5.
19. 2 Chron. 7:14.
20. Ezek. 47:11.
21. Matt. 4:23.
22. Luke, 7:19.
23. John, 7:23.
24. 2 Kings 20:5.
25. Num. 12:14.

IX

Upon Their [the Physicians'] Consultation They Prescribe

Meditation

They have seen me and heard me, arraigned me in these fetters and received the evidence; I have cut up mine own anatomy, dissected myself,
and they are gone to read upon me. O how manifold and perplexed a thing,
nay, how wanton and various a thing, is ruin and destruction! God presented to David three kinds, war, famine and pestilence; Satan left out
these, and brought in fires from heaven and winds from the wilderness. If
there were no ruin but sickness, we see the masters of that art can scarce
number, not name all sicknesses; every thing that disorders a faculty, and
the function of that, is a sickness; the names will not serve them which are
given from the place affected, the pleurisy is so; nor from the effect which
it works, the falling sickness is so; they cannot have names enough, from
what it does, nor where it is, but they must extort names from what it is
like, what it resembles, and but in some one thing, or else they would lack
names; for the wolf, and the canker, and the polypus are so; and that
question whether there be more names or things, is as perplexed in sicknesses as in any thing else; except it be easily resolved upon that side that
there are more sicknesses than names. If ruin were reduced to that one
way, that man could perish no way but by sickness, yet his danger were
infinite; and if sickness were reduced to that one way, that there were no
sickness but a fever, yet the way were infinite still; for it would overload
and oppress any natural, disorder and discompose any artificial, memory,
to deliver the names of several fevers; how intricate a work then have they
who are gone to consult which of these sicknesses mine is, and then which
of these fevers, and then what it would do, and then how it may be
countermined. But even in ill it is a degree of good when the evil will admit
consultation. In many diseases, that which is but an accident, but a symptom of the main disease, is so violent, that the physician must attend the

262

cure of that, though he pretermit (so far as to intermit) the cure of the disease itself. Is it not so in states too? Sometimes the insolency of those that are great puts the people into commotions; the great disease, and the greatest danger to the head, is the insolency of the great ones; and yet they execute martial law, they come to present executions upon the people, whose commotion was indeed but a symptom, but an accident of the main disease; but this symptom, grown so violent, would allow no time for a consultation. Is it not so in the accidents of the diseases of our mind too? Is it not evidently so in our affections, in our passions? If a choleric man be ready to strike, must I go about to purge his choler, or to break the blow? But where there is room for consultation things are not desperate. They consult, so there is nothing rashly, inconsiderately done; and then they prescribe, they write, so there is nothing covertly, disguisedly, unavowedly done. In bodily diseases it is not always so; sometimes, as soon as the physician's foot is in the chamber, his knife is in the patient's arm; the disease would not allow a minute's forbearing of blood, nor prescribing of other remedies. In states and matter of government it is so too; they are sometimes surprised with such accidents, as that the magistrate asks not what may be done by law, but does that which must necessarily be done in that case. But it is a degree of good in evil, a degree that carries hope and comfort in it, when we may have recourse to that which is written, and that the proceedings may be apert, and ingenuous, and candid, and avowable, for that gives satisfaction and acquiescence. They who have received my anatomy of myself consult, and end their consultation in prescribing, and in prescribing physic; proper and convenient remedy; for if they should come in again and chide me for some disorder that had occasioned and induced, or that had hastened and exalted this sickness, or if they should begin to write now rules for my diet and exercise when I were well, this were to antedate or to postdate their consultation, not to give physic. It were rather a vexation than a relief, to tell a condemned prisoner, You might have lived if you had done this; and if you can get your pardon, you shall do well to take this or this course hereafter. I am glad they know (I have hid nothing from them), glad they consult (they hide nothing from one another), glad they write (they hide nothing from the world), glad that they write and prescribe physic, that there are remedies for the present case.

Expostulation

My God, my God, allow me a just indignation, a holy detestation of the insolency of that man who, because he was of that high rank, of whom thou hast said, "They are gods," thought himself more than equal to thee; that king of Aragon, Alphonsus, so perfect in the motions of the heavenly bodies as that he adventured to say, that if he had been of counsel with thee, in the making of the heavens, the heavens should have been disposed in a better order than they are. The king Amaziah would not endure thy prophet to reprehend him, but asked him in anger, "Art thou made of the king's counsel?"[1] When thy prophet Esaias asks that question, "Who hath directed the spirit of the Lord, or being his counsellor, hath taught him?"[2] it is after he had settled and determined that office upon thy Son, and him only, when he joins with those great titles, the mighty God and the Prince of peace, this also, the Counsellor;[3] and after he had settled upon him the spirit of might and of counsel.[4] So that then thou, O God, though thou have no counsel from man, yet dost nothing upon man without counsel. In the making of man there was a consultation; "Let us make man."[5] In the preserving of man, "O thou great Preserver of men,"[6] thou proceedest by counsel; for all thy external works are the works of the whole Trinity, and their hand is to every action. How much more must I apprehend that all you blessed and glorious persons of the Trinity are in consultation now, what you will do with this infirm body, with this leprous soul, that attends guiltily, but yet comfortably, your determination upon it. I offer not to counsel them who meet in consultation for my body now, but I open my infirmities, I anatomize my body to them. So I do my soul to thee, O my God, in an humble confession, that there is no vein in me that is not full of the blood of thy Son, whom I have crucified and crucified again, by multiplying many, and often repeating the same, sins; that there is no artery in me that hath not the spirit of error, the spirit of lust, the spirit of giddiness in it;[7] no bone in me that is not hardened with the custom of sin and nourished and suppled with the marrow of sin; no sinews, no ligaments, that do not tie and chain sin and sin together. Yet, O blessed and glorious Trinity, O holy and whole college, and yet but one physician, if you take this confession into a consultation, my case is not desperate, my destruction is not decreed. If your consultation determine in writing, if you refer me to that which is written, you intend my recovery: for all the way, O my God (ever constant to thine own ways), thou hast proceeded

---

1. 2 Chron. 25:16.
2. Isaiah, 42:13.
3. Isaiah, 9:6.
4. Isaiah, 11:2.
5. Gen. 1:26.
6. Job, 7:20.
7. 1 Tim. 4:1; Hos. 4:12; Isaiah, 19:14.

openly, intelligibly, manifestly by the book. From thy first book, the book of life, never shut to thee, but never thoroughly open to us; from thy second book, the book of nature, where, though sub-obscurely and in shadows, thou hast expressed thine own image; from thy third book, the Scriptures, where thou hadst written all in the Old, and then lightedst us a candle to read it by, in the New, Testament; to these thou hadst added the book of just and useful laws, established by them to whom thou hast committed thy people; to those, the manuals, the pocket, the bosom books of our own consciences; to those thy particular books of all our particular sins; and to those, the books with seven seals, which only "the Lamb which was slain, was found worthy to open";[8] which, I hope, it shall not disagree with the meaning of thy blessed Spirit to interpret the promulgation of their pardon and righteousness who are washed in the blood of that Lamb; and if thou refer me to these books, to a new reading, a new trial by these books, this fever may be but a burning in the hand and I may be saved, though not by my book, mine own conscience, nor by thy other books, yet by thy first, the book of life, thy decree for my election, and by thy last, the book of the Lamb, and the shedding of his blood upon me. If I be still under consultation, I am not condemned yet; if I be sent to these books, I shall not be condemned at all; for though there be something written in some of those books (particularly in the Scriptures) which some men turn to poison, yet upon these consultations (these confessions, these takings of our particular cases into thy consideration) thou intendest all for physic; and even from those sentences from which a too late repenter will suck desperation, he that seeks thee early shall receive thy morning dew, thy seasonable mercy, thy forward consolation.

Prayer

O Eternal and most gracious God, who art of so pure eyes as that thou canst not look upon sin, and we of so unpure constitutions as that we can present no object but sin, and therefore might justly fear that thou wouldst turn thine eyes for ever from us, as, though we cannot endure afflictions in ourselves, yet in thee we can; so, though thou canst not endure sin in us, yet in thy Son thou canst, and he hath taken upon himself, and presented to thee, all those sins which might displease thee in us. There is an eye in nature that kills as soon as it sees, the eye of a serpent; no eye in nature that nourishes us by looking upon us; but thine eye, O Lord, does so. Look

---

8. Rev. 7:1.

therefore upon me, O Lord, in this distress and that will recall me from the borders of this bodily death; look upon me, and that will raise me again from that spiritual death in which my parents buried me when they begot me in sin, and in which I have pierced even to the jaws of hell by multiplying such heaps of actual sins upon that foundation, that root of original sin. Yet take me again into your consultation, O blessed and glorious Trinity; and though the Father know that I have defaced his image received in my creation; though the Son know I have neglected mine interest in the redemption; yet, O blessed Spirit, as thou art to my conscience so be to them, a witness that, at this minute, I accept that which I have so often, so rebelliously refused, thy blessed inspirations; be thou my witness to them that, at more pores than this slack body sweats tears, this sad soul weeps blood; and more for the displeasure of my God, than for the stripes of his displeasure. Take me, then, O blessed and glorious Trinity, into a recon-sultation, and prescribe me any physic. If it be a long and painful holding of this soul in sickness, it is physic if I may discern thy hand to give it; and it is physic if it be a speedy departing of this soul, if I may discern thy hand to receive it.

XVI

From the Bells of the Church Adjoining, I Am Daily Remembered of My Burial in the Funerals of Others

Meditation

We have a convenient author,[1] who writ a discourse of bells when he was prisoner in Turkey. How would he have enlarged himself if he had been my fellow-prisoner in this sick bed, so near to that steeple which never ceases, no more than the harmony of the spheres, but is more heard. When the Turks took Constantinople, thy melted the bells into ordnance; I have heard both bells and ordnance, but never been so much affected with those as with these bells. I have lain near a steeple[2] in which there are said to be more than thirty bells, and near another, where there is one so big, as that the clapper is said to weigh more than six hundred pounds,[3] yet never so affected as here. Here the bells can scarce solemnize the funeral of any person, but that I knew him, or knew that he was my neighbour: we dwelt in houses near to one another before, but now he is gone into that house into which I must follow him. There is a way of correcting the children of great persons, that other children are corrected in their behalf, and in their names, and this works upon them who indeed had more deserved it. And when these bells tell me, that now one, and now another is buried, must not I acknowledge that they have the correction due to me, and paid the debt that I owe? There is a story of a bell in a monastery[4] which, when any of the house was sick to death, rung always voluntarily, and they knew the inevitableness of the danger by that. It rung once when no man was sick,

---

1. Magius.
2. Antwerp.
3. Roan.
4. Roccha.

267

but the next day one of the house fell from the steeple and died, and the bell held the reputation of a prophet still. If these bells that warn to a funeral now, were appropriated to none, may not I, by the hour of the funeral, supply? How many men that stand at an execution, if they would ask, For what dies that man? should hear their own faults condemned, and see themselves executed by attorney? We scarce hear of any man preferred, but we think of ourselves that we might very well have been that man; why might not I have been that man that is carried to his grave now? Could I fit myself to stand or sit in any man's place, and not to lie in any man's grave? I may lack much of the good parts of the meanest, but I lack nothing of the mortality of the weakest; they may have acquired better abilities than I, but I was born to as many infirmities as they. To be an incumbent by lying down in a grave, to be a doctor by teaching mortification by example, by dying, though I may have seniors, others may be older than I, yet I have proceeded apace in a good university, and gone a great way in a little time, by the furtherance of a vehement fever, and whosoever these bells bring to the ground today, if he and I had been compared yesterday, perchance I should have been thought likelier to come to this preferment then than he. God hath kept the power of death in his own hands, lest any man should bribe death. If man knew the gain of death, the ease of death, he would solicit, he would provoke death to assist him by any hand which he might use. But as when men see many of their own professions preferred, it ministers a hope that that may light upon them; so when these hourly bells tell me of so many funerals of men like me, it presents, if not a desire that it may, yet a comfort whensoever mine shall come.

Expostulation

My God, my God, I do not expostulate with thee, but with them who dare do that; who dare expostulate with thee, when in the voice of thy church thou givest allowance to this ceremony of bells at funerals. Is it enough to refuse it, because it was in use among the Gentiles? so were funerals too. Is it because some abuses may have crept in amongst Christians? Is that enough, that their ringing hath been said to drive away evil spirits? Truly, that is so far true, as that the evil spirit is vehemently vexed in their ringing, therefore, because that action brings the congregation together, and unites God and his people, to the destruction of that kingdom which the evil spirit usurps. In the first institution of thy church in this world, in the foundation of thy militant church amongst the Jews, thou didst appoint the calling of the assembly in to be by trumpet;[5] and when they were in, then thou gavest them the sound of bells in the garment of thy priest.[6] In the triumphant church, thou employest both too, but in an inverted order; we enter into the triumphant church by the sound of bells (for we enter when we die); and then we receive our further edification, or consummation, by the sound of trumpets at the resurrection. The sound of thy trumpets thou didst impart to secular and civil uses too, but the sound of bells only to sacred. Lord, let not us break the communion of saints in that which was intended for the advancement of it; let not that pull us asunder from one another, which was intended for the assembling of us in the militant, and associating of us to the triumphant church. But he, for whose funeral these bells ring now, was at home, at his journey's end yesterday; why ring they now? a man, that is a world, is all the things in the world; he is an army, and when an army marches, the van may lodge tonight where the rear comes not till tomorrow. A man extends to his act and to his example; to that which he does, and that which he teaches; so do those things that concern him, so do these bells; that which rung yesterday was to convey him out of the world in his van, in his soul; that which rung today was to bring him in his rear, in his body, to the church; and this continuing of ringing after his entering is to bring him to me in the application. Where I lie I could hear the psalm, and did join with the congregation in it; but I could not hear the sermon, and these latter bells are a repetition sermon to me. But, O my God, my God, do I that have this fever need other remembrances of my mortality? Is not mine own hollow voice, voice enough to pronounce that to me? Need I look upon a death's head in a ring, that have one in my face? or go for death to my neighbour's house, that have him in my bosom? We cannot, we cannot, O my God, take in too many helps for religious duties; I know I cannot have any better image of thee than thy Son, nor any better image of him than his Gospel; yet must not I with thanks confess to thee, that some historical pictures of his have sometimes put me upon better meditations than otherwise I should have fallen upon? I know thy church needed not to have taken in, from Jew, or Gentile, any supplies for the exaltation of thy glory, or our devotion; of absolute necessity I know she needed not; but yet we owe thee our thanks, that thou hast given her leave to do so, and that as, in making us Christians, thou didst not destroy that which we were before,

---

5. Numb. 10:2.
6. Exod. 18:33–4.

natural men, so, in the exalting of our religious devotions now we are Christians, thou hast been pleased to continue to us those assistances which did work upon the affections of natural men before; for thou lovest a good man as thou lovest a good Christian; and though grace be merely from me, yet thou dost not plant grace but in good natures.

Prayer

O eternal and most gracious God, who having consecrated our living bodies to thine own Spirit, and made us temples of the Holy Ghost, dost also require a respect to be given to these temples, even when the priest is gone out of them, to these bodies when the soul is departed from them, I bless and glorify thy name, that as thou takest care in our life of every hair of our head, so dost thou also of every grain of ashes after our death. Neither dost thou only do good to us all in life and death, but also wouldst have us do good to one another, as in a holy life, so in those things which accompany our death. In that contemplation I make account that I hear this dead brother of ours, who is now carried out to his burial, to speak to me, and to preach my funeral sermon in the voice of these bells. In him, O God, thou hast accomplished to me even the request of Dives to Abraham; thou hast sent one from the dead to speak unto me. He speaks to me aloud from the steeple; he whispers to me at these curtains, and he speaks thy words: "Blessed are the dead which die in the Lord from henceforth."[7] Let this prayer therefore, O my God, be as my last gasp, my expiring, my dying in thee; that if this be the hour of my transmigration, I may die the death of a sinner, drowned in my sins, in the blood of thy Son; and if I live longer, yet I may now die the death of the righteous, die to sin; which death is a resurrection to a new life. "Thou killest and thou givest life": which soever comes, it comes from thee; which way soever it comes, let me come to thee.

---

7. Rev. 14:13.

XVII

Now, This Bell Tolling Softly for Another, Says to Me: Thou Must Die

Meditation

Perchance he for whom this bell tolls may be so ill, as that he knows not it tolls for him; and perchance I may think myself so much better than I am, as that they who are about me, and see my state, may have caused it to toll for me, and I know not that. The church is Catholic, universal, so are all her actions; all that she does belongs to all. When she baptizes a child, that action concerns me; for that child is thereby connected to that body which is my head too, and ingrafted into that body whereof I am a member. And when she buries a man, that action concerns me: all mankind is of one author, and is one volume; when one man dies, one chapter is not torn out of the book, but translated into a better language; and every chapter must be so translated; God employs several translators; some pieces are translated by age, some by sickness, some by war, some by justice; but God's hand is in every translation, and his hand shall bind up all our scattered leaves again for that library where every book shall lie open to one another. As therefore the bell that rings to a sermon calls not upon the preacher only, but upon the congregation to come, so this bell calls us all; but how much more me, who am brought so near the door by this sickness. There was a contention as far as a suit (in which both piety and dignity, religion and estimation, were mingled), which of the religious orders should ring to prayers first in the morning; and it was determined, that they should ring first that rose earliest. If we understand aright the dignity of this bell that tolls for our evening prayer, we would be glad to make it ours by rising early, in that application, that it might be ours as well as his, whose indeed it is. The bell doth toll for him that thinks it doth; and though it intermit again, yet from that minute that that occasion wrought upon him, he is united to God. Who casts not up his eye to the sun when it rises? but who

271

takes off his eye from a comet when that breaks out? Who bends not his ear to any bell which upon any occasion rings? but who can remove it from that bell which is passing a piece of himself out of this world? No man is an island, entire of itself; every man is a piece of the continent, a part of the main. If a clod be washed away by the sea, Europe is the less, as well as if a promontory were, as well as if a manor of thy friend's or of thine own were: any man's death diminishes me, because I am involved in mankind, and therefore never send to know for whom the bell tolls; it tolls for thee. Neither can we call this a begging of misery, or a borrowing of misery, as though we were not miserable enough of ourselves, but must fetch in more from the next house, in taking upon us the misery of our neighbours. Truly it were an excusable covetousness if we did, for affliction is a treasure, and scarce any man hath enough of it. No man hath affliction enough that is not matured and ripened by it, and made fit for God by that affliction. If a man carry treasure in bullion, or in a wedge of gold, and have none coined into current money, his treasure will not defray him as he travels. Tribulation is treasure in the nature of it, but it is not current money in the use of it, except we get nearer and nearer our home, heaven, by it. Another man may be sick too, and sick to death, and this affliction may lie in his bowels, as gold in a mine, and be of no use to him; but this bell, that tells me of his affliction, digs out and applies that gold to me: if by this consideration of another's danger I take mine own into contemplation, and so secure myself, by making my recourse to my God, who is our only security.

Expostulation

My God, my God, is this one of thy ways of drawing light out of darkness, to make him for whom this bell tolls, now in this dimness of his sight, to become a superintendent, an overseer, a bishop, to as many as hear his voice in this bell, and to give us a confirmation in this action? Is this one of thy ways, to raise strength out of weakness, to make him who cannot rise from his bed, nor stir in his bed, come home to me, and in this sound give me the strength of healthy and vigorous instructions? O my God, my God, what thunder is not a well-tuned cymbal, what hoarseness, what harshness, is not a clear organ, if thou be pleased to set thy voice to it? And what organ is not well played on if thy hand be upon it? Thy voice, thy hand, is in this sound, and in this one sound I hear this whole concert. I hear thy Jacob call unto his sons and say, "Gather yourselves together, that I may tell you what shall befall you in the last days":[1] he says, That which I am now, you must be then. I hear thy Moses telling me, and all within the compass of this sound, "This is the blessing wherewith I bless you before my death";[2] this, that before your death, you would consider your own in mine. I hear thy prophet saying to Hezekiah, "Set thy house in order, for thou shalt die, and not live":[3] he makes use of his family, and calls this a setting of his house in order, to compose us to the meditation of death. I hear thy apostle saying, "I think it meet to put you in rememberance, knowing that shortly I must go out of this tabernacle":[4] this is the publishing of his will, and this bell is our legacy, the applying of his present condition to our use. I hear that which makes all sounds music, and all music perfect; I hear thy Son himself saying, "Let not your hearts be troubled";[5] only I hear this change, that whereas thy Son says there, "I go to prepare a place for you," this man in this sound says, I send to prepare you for a place, for a grave. But, O my God, my God, since heaven is glory and joy, why do not glorious and joyful things lead us, induce us to heaven? Thy legacies in thy first will, in the Old Testament, were plenty and victory, wine and oil, milk and honey, alliances of friends, ruin of enemies, peaceful hearts and cheerful countenances, and by these galleries thou broughtest them into thy bedchamber, by these glories and joys, to the joys and glories of heaven. Why hast thou changed thine old ways, and carried us by the ways of discipline and mortification, by the ways of mourning and lamentation, by the ways of miserable ends and miserable anticipations of those miseries, in appropriating the exemplar miseries of others to ourselves, and usurping upon their miseries as our own, to our prejudice? Is the glory of heaven no perfecter in itself, but that it needs a foil of depression and ingloriousness in this world, to set it off? Is the joy of heaven no perfecter in itself, but that it needs the sourness of this life to give it a taste? Is that joy and that glory but a comparative glory and a comparative joy? not such in itself, but such in comparison of the joylessness and the ingloriousness of this world? I know, my God, it is far, far otherwise. As thou thyself, who art all, art made of no substances, so the joys and glory which are with thee are made of none of these circum-

1. Gen. 49:1.
2. Deut. 33:1.
3. 2 Kings, 20:1.
4. 2 Pet. 1:13.
5. John, 14:1.

stances, essential joy, and glory essential. But why then, my God, wilt thou not begin them here? Pardon, O God, this unthankful rashness; I that ask why thou dost not, find even now in myself, that thou dost; such joy, such glory, as that I conclude upon myself, upon all, they that find not joys in their sorrows, glory in their dejections in this world, are in a fearful danger of missing both in the next.

Prayer

O eternal and most gracious God, who hast been pleased to speak to us, not only in the voice of nature, who speaks in our hearts, and of thy word, which speaks to our ears, but in the speech of speechless creatures, in Balaam's ass, in the speech of unbelieving men, in the confession of Pilate, in the speech of the devil himself, in the recognition and attestation of thy Son, I humbly accept thy voice in the sound of this sad and funeral bell. And first, I bless thy glorious name, that in this sound and voice I can hear thy instructions, in another man's to consider mine own condition; and to know, that this bell which tolls for another, before it come to ring out, may take me in too. As death is the wages of sin it is due to me; as death is the end of sickness it belongs to me; and though so disobedient a servant as I may be afraid to die, yet to so merciful a master as thou I cannot be afraid to come; and therefore into thy hands, O my God, I commend my spirit, a surrender which I know thou wilt accept, whether I live or die; for thy servant David made it,[6] when he put himself into thy protection for his life; and thy blessed Son made it, when he delivered up his soul at his death: declare thou thy will upon me, O Lord, for life or death in thy time; receive my surrender of myself now; into thy hands, O Lord, I commend my spirit. And being thus, O my God, prepared by thy correction, mellowed by thy chastisement, and conformed to thy will by thy Spirit, having received thy pardon for my soul, and asking no reprieve for my body, I am bold, O Lord, to bend my prayers to thee for his assistance, the voice of whose bell hath called me to his devotion. Lay hold upon his soul, O God, till that soul have thoroughly considered his account; and how few minutes soever it have to remain in that body, let the power of thy Spirit recompense the shortness of time, and perfect his account before he pass away; present his sins so to him, as that he may know what thou forgivest, and not doubt of thy forgiveness, let him stop upon the infiniteness of those sins, but dwell upon the infiniteness of thy mercy; let him discern his own

---

6. Psalm 31:5.

demerits, but wrap himself up in the merits of thy Son Christ Jesus; breathe inward comforts to his heart, and afford him the power of giving such outward testimonies thereof, as all that are about him may derive comforts from thence, and have this edification, even in this dissolution, that though the body be going the way of all flesh, yet that soul is going the way of all saints. When thy Son cried out upon the cross, "My God, my God, why hast thou forsaken me?" he spake not so much in his own person, as in the person of the church, and of his afflicted members, who in deep distresses might fear thy forsaking. This patient, O most blessed God, is one of them; in his behalf, and in his name, hear thy Son crying to thee, "My God, my God, why hast thou forsaken me?" and forsake him not; but with thy left hand lay his body in the grave (if that be thy determination upon him), and with thy right hand receive his soul into thy kingdom, and unite him and us in one communion of saints. Amen.

XX

Upon These Indications of Digested Matter, They Proceed to Purge

Meditation

Though counsel seem rather to consist of spiritual parts than action, yet action is the spirit and the soul of counsel. Counsels are not always determined in resolutions, we cannot always say, this was concluded; actions are always determined in effects, we can say, this was done. Then have laws their reverence and their majesty, when we see the judge upon the bench executing them. Then have counsels of war their impressions and their operations, when we see the seal of an army set to them. It was an ancient way of celebrating the memory of such as deserved well of the state, to afford them that kind of statuary representation, which was then called Hermes, which was the head and shoulders of a man standing upon a cube, but those shoulders without arms and hands. Altogether it figured a constant supporter of the state, by his counsel; but in this hieroglyphic, which they made without hands, they pass their consideration no farther but that the counsellor should be without hands, so far as not to reach out his hand to foreign temptations of bribes, in matters of counsel, and that it was not necessary that the head should employ his own hand; that the same men should serve in the execution which assisted in the counsel; but that there should not belong hands to every head, action to every counsel, was never intended so much as in figure and representation. For as matrimony is scarce to be called matrimony where there is a resolution against the fruits of matrimony, against the having of children,[1] so counsels are not counsels, but illusions, where there is from the beginning no purpose to execute the determinations of those counsels. The arts and sciences are most properly referred to the head; that is their proper element and sphere;

---

1. August.

but yet the art of proving, logic, and the art of persuading, rhetoric, are deduced to the hand, and that expressed by a hand contracted into a fist, and this by a hand enlarged and expanded; and evermore the power of man, and the power of God, himself is expressed so. All things are in his hand; neither is God so often presented to us, by names that carry our consideration upon counsel, as upon execution of counsel; he oftener is called the Lord of Hosts than by all other names, that may be referred to the other signification. Hereby therefore we take into our meditation the slippery condition of man, whose happiness in any kind, the defect of any one thing conducing to that happiness, may ruin; but it must have all the pieces to make it up. Without counsel, I had not got thus far; without action and practice, I should go no farther towards health. But what is the present necessary action? Purging; a withdrawing, a violating of nature, a farther weakening. O dear price, and O strange way of addition, to do it by subtraction; of restoring nature, to violate nature; of providing strength, by increasing weakness. Was I not sick before? And is it a question of comfort to be asked now, did your physic make you sick? Was that it that my physic promised, to make me sick? This is another step upon which we may stand, and see farther into the misery of man, the time, the season of his misery; it must be done now. O over-cunning, over-watchful, over-diligent, and over-sociable misery of man, that seldom comes alone, but then when it may accompany other miseries, and so put one another into the higher exaltation, and better heart. I am ground even to an attenuation and must proceed to evacuation, all ways to exinanition and annihilation.

Expostulation

My God, my God, the God of order, but yet not of ambition, who assignest place to every one, but not contention for place, when shall it be thy pleasure to put an end to all quarrels for spiritual precedences? When shall men leave their uncharitable disputations, which is to take place, faith or repentance, and which, when we consider faith and works? The head and the hand too are required to a perfect natural man; counsel and action too, to a perfect civil man; faith and works too, to him that is perfectly spiritual. But because it is easily said, I believe, and because it doth not easily lie in proof, nor is easily demonstrable by any evidence taken from my heart (for who sees that, who searches those rolls?) whether I do believe or no, is it not therefore, O my God, that thou dost so frequently, so earnestly, refer us to the hand, to the observation of actions? There is a little suspicion, a little imputation laid upon over-tedious and dilatory counsels. Many good occasions slip away in long consultations; and it may be a degree of sloth, to be too long in mending nets, though that must be done. "He that observeth the wind shall not sow, and he that regardeth the clouds shall not reap";[2] that is, he that is too dilatory, too superstitious in these observations, and studies but the excuse of his own idleness in them; but that which the same wise and royal servant of thine says in another place, all accept, and ask no comment upon it, "He becometh poor that dealeth with a slack hand, but the hand of the diligent maketh rich";[3] all evil imputed to the absence, all good attributed to the presence of the hand. I know, my God (and I bless thy name for knowing it, for all good knowledge is from thee), that thou considerest the heart; but thou takest not off thine eye till thou come to the hand. Nay, my God, doth not thy Spirit intimate that thou beginnest where we begin (at least, that thou allowest us to begin there), when thou orderest thine own answer to thine own question, "Who shall ascend into the hill of the Lord?" thus, "He that hath clean hands, and a pure heart?"[4] Dost thou not (at least) send us first to the hand? And is not the work of their hands that declaration of their holy zeal, in the present execution of manifest idolators, called a consecration of themselves,[5] by thy Holy Spirit? Their hands are called all themselves; for even counsel itself goes under that name in thy word, who knowest best how to give right names: because the counsel of the priests assisted David,[6] Saul says the hand of the priest is with David. And that which is often said by Moses, is very often repeated by thy other prophets, "These and these things the Lord spake,"[7] and "the Lord said," and "the Lord commanded," not by the counsels, not by the voice, but by the "hand of Moses," and by the "hand of the prophets." Evermore we are referred for our evidence of others, and of ourselves, to the hand, to action, to works. There is something before it, believing; and there is something after it, suffering; but in the most eminent, and obvious, and conspicuous place stands doing. Why then, O my God, my blessed God, in the ways of my spiritual strength, come I so slow to action? I was whipped by thy rod, before I came to consultation, to consider my state; and shall I go no farther? As he that would describe a circle in paper, if he have brought that circle within one inch of finishing, yet if he remove his compass he cannot make it up a perfect circle except he fall to work again, to find out the same centre, so, though setting that foot of my compass upon thee, I have gone so far as to

2. Eccles. 11:4.
3. Prov. 10:4.
4. Psalm 24:3.
5. Exod. 32:29.
6. 1 Sam. 22:17.
7. Lev. 8:36.

the consideration of myself, yet if I depart from thee, my centre, all is imperfect. This proceeding to action, therefore, is a returning to thee, and a working upon myself by thy physic, by thy purgative physic, a free and entire evacuation of my soul by confession. The working of purgative physic is violent and contrary to nature. O Lord, I decline not this potion of confession, however it may be contrary to a natural man. To take physic, and not according to the right method, is dangerous.[8] O Lord, I decline not that method in this physic, in things that burthen my conscience, to make my confession to him, into whose hands thou hast put the power of absolution. I know that "physic may be made so pleasant as that it may easily be taken; but not so pleasant as the virtue and nature of the medicine be extinguished."[9] I know I am not submitted to such a confession as is a rack and torture of the conscience; but I know I am not exempt from all. If it were merely problematical, left merely indifferent whether we should take this physic, use this confession, or no, a great physician acknowledges this to have been his practice, to minister to many things which he was not sure would do good, but never any other thing but such as he was sure would do no harm.[10] The use of this spiritual physic can certainly do no harm; and the church hath always thought that it might, and, doubtless, many humble souls have found, that it hath done them good. "I will therefore take the cup of salvation, and call upon thy name."[11] I will find this cup of compunction as full as I have formerly filled the cups of worldly confections, that so I may escape the cup of malediction and irrecoverable destruction that depends upon that. And since thy blessed and glorious Son, being offered, in the way to his execution, a cup of stupefaction,[12] to take away the sense of his pain (a charity afforded to condemned persons ordinarily in those places and times), refused that ease, and embraced the whole torment, I take not this cup, but this vessel of mine own sins into my contemplation, and I pour them out here according to the motions of thy Holy Spirit, and any where according to the ordinances of thy holy church.

Prayer

O eternal and most gracious God, who having married man and woman together, and made them one flesh, wouldst have them also to become one

---

8. Galen.
9. Galen.
10. Galen.
11. Psalm 116:13.
12. Mark 15:23.

soul, so as that they might maintain a sympathy in their affections, and have a conformity to one another in the accidents of this world, good or bad; so having married this soul and this body in me, I humbly beseech thee that my soul may look and make her use of thy merciful proceedings towards my bodily restitution, and go the same way to a spiritual. I am come, by thy goodness, to the use of thine ordinary means for my body, to wash away those peccant humours that endangered it. I have, O Lord, a river in my body, but a sea in my soul, and a sea swollen into the depth of a deluge, above the sea. Thou hast raised up certain hills in me heretofore, by which I might have stood safe from these inundations of sin. Even our natural faculties are a hill and might preserve us from some sin. Education, study, observation, example, are hills too, and might preserve us some. Thy church, and thy word, and thy sacraments, and thine ordinances are hills above these; thy spirit of remorse, and compunction, and repentance for former sin, are hills too; and to the top of all these hills thou hast brought me heretofore; but this deluge, this inundation, is got above all my hills; and I have sinned and sinned, and multiplied sin to sin, after all these thy assistances against sin, and where is there water enough to wash away this deluge? There is a red sea, greater than this ocean, and there is a little spring, through which this ocean may pour itself into that red sea. Let thy spirit of true contrition and sorrow pass all my sins, through these eyes, into the wounds of thy Son, and I shall be clean, and my soul so much better purged than my body, as it is ordained for better and a longer life.

XXI

God Prospers Their Practice,
and He, by Them,
Calls Lazarus out of His Tomb,
Me out of My Bed

Meditation

If man had been left alone in this world at first, shall I think that he would not have fallen? If there had been no woman, would not man have served to have been his own tempter? When I see him now subject to infinite weaknesses, fall into infinite sin without any foreign temptations, shall I think he would have had none, if he had been alone? God saw that man needed a helper, if he should be well; but to make woman ill, the devil saw that there needed no third. When God and we were alone in Adam, that was not enough; when the devil and we were alone in Eve, it was enough. O what a giant is man when he fights against himself, and what a dwarf when he needs or exercises his own assistance for himself? I cannot rise out of my bed till the physician enable me, nay, I cannot tell that I am able to rise till he tell me so. I do nothing, I know nothing of myself; how little and how impotent a piece of the world is any man alone? And how much less a piece of himself is that man? So little as that when it falls out (as it falls out in some cases) that more misery and more oppression would be an ease to a man, he cannot give himself that miserable addition of more misery. A man that is pressed to death, and might be eased by more weights, cannot lay those more weights upon himself: he can sin alone, and suffer alone, but not repent, not be absolved, without another. Another tells me, I may rise; and I do so. But is every raising a preferment? or is every present preferment a station? I am readier to fall to the earth, now I am up, than I was when I lay in the bed. O perverse way, irregular motion of man; even rising itself is the way to ruin! How many men are raised, and then do not fill the place they are raised to? No corner of any place can be

281

empty; there can be no vacuity. If that man do not fill the place, other men will; complaints of his insufficiency will fill it; nay, such an abhorring is there in nature of vacuity, that if there be but an imagination of not filling, in any man, that which is but imagination, neither will fill it, that is, rumour and voice, and it will be given out (upon no ground but imagination, and no man knows whose imagination), that he is corrupt in his place, or insufficient in his place, and another prepared to succeed him in his place. A man rises sometimes and stands not, because he doth not or is not believed to fill his place; and sometimes he stands not because he over-fills his place. He may bring so much virtue, so much justice, so much integrity to the place, as shall spoil the place, burthen the place; his integrity may be a libel upon his predecessor and cast an infamy upon him, and a burthen upon his successor to proceed by example, and to bring the place itself to an undervalue and the market to an uncertainty. I am up, and I seem to stand, and I go round, and I am a new argument of the new philosophy, that the earth moves round; why may I not believe that the whole earth moves, in a round motion, though that seem to me to stand, when as I seem to stand to my company, and yet am carried in a giddy and circular motion as I stand? Man hath no centre but misery; there, and only there, he is fixed, and sure to find himself. How little soever he be raised, he moves, and moves in a circle giddily; and as in the heavens there are but a few circles that go about the whole world, but many epicycles, and other lesser circles, but yet circles; so of those men which are raised and put into circles, few of them move from place to place, and pass through many and beneficial places, but fall into little circles, and, within a step or two, are at their end, and not so well as they were in the centre, from which they were raised. Every thing serves to exemplify, to illustrate man's misery. But I need go no farther than myself: for a long time I was not able to rise; at last I must be raised by others; and now I am up, I am ready to sink lower than before.

Expostulation

My God, my God, how large a glass of the next world is this! As we have an art, to cast from one glass to another, and so to carry the species a great way off, so hast thou, that way, much more; we shall have a resurrection in heaven; the knowledge of that thou castest by another glass upon us here; we feel that we have a resurrection from sin, and that by another glass too; we see we have a resurrection of the body from the miseries and calamities of this life. This resurrection of my body shows me the resurrection of my soul; and both here severally, of both together hereafter. Since thy martyrs under the altar press thee with their solicitation for the resurrection of the body to glory, thou wouldst pardon me, if I should press thee by prayer for the accomplishing of this resurrection, which thou hast begun in me, to health. But, O my God, I do not ask, where I might ask amiss, nor beg that which perchance might be worse for me. I have a bed of sin; delight in sin is a bed: I have a grave of sin; senselessness of sin is a grave: and where Lazarus had been four days, I have been fifty years in this putrefaction; why dost thou not call me, as thou didst him, "with a loud voice,"[1] since my soul is as dead as his body was? I need thy thunder, O my God; thy music will not serve me. Thou hast called thy servants, who are to work upon us in thine ordinance, by all these loud names—winds, and chariots, and falls of waters; where thou wouldst be heard, thou wilt be heard. When thy Son concurred with thee to the making of man, there it is but a speaking, but a saying. There, O blessed and glorious Trinity, was none to hear but you three, and you easily hear one another, because you say the same things. But when thy Son came to the work of redemption, thou spokest,[2] and they that heard it took it for thunder; and thy Son himself cried with a loud voice upon the cross twice,[3] as he who was to prepare his coming, John Baptist, was the voice of a crier, and not of a whisperer. Still, if it be thy voice, it is a loud voice. "These words," says thy Moses, "thou spokest with a great voice, and thou addedst no more,"[4] says he there. That which thou hast said is evident, and it is evident that none can speak so loud; none can bind us to hear him, as we must thee. "The Most High uttered his voice." What was his voice? "The Lord thundered from heaven,"[5] it might be heard; but this voice, thy voice, is also a "mighty voice";[6] not only mighty in power, it may be heard, nor mighty in obligation, it should be heard; but mighty in operation, it will be heard; and therefore hast thou bestowed a whole psalm[7] upon us, to lead us to the consideration of thy voice. It is such a voice as that thy Son says, "the dead shall hear it";[8] and that is my state. And why, O God, dost thou not speak to me, in that effectual loudness? Saint John heard a voice, and "he turned about to see the voice":[9] sometimes we are too curious of the instrument by what man God speaks; but thou speakest loudest when thou speakest to

1. John, 11:43.
2. John 12:28.
3. Matt. 27:46,50.
4. Deut. 5:22.
5. 2 Sam. 22:14.
6. Psalm 68:33.
7. Psalm 29.
8. John, 5:25.
9. Rev. 1:12.

283

JOHN DONNE

the heart. "There was silence, and I heard a voice," says one, to thy servant Job.[10] I hearken after thy voice in thine ordinances, and I seek not a whispering in conventicles; but yet, O my God, speak louder, that so, though I do hear thee now, then I may hear nothing but thee. My sins cry aloud; Cain's murder did so: my afflictions cry aloud; the "floods have lifted up their voice" (and waters are afflictions), "but thou, O Lord, art mightier than the voice of many waters";[11] than many temporal, many spiritual afflictions, than any of either kind: and why dost thou not speak to me in that voice? "What is man, and whereto serveth he? What is his good and what is his evil?"[12] My bed of sin is not evil, not desperately evil, for thou dost call me out of it; but my rising out of it is not good (not perfectly good), if thou call not louder, and hold me now I am up. O my God, I am afraid of a fearful application of those words, "When a man hath done, then he beginneth";[13] when this body is unable to sin, his sinful memory sins over his old sins again; and that which thou wouldst have us to remember for compunction, we remember with delight. "Bring him to me in his bed, that I may kill him,"[14] says Saul of David: thou hast not said so, that is not thy voice. Joash's own servants slew him when he was sick in his bed:[15] thou hast not suffered that, that my servants should so much as neglect me, or be weary of me in my sickness. Thou threatenest, that "as a shepherd takes out of the mouth of the lion two legs, or a piece of an ear, so shall the children of Israel, that dwell in Samaria, in the corner of a bed, and in Damascus, in a couch, be taken away";[16] and even they that are secure from danger shall perish. How much more might I, who was in the bed of death, die? But thou hast not so dealt with me. As they brought out sick persons in beds, that thy servant Peter's shadow might over-shadow them,[17] thou hast, O my God, over-shadowed me, refreshed me; but when wilt thou do more? When wilt thou do all? When wilt thou speak in thy loud voice? When wilt thou bid me "take up my bed and walk?"[18] As my bed is my affections, when shall I bear them so as to subdue them? As my bed is my afflictions, when shall I bear them so as not to murmur at them?

---

10. Job, 4:16.
11. Psalm 93:3,4.
12. Ecclus. 18:8.
13. Ecclus. 5:7.
14. 1 Sam. 19:15.
15. 2 Chron. 24:25.
16. Amos, 3:12.
17. Acts, 5:15.
18. Matt. 9:6.

When shall I take up my bed and walk? Not lie down upon it, as it is my pleasure, not sink under it, as it is my correction? But O my God, my God, the God of all flesh, and of all spirit, which thou declarest in this decayed flesh, that as this body is content to sit still, that it may learn to stand, and to learn by standing to walk, and by walking to travel, so my soul, by obeying this thy voice of rising, may by a farther and farther growth of thy grace proceed so, and be so established, as may remove all suspicions, all jealousies between thee and me, and may speak and hear in such a voice, as that still I may be acceptable to thee, and satisfied from thee.

Prayer

O eternal and most gracious God, who hast made little things to signify great, and conveyed the infinite merits of thy Son in the water of baptism, and in the bread and wine of thy other sacrament, unto us, receive the sacrifice of my humble thanks, that thou hast not only afforded me the ability to rise out of this bed of weariness and discomfort, but hast also made this bodily rising, by thy grace, an earnest of a second resurrection from sin, and of a third, to everlasting glory. Thy Son himself, always infinite in himself, and incapable of addition, was yet pleased to grow in the Virgin's womb, and to grow in stature in the sight of men. Thy good purposes upon me, I know, have their determination and perfection in thy holy will upon me; there thy grace is, and there I am altogether; but manifest them so unto me, in thy seasons, and in thy measures and degrees, that I may not only have that comfort of knowing thee to be infinitely good, but that also of finding thee to be every day better and better to me; and that as thou gavest Saint Paul the messenger of Satan, to humble him so for my humiliation, thou mayst give me thyself in this knowledge, that what grace soever thou afford me today, yet I should perish tomorrow if I had not had tomorrow's grace too. Therefore I beg of thee my daily bread; and as thou gavest me the bread of sorrow for many days, and since the bread of hope for some, and this day the bread of possessing, in rising by that strength, which thou the God of all strength hast infused into me, so, O Lord, continue to me the bread of life: the spiritual bread of life, in a faithful assurance in thee; the sacramental bread of life, in a worthy receiving of thee; and the more real bread of life in an everlasting union to thee. I know, O Lord, that when thou hast created angels, and they saw thee produce fowl, and fish, and beasts, and worms, they did not importune thee, and say, Shall we have no better creatures than these, no better companions than these? but stayed thy leisure, and then had man delivered over to them, not much inferior in nature to themselves. No more do I, O God, now that by thy first mercy I am able to rise, importune thee for present confirmation of health; nor now, that by thy mercy I am brought to see that thy correction hath wrought medicinally upon me, presume I upon that spiritual strength I have; but as I acknowledge that my bodily strength is subject to every puff of wind, so is my spiritual strength to every blast of vanity. Keep me therefore still, O my gracious God, in such a proportion of both strengths, as I may still have something to thank thee for, which I have received, and still something to pray for and ask at thy hand.

Prayers

I

From *Essays in Divinity*

1

O ETERNAL AND ALMIGHTY POWER, which being infinite, hast enabled a limited creature, faith, to comprehend thee; and being, even to angels but a passive mirror and looking-glass, art to us an active guest and domestic, (for thou hast said, "I stand at the door and knock, if any man hear me, and open the door, I will come unto him, and sup with him, and he with me"), and so thou dwellest in our hearts; and not there only, but even in our mouths; for though thou beest greater, and more removed, yet humbler and more communicable then the Kings of Egypt, or Roman Emperors, which disdained their particular distinguishing names, for Pharaoh and Caesar, names of confusion; hast contracted thine immensity, and shut thy self within syllables, and accepted a Name from us. O keep and defend my tongue from misusing that Name in lightness, passion, or falsehood; and my heart, from mistaking thy nature, by an inordinate preferring thy justice before thy mercy, or advancing this before that. And as, though thy self hadst no beginning thou gavest a beginning to all things in which thou wouldst be served and glorified; so, though this soul of mine, by which I partake thee, begin not now, yet let this minute, O God, this happy minute of thy visitation, be the beginning of her conversion, and shaking away confusion, darkness, and barrenness; and let her now produce creatures, thoughts, words, and deeds agreeable to thee. And let her not produce them, O God, out of any contemplation, or (I cannot say, Idea, but) chimera of my worthiness, either because I am a man and no worm, and within the pale of thy Church, and not in the wild forest, and enlightened with some glimmerings of natural knowledge; but merely out of nothing: nothing pre-existent in her self, but by power of thy divine will and word. By which, as thou didst so make heaven, as thou didst not neglect earth, and madest them answerable and agreeable to one another, so let my soul's creatures have that temper and harmony, that they be not by a misdevout consideration of the next life, stupidly and treacherously negligent of the offices and duties which thou enjoinest amongst us in this life; nor so anxious in these, that the other (which is our better business, though this also must be attended) be the less endeavored. Thou hast, O God, denied even to angels, the ability of arriving from one extreme to another, without passing the mean way between. Nor can we pass from the prison of our mother's womb, to thy palace, but we must walk (in that pace whereto thou hast enabled us) through the street of this life, and not sleep at the first corner, nor in the midst. Yet since my soul is sent immediately from thee, let me (for her return) rely, not principally but wholly upon thee and thy word: and for this body, made of preordained matter, and instruments, let me so use the material means of her sustaining, that I neither neglect the seeking, nor grudge the missing of the conveniencies of this life: And that for fame, which is a mean nature between them, I so esteem opinion, that I despise not others' thoughts of me, since most men are such, as most men think they be: nor so reverence it, that I make it always the rule of my actions. And because in this world my body was first made, and then my soul, but in the next my soul shall be first, and then my body, in my exterior and moral conversation let my first and presentest care be to give them satisfaction with whom I am mingled, because they may be scandalized, but thou, which seest hearts, canst not: but for my faith, let my first relation be to thee, because of that thou art justly jealous, which they cannot be. Grant these requests, O God, if I have asked fit things fitly, and as many more, under the same limitations, as are within that prayer which (as thy manna, which was meat for all tastes, and served to the appetite of him which took it, and was that which ever man would) includes all which all can ask, "Our Father which art," etc.

2

O ETERNAL GOD, as thou didst admit thy faithfull servant Abraham, to make the granting of one petition an encouragement and rise to another, and gavest him leave to gather upon thee from fifty to ten; so I beseech thee, that since by thy grace, I have thus long meditated upon thee, and spoken of thee, I may now speak to thee. As thou hast enlightened and enlarged me to contemplate thy greatness, so, O God, descend thou and stoop down to see my infirmities and the Egypt in which I live; and (if thy good pleasure be such) hasten mine Exodus and deliverance, for I desire to be dissolved, and be with thee. O Lord, I most humbly acknowledge and confess thine infinite mercy, that when thou hadst almost broke the staff of bread, and called a famine of thy word almost upon all the world, then thou broughtest me into this Egypt, where thou hadst appointed thy stewards to husband thy blessings, and to feed thy flock. Here also, O God, thou hast multiplied thy children in me, by begetting and cherishing in me reverent devotions, and pious affections towards thee, but that mine own corruption, mine own Pharaoh hath ever smothered and strangled them. And thou hast put me in my way towards thy land of promise, thy heavenly Canaan, by removing me from the Egypt of frequented and populous, glorious places, to a more solitary and desert retiredness, where I may more safely feed upon both thy mannas, thy self in thy Sacrament, and that other, which is true angel's food, contemplation of thee. O Lord, I most humbly acknowledge and confess, that I feel in me so many strong effects of thy power, as only for the ordinariness and frequency thereof, they are not miracles. For hourly thou rectifiest my lameness, hourly thou restorest my sight, and hourly not only deliverest me from the Egypt, but raisest me from the death of sin. My sin, O God, hath not only caused thy descent hither, and passion here; but by it I am become that hell into which thou descendest after thy passion; yea, after thy glorification: for hourly thou in thy Spirit descendest into my heart, to overthrow there legions of spirits of disobedience, and incredulity, and murmuring. O Lord, I most humbly acknowledge and confess, that by thy mercy I have a sense of thy justice; for not only those afflictions with which it pleaseth thee to exercise me, awaken me to consider how terrible thy severe justice is; but even the rest and security which thou affordest me, puts me often into fear, that thou reservest and sparest me for a greater measure of punishment. O Lord, I most humbly acknowledge and confess, that I have understood sin, by misunderstanding thy laws and judgements; but have done against thy known and revealed will. Thou hast set up many candlesticks, and kindled many lamps in me; but I have either blown them out, or carried them to guide me in by and forbidden ways. Thou hast given me a desire of knowledge, and some means to it, and some possession of it; and I have armed my self with thy weapons against thee: Yet, O God, have mercy upon me, for thine own sake have mercy upon me. Let not sin and me be able to exceed thee, nor to defraud thee, nor to frustrate thy purposes: But let me, in despite of me, be of so much use to thy glory, that by thy mercy to my sin, other sinners may see how much sin thou canst pardon. Thus show mercy to many in one: And show thy power and almightiness upon thy self, by casting manacles upon thine own hands, and calling back those thunder-bolts which thou hadst thrown against me. Show thy justice upon the common seducer and devourer of us all: and show to us so much of thy judgements, as may instruct, not condemn us. Hear us, O God, hear us, for this contrition which thou hadst put into us, who come to thee with that watch-word, by which thy Son hath assured us of access. "Our Father which art in heaven," etc.

3

O ETERNAL GOD, who art not only first and last, but in whom, first and last is all one; who in the height of thy justice, wouldest not spare thine own, and only most innocent Son; and yet in the depth of thy mercy, wouldst not have the wretchedest liver come to destruction; behold us, O God, here gathered together in thy fear, according to thine ordinance, and in confidence of thy promise, that when two or three are gathered together in thy name, thou wilt be in the midst of them, and grant them their petitions. We confess, O God, that we are not worthy so much as to confess, less to be heard, least of all to be pardoned our manifold sins and transgressions against thee. We have betrayed thy temples to prophaneness, our bodies to sensuality, thy fortresses to thine enemy, our souls to Satan. We have armed him with thy munition to fight against thee, by surrendering our eyes and ears, all our senses, all our faculties to be exercised and wrought upon, and tyrannized by him. Vanities and disguises have covered us, and thereby we are naked; licentiousness hath inflamed us, and thereby we are frozen; voluptuousness hath fed us, and thereby we are starved; the fancies and traditions of men have taught and instructed us, and thereby we are ignorant. These distempers thou only, O God, who art true and perfect harmony, canst tune and rectify and set in order again. Do so then, O most merciful Father, for thy most innocent Son's sake: and since he hath spread his arms upon the cross to receive the whole world, O Lord, shut out none of us (who are now fallen before the throne of thy majesty and thy mercy) from the benefit of his merits; but with as many of us as begin their conversion and newness of life this minute, this minute, O God, begin thou thy account with them, and put all that is past out of thy remembrance. Accept our humble thanks for all thy mercies; and continue and enlarge them upon the whole Church, etc.

4

O MOST GLORIOUS AND MOST GRACIOUS GOD, into whose presence our own consciences make us afraid to come, and from whose presence we cannot hide our selves, hide us in the wounds of thy Son, our

Savior Christ Jesus; and though our sins be as red as scarlet, give them there another redness, which may be acceptable in thy sight. We renounce, O Lord, all our confidence in this world; for this world passeth away, and the lusts thereof. We renounce all our confidence in our own merits, for we have done nothing in respect of that which we might have done; neither could we ever have done any such thing, but that still we must have remained unprofitable servants to thee. We renounce all confidence, even in our own confessions and accusations of ourselves; for our sins are above number if we would reckon them; above weight and measure, if we would weigh and measure them; and past finding out, if we would seek them in those dark corners in which we have multiplied them against thee. Yea we renounce all confidence even in our repentances, for we have found by many lamentable experiences that we never perform our promises to thee, never perfect our purposes in our selves, but relapse again and again into those sins which again and again we have repented. We have no confidence in this world, but in him who hath taken possession of the next world for us, by sitting down at thy right hand. We have no confidence in our merits, but in him whose merits thou hast been pleased to accept for us, and to apply to us, we have no confidence in our own confessions and repentances, but in that blessed Spirit, who is the author of them and loves to perfect his own works and build upon his own foundations, we have. Accept them therefore, O Lord, for their sakes whose they are; our poor endeavors, for thy glorious Son's sake, who gives them their root, and so they are his; our poor beginnings of sanctification, for thy blessed Spirit's sake, who gives them their growth, and so they are his: and for thy Son's sake, in whom only our prayers are acceptable to thee: and for thy Spirit's sake which is now in us, and must be so whensoever we do pray acceptably to thee; accept our humble prayers for, etc.

5

O ETERNAL AND MOST MERCIFUL GOD, against whom, as we know and acknowledge that we have multiplied contemptuous and rebellious sins, so we know and acknowledge too, that it were a more sinful contempt and rebellion then all those to doubt of thy mercy for them; have mercy upon us. In the merits and mediation of thy Son, our Savior Christ Jesus, be merciful unto us. Suffer not, O Lord, so great a waste as the effusion of his blood, without any return to thee; suffer not the expense of so rich a treasure as the spending of his life, without any purchase to thee; but as thou didst empty and evacuate his glory here upon earth, glorify us with that glory which his humiliation purchased for us in the kingdom of Heaven. And as thou didst empty that kingdom of thine, in a great part, by the banishment of those angels whose pride threw them into everlasting ruin, be pleased to repair that kingdom which their fall did so far depopulate, by assuming us into their places and making us rich with their confiscations. And to that purpose, O Lord, make us capable of that succession to thine angels there; begin in us here in this life an angelical purity, an angelical chastity, an angelical integrity to thy service, an angelical acknowledgement that we always stand in thy presence and should direct all our actions to thy glory. Rebuke us not, O Lord, in thine anger, that we have not done so till now; but enable us now to begin that great work; and imprint in us an assurance that thou receivest us now graciously, as reconciled, though enemies; and fatherly, as children, though prodigals; and powerfully, as the God of our salvation, though our own consciences testify against us. Continue and enlarge thy blessings upon the whole Church, etc.

II

Selections from *Devotions Upon Emergent Occasions*

1

O MOST MIGHTY AND MOST MERCIFUL GOD, who, though thou have taken me off of my feet, hast not taken me off of my foundation, which is thyself; who, though thou have removed me from that upright form in which I could stand and see thy throne, the heavens, yet hast not removed from me that light by which I can lie and see thyself; who, though thou have weakened my bodily knees, that they cannot bend to thee, hast yet left me the knees of my heart; which are bowed unto thee evermore; as thou hast made this bed thine altar, make me thy sacrifice; and as thou makest thy Son Christ Jesus the priest, so make me his deacon, to minister to him in a cheerful surrender of my body and soul to thy pleasure, by his hands. I come unto thee, O God, my God, I come unto thee, so as I can come, I come to thee, by embracing thy coming to me, I come in the confidence, and in the application of thy servant David's promise, "that thou wilt make all my bed in my sickness";[1] all my bed; that which way soever I turn, I may turn to thee; and as I feel thy hand upon all by body, so I may find it upon all my bed, and see all my corrections, and all my refreshings to flow from one and the same, and all from thy hand. As thou hast made these feathers thorns, in the sharpness of this sickness, so, Lord, make these thorns feathers again, feathers of thy dove, in the peace of conscience, and in a holy recourse to thine ark, to the instruments of true comfort, in thy institutions and in the ordinances of thy church. Forget my bed, O Lord, as it hath been a bed of sloth, and worse than sloth; take me not, O Lord, at this advantage, to terrify my soul with saying, Now I have met thee there where thou hast so often departed from me; but having

---

1. Psalm 41:3.

295

burnt up that bed by these vehement heats, and washed that bed in these abundant sweats, make my bed again, O Lord, and enable me, according to thy command, "to commune with mine own heart upon my bed, and be still";[2] to provide a bed for all my former sins whilst I lie upon this bed, and a grave for my sins before I come to my grave; and when I have deposited them in the wounds of thy Son, to rest in that assurance, that my conscience is discharged from further anxiety, and my soul from further danger, and my memory from further calumny. Do this, O Lord, for his sake, who did and suffered so much, that thou mightest, as well in thy justice as in thy mercy, do it for me, thy Son, our Saviour, Christ Jesus.

2

O MOST MIGHTY GOD, and merciful God, the God of all true sorrow, and true joy too, of all fear, and of all hope too, as thou hast given me a repentance, not to be repented of, so give me, O Lord, a fear, of which I may not be afraid. Give me tender and supple and conformable affections, that as I joy with them that joy, and mourn with them that mourn, so I may fear with them that fear. And since thou hast vouchsafed to discover to me, in his fear whom thou hast admitted to be my assistance in this sickness, that there is danger therein, let me not, O Lord, go about to overcome the sense of that fear, so far as to pretermit the fitting and preparing of myself for the worst that may be feared, the passage out of this life. Many of thy blessed martyrs have passed out of this life without any show of fear; but thy most blessed Son himself did not so. Thy martyrs were known to be but men, and therefore it pleased thee to fill them with thy Spirit and thy power, in that they did more than men; thy Son was declared by thee, and by himself, to be God; and it was requisite that he should declare himself to be man also, in the weaknesses of man. Let me not therefore, O my God, be ashamed of these fears, but let me feel them to determine where his fear did, in a present submitting of all to thy will. And when thou shalt have inflamed and thawed my former coldnesses and indevotions with these heats, and quenched my former heat with these sweats and inundations, and rectified my former presumptions and negligences with these fears, be pleased, O Lord, as one made so by thee, to think me fit for thee; and whether it be thy pleasure to dispose of this body, this garment, so as to put

2. Psalm 4:4.

it to a farther wearing in this world, or to lay it up in the common wardrobe, the grave, for the next, glorify thyself in thy choice now, and glorify it then, with that glory, which thy Son, our Saviour Christ Jesus, hath purchased for them whom thou makest partakers of his resurrection. Amen.

3

O ETERNAL AND MOST GRACIOUS GOD, who, though thou have reserved thy treasure of perfect joy and perfect glory to be given by thine own hands then, when, by seeing thee as thou art in thyself, and knowing thee as we are known, we shall possess in an instant, and possess for ever, all that can any way conduce to our happiness, yet here also, in this world, givest us such earnests of that full payment, as by the value of the earnest we may give some estimate of the treasure, humbly and thankfully I acknowledge, that thy blessed Spirit instructs me to make a difference of thy blessings in this world, by that difference of the instruments by which it hath pleased thee to derive them unto me. As we see thee here in a glass, so we receive from thee here by reflection and by instruments. Even casual things come from thee; and that which we call fortune here hath another name above. Nature reaches out her hand and gives us corn, and wine, and oil, and milk; but thou fillest her hand before, and thou openest her hand that she may rain down her showers upon us. Industry reaches out her hand to us and gives us fruits of our labour for ourselves and our posterity; but thy hand guides that hand when it sows and when it waters, and the increase is from thee. Friends reach out their hands and prefer us; but thy hand supports that hand that supports us. Of all these thy instruments have I received thy blessing, O God; but bless thy name most for the greatest; that, as a member of the public, and as a partaker of private favours too, by thy hand, thy powerful hand set over us, I have had my portion not only in the hearing, but in the preaching of thy Gospel. Humbly beseeching thee, that as thou continuest thy wonted goodness upon the whole world by the wonted means and instruments, the same sun and moon, the same nature and industry, so to continue the same blessings upon this state and this church by the same hand, so long as that thy Son, when he comes in the clouds, may find him, or his son, or his son's sons ready to give an account and able to stand in that judgment, for their faithful stewardship and dispensation of thy talents so abundantly committed to them; and be to him, O God, in all distempers of his body, in all anxieties of spirit, in all holy sadnesses of soul, such a physician in thy proportion, who are the greatest in heaven, as he hath been in soul and body to me, in his proportion, who is the greatest upon earth.

4

O ETERNAL AND MOST GRACIOUS GOD, I have a new occasion of thanks, and a new occasion of prayer to thee from the ringing of this bell. Thou toldest me in the other voice that I was mortal and approaching to death; in this I may hear thee say that I am dead in an irremediable, in an irrecoverable state for bodily health. If that be thy language in this voice, how infinitely am I bound to thy heavenly Majesty for speaking so plainly unto me? for even that voice, that I must die now, is not the voice of a judge that speaks by way of condemnation, but of a physician that presents health in that. Thou presentest me death as the cure of my disease, not as the exaltation of it; if I mistake thy voice herein, if I overrun thy pace, and prevent thy hand, and imagine death more instant upon me than thou hast bid him be, yet the voice belongs to me; I am dead, I was born dead, and from the first laying of these mud walls in my conception, they have mouldered away, and the whole course of life is but an active death. Whether this voice instruct me that I am a dead man now, or remember me that I have been a dead man all this while, I humbly thank thee for speaking in this voice to my soul; and I humbly beseech thee also to accept my prayers in his behalf, by whose occasion this voice, this sound, is come to me. For though he be by death transplanted to thee, and so in possession of inexpressible happiness there, yet here upon earth thou hast given us such a portion of heaven, as that though men dispute whether thy saints in heaven do know what we in earth in particular do stand in need of, yet, without all disputation, we upon earth do know what thy saints in heaven lack yet for the consummation of their happiness, and therefore thou hast afforded us the dignity that we may pray for them. That therefore this soul, now newly departed to thy kingdom, may quickly return to a joyful reunion to that body which it hath left, and that we with it may soon enjoy the full consummation of all in body and soul, I humbly beg at thy hand, O our most merciful God, for thy Son Christ Jesus' sake. That that blessed Son of thine may have the consummation of his dignity, by entering into his last office, the office of a judge, and may have society of human bodies in heaven, as well as he hath had ever of souls; and that as thou hatest sin itself, thy hate to sin may be expressed in the abolishing of all instruments of sin, the allurements of this world, and the world itself; and all the temporary revenges of sin, the stings of sickness and of death; and all the castles, and prisons, and monuments of sin, in the grave. That time may be swallowed up in eternity, and hope swallowed in possession, and ends swallowed in infiniteness, and all men ordained to salvation in body and soul be one entire and everlasting sacrifice to thee, where thou mayst receive delight from them, and they glory from thee, for evermore. Amen.

5

O ETERNAL AND MOST GRACIOUS GOD, the God of security, and the enemy of security too, who wouldst have us always sure of thy love, and yet wouldst have us always doing something for it, let me always so apprehend thee as present with me, and yet so follow after thee, as though I had not apprehended thee. Thou enlargedst Hezekiah's lease for fifteen years; thou renewedst Lazarus's lease for a time which we know not; but thou didst never so put out any of these fires as that thou didst not rake up the embers, and wrap up a future mortality in that body, which thou hadst then so reprieved. Thou proceedest no otherwise in our souls, O our good but fearful God; thou pardonest no sin, so as that that sinner can sin no more; thou makest no man so acceptable as that thou makest him impeccable. Though therefore it were a diminution of the largeness, and derogatory to the fulness of thy mercy, to look back upon the sins which in a true repentance I have buried in the wounds of thy Son, with a jealous or suspicious eye, as though they were now my sins, when I had so transferred them upon thy Son, as though they could now be raised to life again, to condemn me to death, when they are dead in him who is the fountain of life, yet were it an irregular anticipation, and an insolent presumption, to think that thy present mercy extended to all my future sins, or that there were no embers, no coals, of future sins left in me. Temper therefore thy mercy so to my soul, O my God, that I may neither decline to any faintness of spirit, in suspecting thy mercy now to be less hearty, less sincere, than it used to be, to those who are perfectly reconciled to thee, nor presume so of it as either to think this present mercy an antidote against all poisons, and so expose myself to temptations, upon confidence that this thy mercy shall preserve me, or that when I do cast myself into new sins, I may have new mercy at any time, because thou didst so easily afford me this.

6

O ETERNAL AND MOST GRACIOUS GOD, who, though thou beest ever infinite, yet enlargest thyself by the number of our prayers, and takest our often petitions to thee to be an addition to thy glory and thy greatness, as ever upon all occasions, so now, O my God, I come to thy majesty with two prayers, two supplications. I have meditated upon the jealousy which thou hast of thine own honour, and considered that nothing comes nearer a violating of that honour, nearer to the nature of a scorn to thee, than to sue out thy pardon, and receive the seals of reconciliation to thee, and then return to that sin for which I needed and had thy pardon before. I know that this comes too near to a making thy holy ordinances, thy word, thy sacraments, thy seals, thy grace, instruments of my spiritual fornications. Since therefore thy correction hath brought me to such a participation of thyself (thyself, O my God, cannot be parted), to such an entire possession of thee, as that I durst deliver myself over to thee this minute, if this minute thou wouldst accept my dissolution, preserve me, O my God, the God of constancy and perseverance, in this state, from all relapses into those sins which have induced thy former judgments upon me. But because, by too lamentable experience, I know how slippery my customs of sin have made my ways of sin, I presume to add this petition too, that if my infirmity overtake me, thou forsake me not. Say to my soul, "My son, thou hast sinned, do so no more";[1] but say also, that though I do, thy spirit of remorse and compunction shall never depart from me. Thy holy apostle, St. Paul, was shipwrecked thrice,[2] and yet still saved. Though the rocks and the sands, the heights and the shallows, the prosperity and the adversity of this world, do diversely threaten me, though mine own leaks endanger me, yet, O God, let me never put myself aboard with Hymenaeus, nor "make shipwreck of faith and a good conscience,"[3] and then thy long-lived, thy everlasting mercy, will visit me, though that which I most earnestly pray against, should fall upon me, a relapse into those sins which I have truly repented, and thou hast fully pardoned.

1. Ecclus. 1:21.
2. 2 Cor. 11:25.
3. 1 Tim. 1:19.

Bibliography

A select list of books and articles, indicating works used in the preparation of this edition, and works that may be of assistance to readers.

I. Bibliographies

Keynes, Sir Geoffrey. *A Bibliography of Dr. John Donne.* Fourth edition. Oxford: Clarendon, 1973.

Roberts, John R. *John Donne: An Annotated Bibliography of Modern Criticism, 1912–1967.* Columbia: University of Missouri Press, 1975.

White, William. "John Donne Since 1900: A Bibliography of Periodical Articles," *Bulletin of Bibliography,* 17:86–9, 113, 165–71, 192–5 (1941). Published as a pamphlet: Boston: F. W. Faxon, 1942.

II. Biography

Walton, Izzak. *The Life of John Donne, Dr. in Divinity, and Late Dean of Saint Pauls Church, London.* London: J. G. for R. Marriot, 1658. Available in numerous subsequent editions.

Novarr, David. *The Making of Walton's Lives.* Cornell Studies in English, 41. Ithaca, N.Y.: Cornell University Press, 1958. Should be read with the above.

Gosse, Edmund. *The Life and Letters of John Donne ... revised and collected ... in two volumes.* London: 1899. The old standard.

Bald, R. C. *John Donne. A Life.* New York and Oxford: Oxford University Press, 1970. Basis for life in this volume.

III. Donne's Works (as used in this volume)

Donne, John. *Devotions Upon Emergent Occasions.* Edited with commentary by Anthony Raspa. New York and Oxford: Oxford University Press, 1987. First published 1975.

301

BIBLIOGRAPHY

————*Devotions Upon Emergent Occasions*. Edited by John Sparrow, with a bibliographical note by Geoffrey Keynes. Cambridge: Cambridge University Press, 1923.

————*Devotions Upon Emergent Occasions*. Ann Arbor: University of Michigan Press, 1959. Bound with *Death's Duell*.

————*Essays in Divinity*. Edited by Evelyn Simpson. Oxford: Clarendon, 1952 (and 1965).

————*The Poems of John Donne*. Edited by H.J.C. Grierson. London: Oxford University Press, 1929, based on the larger edition of 1919.

————*Complete Poetry*. Edited by John T. Shawcross. Garden City, New York: Doubleday, Anchor, 1967.

————*The Divine Poems*. Edited with an introduction and commentary by Helen Gardner. Oxford: Clarendon, 1952 (reprinted 1959). Basic.

————*The Prayers of John Donne*. Selected and edited from the Earliest Sources, with an Essay on Donne's Idea of Prayer, by Herbert H. Umbach. New York: Bookman Associates, 1951 (reprinted 1962).

————*The Sermons of John Donne*. Edited with Introductions and Critical Apparatus by George R. Potter and Evelyn M. Simpson. Berkeley and Los Angeles: University of California Press, 1953–1962. 10 volumes. Basic.

————*Donne's Sermons: Selected Passages*. With an essay by Logan Pearsall Smith. Oxford: Clarendon, 1919.

————*Sermons on the Psalms and Gospels; With a Selection of Prayers and Meditations*. Edited with an introduction by Evelyn M. Simpson. Berkeley: University of California Press, 1963.

————*The Sermons of John Donne*. Selected and edited by Theodore Gill. Living Age Books. New York: Meridian, 1958.

————*The Showing forth of Christ. Sermons of John Donne*. Selected and edited by Edmund Fuller. New York, Evanston, and London: Harper and Row, 1964.

————*Donne's Prebend Sermons*. Edited with an introduction and commentary by Janel M. Mueller. Cambridge, Mass.: Harvard University Press, 1971.

IV. General Criticism, Background, Context

Andrewes, Lancelot. *Ninety-six Sermons*. Library of Anglo-Catholic Theology. 5 volumes. Oxford, 1841.

Baker, Herschel. *The Wars of Truth: Studies in the Decay of Christian Humanism in the Earlier Seventeenth Century*. Cambridge, Mass.: Harvard University Press, 1952.

Bethell, S. L. *The Cultural Revolution of the Seventeenth Century*. London: Denis Dobson, 1951.

Booty, John E., ed. *The Book of Common Prayer 1559. The Elizabethan Prayer Book*. Folger Documents in Tudor and Stuart Civilization. Charlottesville, Va.: University of Virginia Press, for the Folger Shakespeare Library, 1976. Text, notes and historical essay.

Gardner, Helen. "Seventeenth Century Religious Poetry," *Religion and Literature*. New York: Oxford University Press, 1971, pp. 171ff.

Hall, Joseph. *Works*. Edited by Josiah Pratt. 10 volumes. London, 1808.

Hardison, O. B. *The Enduring Moment. A Study in the Idea of Praise in Renaissance Literary Theory and Practice*. Chapel Hill: University of North Carolina Press, 1962.

Hooker, Richard. *The Folger Library Edition of the Works of—*. W. Speed Hill, general editor. 6 volumes. Cambridge, Mass.: The Belnap Press of Harvard University Press, 1977–.

Husain, Itrat. *The Mystical Element in the Metaphysical Poets of the Seventeenth Century*. Edinburgh: Oliver and Boyd, 1948.

Johnson, C. H. *Reason's Double Agents*. Chapel Hill: University of North Carolina Press, 1966.

Lewalski, Barbara Kiefer. *Protestant Poetics and the Seventeenth Century Religious Lyric*. Princeton, N.J.: Princeton University Press, 1979.

Lewis, C. S. *Oxford History of English Literature*. Oxford: Oxford University Press, 1954.

Martz, Louis L. *The Poetry of Meditation: A Study in English Religious Literature of the Seventeenth Century*. Yale Studies in English, 125. New Haven: Yale University Press, 1954.

Peterson, Douglas. *The English Lyric*. Princeton, N.J.: Princeton University Press, 1967.

Webber, J. M. *The Eloquent I. Style and Self in Seventeenth Century Prose*. Madison, Wisc.: University of Wisconsin Press, 1968.

White, Helen C. *The Metaphysical Poets: A Study in Religious Experience*. New York: Macmillan, 1936.

V. Donne Criticism: General

Andreason, N. J. C. *John Donne: Conservative Revolutionary*. Princeton, N.J.: Princeton University Press, 1967.

Carey, John. *John Donne. Life, Mind, Art*. New York: Oxford University Press, 1981. Important but controversial.

Cathcart, Dwight. *Doubting Conscience. Donne and the Poetry of Moral Argument*. Ann Arbor: University of Michigan Press, 1975.

Coffin, Charles Monroe. *John Donne and the New Philosophy*. New York: Columbia University Press, 1937 (reprinted 1958).

Gardner, Helen, ed. *John Donne: A Collection of Critical Essays*. Spectrum Book, 20th century views. Englewood Cliffs, N.J.: Prentice Hall, 1962 (reprinted 1963).

Kermode, Frank, ed. *Discussions of John Donne*. Boston: Heath, 1962.

Lewalski, Barbara Kiefer. *Donne's Anniversaries and the Poetry of Praise: The Creation of a Symbolic Mode*. Princeton, N.J.: Princeton University Press, 1973.

Maloney, Michael Francis. *John Donne: His Flight from Mediaevalism*. Illinois Studies in Language and Literature, 29, No. 2–3. Urbana: University of Illinois Press, 1944.

Rosten, Murray. *The Soul of Wit. A Study of John Donne*. Oxford: Clarendon, 1974. Important.

BIBLIOGRAPHY

Simpson, Evelyn M. *A Study of the Prose Works of John Donne*. 2nd ed. Oxford: Clarendon, 1962. 1st ed. 1924.

Stampfer, Judah. *John Donne and the Metaphysical Gesture*. New York: Funk and Wagnalls, 1970. A major study.

VI.   Donne Criticism: Specifically Religious

Baker-Smith, D. "John Donne and the Mysterium Crucis," *English Miscell.*, 19(1968):65–82.

———"John Donne's Critique of True Religion," *John Donne: Essays in Criticism*. Edited by A. J. Smith. London: Methuen, 1972, pp. 404–432.

Bredvoid, Louis I. "The Religious Thought of Donne in Relation to Medieval and Later Traditions," *Studies in Shakespeare, Milton and Donne*, University of Michigan Publications, Language and Literature, 1. New York: Macmillan, 1925, pp. 191–232.

Daniel, E. Randolph. "Reconciliation, Covenant, and Election: A Study in the Theology of John Donne," *Anglican Theological Review*, 48(1966):14–30.

Gardner, Helen. "The Historical Sense," *The Limits of Criticism: Reflections on the Interpretation of Poetry and Scripture*. London: Oxford University Press, 1956, pp. 40–63.

Grierson, H. J. C. "John Donne and the 'Via Media,'" *Modern Language Review*, 43(1948):305–14.

Hughes, R. E. *The Progress of the Soul. The Interior Career of John Donne*. New York and Toronto: W. Morrow, 1968.

Husain, Itrat. *The Dogmatic and Mystical Theology of John Donne*. London: S.P.C.K., 1938.

Jackson, Robert S. *John Donne's Christian Vocation*. Evanston: Northwestern University Press, 1970.

Merrill, T. F. "John Donne and the Word of God," *Neuphilol. Mitteil.*, 69(1968):597–616.

Quinn, Dennis B. "John Donne's Principles of Biblical Exegesis," *Journal of English and Germanic Philology*, 41(1962):313–29.

Sculpholme, A. C. "Anniversary Study of John Donne. Pt. 1: Anglican Wit. Pt. 2: Fraited With Salvation," *Theology*, 75(1972):21–26; 72–78.

Sellin, Paul R. *John Donne and 'Calvinist' Views of Grace*. Amsterdam: VU Boekhandel/Uitgeverij, 1983.

Shaw, Robert B. *The Call of God. The Theme of Vocation in the Poetry of Donne and Herbert*. Cambridge, Mass.: Cowley Publications, 1981. Valuable for Donne's spirituality.

Smith, R. G. "Augustine and Donne: A Study in Conversion," *Theology*, 45(1942):147–59.

Stanwood, P. G., and Asals, Heather Ross, eds. *John Donne and the Theology of Language*. Columbia: University of Missouri Press, 1986.

Webber, Joan. *Contrary Music: The Prose Style of John Donne*. Madison, Wisc.: University of Wisconsin Press, 1964.

BIBLIOGRAPHY

VII. Donne Criticism: The Sonnets

Archer, Stanley. "Meditation and the Structure of Donne's Holy Sonnets," *Journal of English Lit. Hist.*, 28(1961):137–47. Challenges views of Martz and Gardner.

Hester, M. Thomas. "Re-signing the Text of the Self: Donne's 'As due by many titles,' " *Bright Shootes of Everlastingnesse, The Seventeenth-Century Religious Lyric*. Edited by C. J. Summers and T.-L. Pebworth. Columbia: University of Missouri Press, 1987, pp. 59–71.

Leishman, J. B. *The Monarch of Wit: An Analytical and Comparative Study of the Poetry of John Donne*. London: Hutchinson, 1951.

Peterson, Douglas L. "John Donne's Holy Sonnets and the Anglican Doctrine of Contrition," *Studies in Philology*, 56(1959):504–18. See his *The English Lyric* (1967).

Rollin, Roger B. " 'Fantastique Ague,' The Holy Sonnets and Religious Melancholy," *The Eagle and the Dove, Reassessing John Donne*. Edited by C. J. Summers and T.-L. Pebworth. Columbia: University of Missouri Press, 1986, pp. 131–146.

Sanders, Wilbur. *John Donne's Poetry*. Cambridge: At the University Press, 1971. Espec. ch. 6.

Young, R. V. "Donne's Holy Sonnets and the Theology of Grace," *Bright Shootes of Everlastingnesse*, Summers and Pebworth, eds. See Hester above. An important corrective to Lewalaski and Sellin.

VIII. Donne Criticism: The *Devotions*

Andreason, N. J. C. "Donne's Devotions and Psychology of Assent," *Modern Philology*, 62(1965):207–216.

Cox, G. H., III. "Donne's Devotions; a meditative sequence on repentance," *Harvard Theological Review*, 66(1973):331–51.

Harding, D. W. "The Devotions Now," *John Donne, Essays in Criticism*. Edited by A. J. Smith. London: Methuen, 1972, pp. 385–403.

Mueller, Janel M. "The Exegesis of Experience. Dean Donne's Devotions," *Journal of English and German Philology*, 67(1968):1–19.

Webber, Joan. "The Prose Style of John Donne's Devotions upon Emergent Occasions," *Anglia*, 79(1961):138–152. Appears, expanded, in her *Contrary Music* (1963).

IX. Donne Criticism: The Sermons

Carrithers, Gale H., Jr. *Donne at Sermons. A Christian Existential World.* Albany: State University of New York Press, 1972.

Davies, Horton. *Like Angels from a Cloud. The English Metaphysical Preachers, 1588–1645.* San Marino, Calif.: Huntington Library, 1986. Valuable.

Davis, Walter R. "Meditation, Typology, and the Structure of John Donne's Sermons," *The Eagle and the Dove*. C. J. Summers and T.-L. Pebworth, eds. Columbia: University of Missouri Press, 1986, pp. 166–88.

BIBLIOGRAPHY

Doebler, Bettie Anne. *The Quickening Seed: Death in the Sermons of John Donne.* Salzburg: Institut für Englische Sprache, 1974.

Eliot, T. S. "Lancelot Andrewes," *Times Lit. Sup.*, 23 September 1926, pp. 621–22. Often reprinted.

———"The Prose of the Preacher: The Sermons of John Donne," *Listener* 2 (July 3, 1929):22–23.

Hayward, John. "A Note on Donne the Preacher," *A Garland for John Donne, 1631–1931.* Edited by Theodore Spencer. Cambridge, Mass.: Harvard University Press, 1931, pp. 73–97.

Hickey, Robert L. "Donne's Delivery," *Tenn. Studies in Lit.*, 19(1964):39–47.

Kuhnre, W. William. "The Exposition of Sin in the Sermons of John Donne," *Lutheran Quarterly*, 12(1960):217–34.

Merchant, W. Moelwyn. "Donne's Sermon to the Virginia Company," *John Donne: Essays in Criticism.* Edited by A. J. Smith. London: Methuen, 1972, pp. 433–52.

Mitchell, W. Fraser. *English Pulpit Oratory from Andrewes to Tillotson: A Study of Its Literary Aspects.* London: S.P.C.K., 1932.

Mueller, William R. *John Donne: Preacher.* Princeton: Princeton University Press, 1962.

Potter, George Reuben. "John Donne: Poet to Priest," *Five Gayley Lectures, 1947–1954.* Edited by L. B. Bennison and G. R. Potter. Berkeley and Los Angeles: University of California Press, 1954, pp. 105–26.

Schleiner, Winifred. *The Imagery of John Donne's Sermons.* Providence: Brown University Press, 1970.

Sparrow, John. "John Donne and Contemporary Preachers: Their Preparation of Sermons for Delivery and Publication," *Essays and Studies by Members of the English Association*, 16(1931):144–78.

Umbach, Herbert H. "The Rhetoric of Donne's Sermons," *PMLA* 52(1937): 354–58.

Index

INDEX

Devotions Upon Emergent Occasions (Donne), 1, 2, 7, 18, 29, 50, 56–60, 66; Augustine's *Confessions* compared, 28; "No Man is an Iland, intire of it selfe," 1–2, 58, 60; texts, 66, 253–86, 295–300

Divine Poems (Donne), 32–44, 60, 63, 65; texts, 65, 73–106; *see also* specific poems, e.g.: *Corona, La* (Donne), *Holy Sonnets* (Donne); *Litany, A* (Donne)

Donne, Ann (More), 14–15, 16, 26; death, 17, 63–64

Donne, Elizabeth (Heywood), 11, 13, 19

Donne, Henry, 11, 12

Donne, John, 11–20; birth and parentage, 11; conversion to Church of England, 12; dean of St. Paul's, 18; death, 19–20; education, 11–12; illness, 7, 16, 18, 19, 56; imprisonment, 14; marriage, 14–15; ordination, 16, 17; secretary to Sir Thomas Egerton, 13–14; spiritual development, 12, 21–31; *see also* specific topics and works, e.g.: Incarnation; *Holy Sonnets* (Donne)

Drury, Elizabeth, 16

Drury, Robert, Sir, 16

Egerton, Elizabeth, Lady, 14

Egerton, Thomas, 13

Egerton, Thomas, the elder, 13–14, 14–15

"Elegie upon the death of the Deane of Pauls, Dr. Iohn Donne, An" (Carey), 19–20

Eliot, T.S., 23, 36, 54

Essays in Divinity (Donne), 17, 63; text, 289–94

Essex, Earl of, 13

Exercitia Spiritualia (Ignatius of Loyola), 32, 56

"Expiration, The" (Donne), 21

"Extasie, The" (Donne), 22

First Anniversary (Donne), 33

Fish, Stanley, 35

Four Quartets (Eliot), 36

Francis de Sales, 22, 32–33

Fuller, Edmund, 66

Gansfort, Wessell, 33

Gardner, Helen, 24, 32, 36, 65, 66

Gill, Theodore, 66

"Good-Morrow" (Donne), 30

"Goodfriday, 1613. Riding Westward" (Donne), 4, 6, 41; text, 100–01

"Grace of Repentance, The" (sermon) (Donne), 54; text, 218–32

Grierson, Herbert, Sir, 65

Hall, Joseph, 33, 44, 49, 57

Harding, D.W., 59, 60

Harrington, William, 12

Hay, James (Viscount Doncaster), 17

Herbert, George, 3; "Church Porch," 40; "Love (III)," 18, 44; mood of endless struggle, 26; prayer, definition of, 53; *The Temple*, 1, 35

Herbert, Magdalen (Lady Danvers), 15, 19

Herrick, Robert, 3

Heywood, Elizabeth, 11

Heywood, Ellis, 11

Heywood, Jasper, 11

Heywood, John (father of John Donne), 11

Heywood, John (grandfather of John Donne), 11

Holy Sonnets (Donne), 15, 26–27, 37–40, 41; doctrine of prevenient grace, 29; meditative style, 32–35; text, 78–85

Hooker, Richard, 3, 47, 58, 60: on eucharist, 51; on holy fear, 25, 26, 57; on nature, 22–23, 24; on over-scrupulosity, 27; on reason and revelation, 23–24; on repentance, 33–34, 38, 48–49, 57; view of the church, 30

"Hymne to Christ, at the Authors last going into Germany" (Donne), 17, 42–43; text, 104

"Hymne to God my God, in my sicknesse" (Donne), 18, 27, 28, 30, 43; text, 205

"Hymne to God the father" (Donne), 18, 28, 43; text, 106

Ignatius his Conclave (Donne), 15

Ignatius of Loyola, 32, 56

308

INDEX

Other Volumes in this Series

Francis and Clare • THE COMPLETE WORKS
Gregory Palamas • THE TRIADS
Pietists • SELECTED WRITINGS
The Shakers • TWO CENTURIES OF SPIRITUAL REFLECTION
Zohar • THE BOOK OF ENLIGHTENMENT
Luis de León • THE NAMES OF CHRIST
Quaker Spirituality • SELECTED WRITINGS
Emanuel Swedenborg • THE UNIVERSAL HUMAN AND SOUL-BODY INTERACTION
Augustine of Hippo • SELECTED WRITINGS
Safed Spirituality • RULES OF MYSTICAL PIETY, THE BEGINNING OF WISDOM
Maximus Confessor • SELECTED WRITINGS
John Cassian • CONFERENCES
Johannes Tauler • SERMONS
John Ruusbroec • THE SPIRITUAL ESPOUSALS AND OTHER WORKS
Ibn 'Abbād of Ronda • LETTERS ON THE SŪFĪ PATH
Angelus Silesius • THE CHERUBINIC WANDERER
The Early Kabbalah •
Meister Eckhart • TEACHER AND PREACHER
John of the Cross • SELECTED WRITINGS
Pseudo-Dionysius • THE COMPLETE WORKS
Bernard of Clairvaux • SELECTED WORKS
Devotio Moderna • BASIC WRITINGS
The Pursuit of Wisdom • AND OTHER WORKS BY THE AUTHOR OF THE CLOUD
    OF UNKNOWING
Richard Rolle • THE ENGLISH WRITINGS
Francis de Sales, Jane de Chantal • LETTERS OF SPIRITUAL DIRECTION
Albert and Thomas • SELECTED WRITINGS
Robert Bellarmine • SPIRITUAL WRITINGS
Nicodemos of the Holy Mountain • A HANDBOOK OF SPIRITUAL COUNSEL
Henry Suso • THE EXEMPLAR, WITH TWO GERMAN SERMONS
Bérulle and the French School • SELECTED WRITINGS
The Talmud • SELECTED WRITINGS
Ephrem the Syrian • HYMNS
Hildegard of Bingen • SCIVIAS
Birgitta of Sweden • LIFE AND SELECTED REVELATIONS